WHY WE FIGHT

HUMAN DIMENSIONS IN FOREIGN POLICY, MILITARY
STUDIES, AND SECURITY STUDIES

Series editors: Stéphanie A.H. Bélanger, Pierre Jolicoeur,
and Stéfanie von Hlatky

Books published in the Human Dimensions in Foreign Policy, Military
Studies, and Security Studies series offer fresh perspectives on foreign
affairs and global governance. Titles in the series illuminate critical issues
of global security in the twenty-first century and emphasize the human
dimensions of war such as the health and well-being of soldiers, the factors that influence operational effectiveness, the civil-military relations
and decisions on the use of force, as well as the ethical, moral, and legal
ramifications of ongoing conflicts and wars. Foreign policy is also analyzed both in terms of its impact on human rights and the role the public
plays in shaping policy directions.

With a strong focus on definitions of security, the series encourages
discussion of contemporary security challenges and welcomes works that
focus on issues including human security, violent conflict, terrorism, military cooperation, and foreign and defence policy. This series is published
in collaboration with Queen's University and the Royal Military College
of Canada with the Centre for International and Defence Policy, the
Canadian Institute for Military and Veteran Health Research, and the
Centre for Security, Armed Forces, and Society.

Why We Fight

New Approaches
to the Human Dimension
of Warfare

Edited by

ROBERT C. ENGEN,
H. CHRISTIAN BREEDE,
and
ALLAN ENGLISH

McGill-Queen's University Press
Montreal & Kingston • London • Chicago

© McGill-Queen's University Press 2020

ISBN 978-0-2280-0386-1 (cloth)
ISBN 978-0-2280-0387-8 (paper)
ISBN 978-0-2280-0447-9 (ePDF)
ISBN 978-0-2280-0448-6 (ePUB)

Legal deposit fourth quarter 2020
Bibliothèque nationale du Québec

Printed in Canada on acid-free paper that is 100% ancient forest free
(100% post-consumer recycled), processed chlorine free

This book has been published with the help of a grant from the Canadian
Federation for the Humanities and Social Sciences, through the Awards to
Scholarly Publications Program, using funds provided by the Social Sciences
and Humanities Research Council of Canada. Funding was also received
from the Battle of Hill 70 Memorial Project.

Funded by the Government of Canada   Financé par le gouvernement du Canada   Canada   Canada Council for the Arts   Conseil des arts du Canada

We acknowledge the support of the Canada Council for the Arts.

Nous remercions le Conseil des arts du Canada de son soutien.

Library and Archives Canada Cataloguing in Publication

Title: Why we fight: new approaches to the human dimension of warfare / edited
by Robert C. Engen, H. Christian Breede, and Allan English.

Other titles: Why we fight (2020)

Names: Engen, Robert C. (Robert Charles), editor. | Breede, H. Christian, editor. |
English, Allan D. (Allan Douglas), 1949– editor.

Series: Human dimensions in foreign policy, military studies, and security studies;
13.

Description: Series statement: Human dimensions in foreign policy, military
studies, and security studies; 13 | Includes bibliographical references and index.

Identifiers: Canadiana (print) 2020031789X | Canadiana (ebook) 20200318039 |
ISBN 9780228003861 (hardcover) | ISBN 9780228003878 (softcover) |
ISBN 9780228004479 (PDF) | ISBN 9780228004486 (ePUB)

Subjects: LCSH: Psychology, Military. | LCSH: Combat—Psychological aspects. |
LCSH: Military morale—Canada. | LCSH: Military art and science—Canada. |
LCSH: Military education—Canada. | LCSH: Motivation (Psychology) |
LCSH: Canada—Armed Forces.

Classification: LCC U22.3 .W49 2020 | DDC 355.001/9—dc23

This book was typeset by Marquis Interscript in 10.5/13 Sabon.

Dedicated to the memory of
Professor Roger J. Spiller, 1944–2017

Contents

Figures and Tables

FIGURES

TABLES

WHY WE FIGHT

The Human Dimensions of War

Robert C. Engen

There has never been a dull time to study the human dimensions of warfare. From the drilling of soldiers into human *automata* during the seventeenth century to the most recent observations on post-traumatic stress disorder and cohesion, it is fascinating to explore and debate what shapes the behaviour of the soldier. It is important, too, because we have such limited access to the internal states of those who fight, and because concrete answers to the existential questions of why they go to battle, and how they behave once there, are elusive.

This present volume, *Why We Fight*, is a book about the Canadian experience of the human dimension of warfare, both contemporary and historical. It is a compilation of papers that were presented at the Queen's University Centre for International and Defence Policy (CIDP) workshop "Combat Motivation: Past, Present, and Future," held at the Canadian Army Command and Staff College in Kingston in November 2016. The gathering brought together military historians, political scientists, and serving members of the Canadian Armed Forces for discussion and debate. The workshop's objective was to showcase contemporary Canadian approaches to the study of motivation, cohesion, leadership, and the human dimension of warfare. By "human dimension," we mean the cognitive, physical, social, and cultural components of combatants, leaders, and supporters. This is wider than – though inclusive of – the idea of combat motivation ("the process involving a soldier's decision to fight, and to keep fighting, in combat") that originally formed the workshop's conceptual framework.[1] The question of "why we fight" is inextricably linked to that of "how we fight," and new insights on both of these topics are unpacked in this volume.

The literature surrounding the study of the human being in warfare has, in the past thirty years, become highly contentious. Colonel Ardant du Picq's *Études sur le combat (Battle Studies)*, published posthumously in 1870, initiated the field,[2] but as an academic concern, the human dimension of war came into its own after the global carnage of the Second World War. The field has been shaped disproportionately by that war. Three works, in particular, made seminal contributions: Samuel A. Stouffer's *The American Soldier*, Edward Shils and Morris Janowitz's "Cohesion and Disintegration in the Wehrmacht in World War II," and S.L.A. Marshall's *Men Against Fire*.[3] Of these works, Marshall's was the least thorough, yet has become the most influential; throughout the Cold War in the United States, his books defined the parameters for understanding human behaviour in war. Marshall's approach was given fresh life in the 1990s by Dave Grossman's popular book *On Killing*, despite serious academic questions that had been raised.[4] Thirty years after Roger Spiller's incisive critique of Marshall's *Men Against Fire* and its author's postulation that most soldiers in war do not fight, Marshall's work has been enjoying another renaissance of credibility, this time centred in the UK: Christopher Coker wrote that Marshall's findings are "now a universally recognised truth."[5] Sociologist Anthony King's *The Combat Soldier* and historian Jonathan Fennell's *Combat and Morale in the North African Campaign* have both treated Marshall's findings as credible.[6] It seems likely, therefore, that some beliefs about the fundamental facts of behaviour are going to remain contested for the foreseeable future.

Less work exists on the human dimension, specifically from a Canadian point of view, and, as will be shown, reliance upon foreign literature for discussions of human behaviour in war has not benefitted Canada or its military. Defence researcher Anthony Kellett wrote an excellent but little-known book on the subject, *Combat Motivation: The Behaviour of Men in Battle*.[7] Terry Copp and Bill McAndrew's *Battle Exhaustion* has become a classic both in Canada and internationally, and contains many thoughts on the individual psychology of Canadian soldiers facing mental collapse during the Second World War; it is, however, a short book with a lot of ground to cover.[8] A cluster of other books on the human dimension of warfare with a focus on Canada during the Second World War have recently appeared, my own books *Canadians Under Fire* and *Strangers in Arms* among them.[9] Geoff Hayes's excellent *Crerar's Lieutenants*, on officership in the Second World War, is a groundbreaking look at the creation of junior officers at the intersection of gender and class in Canada.[10] Caroline D'Amours has contributed important insights on NCMs and the process of infantry training.[11] Doug Delaney's *The Soldiers' General* is a study of both junior and senior leadership through the case of one prominent Canadian soldier, while his more recent *The Imperial Army Project* locates the war effort at the nexus of imperial coalition building.[12] Jonathan Fennell has recently produced a new work, *Fighting the People's War*, a combined, in-depth study of the human dimension of war in the Commonwealth armies during the Second World War, and includes plenty of insight on the Canadian experience in its comparative framework.[13] Systematic Canadian studies of the human dimension are more sparing for the post-1945 period. Meghan Fitzpatrick's *Invisible Scars* examines mental trauma in the Korean War, and Adam Montgomery's *The Invisible Injured* maps similar terrain with an emphasis on Cold War and modern experience.[14] Gazing past the present and into the future is *Transhumanizing War*, edited by H. Christian Breede, Stéfanie von Hlaky, and Stéphanie A.H. Bélanger, which examines the human dimension of enhancing the warfighting capacity of soldiers beyond its natural limits.[15] All are highly valuable contributions, but more is still needed – in particular, studies that tie historical examples to recent experiences and elucidate what makes a person stand up and take action in the face of almost certain harm or even death. The CIDP workshop and this present volume seek to address this shortfall and inject energy into what deserves to be a vital realm of inquiry for Canada's armed forces.

This volume also features work that explores new facets of the human dimension of warfare. In the past, the field was largely dominated by questions of combat motivation: why soldiers fight, what they think, how they act. However, one of the most interesting things about the CIDP workshop was that while participants organized their presentations around a broad theme of combat motivation, the topics went much deeper in questioning human behaviour in combat. The workshop contained several studies that were definitively part of the traditional conversations about combat motivation: my own, as well as those of Allan English, Roger Spiller, and Ian Hope. So many fundamental questions remain unanswered when it comes to the behaviour of soldiers in battle. But the CIDP workshop also revealed the importance of expanding our ideas about how behaviour in war is manifested and which new directions demand our consideration. The prevailing orthodoxy about motivation and behaviour has to do with camaraderie, cohesion, and the primary group. Many of our workshop attendees – who subsequently became contributors to this volume – have introduced problematic and challenging concepts into the discussion of human behaviour. Claire Cookson-Hills's work on sexual violence during the Second World War, which asks whether such behaviour may be intrinsic to motivation in war, raises extremely troubling questions, particularly in a country struggling with similar issues within its own military. The neglected dimension of religious belief and fervour, discussed in chapters by Robert Martyn and by Victoria Tait, Joshua Clark, and Lena Saleh, likewise demands reconsideration in an age where extremism and radicalization are among the greatest challenges for the Canadian Armed Forces (CAF). Where does religion fit within our traditional paradigms for motivation and behaviour in war? Religion has and continues to be used to promote war, especially against those labelled "non-believers," but has not been fundamental to the study (in the West) of cohesion and motivation in a long time. How can we better frame religious fervour in our modelling of behaviour in war? Robert Williams's work on mutual comprehension flags fundamental problems with behaviour in coalition partnerships – the kind of partnership that Canada invariably cleaves toward in war – when allies seem to lack the basic ability to share understanding. H. Christian Breede and Karen D. Davis offer a critical examination of the "warrior culture" that has been actively promoted within the CAF, demonstrating how toxic and self-destructive elements of a culture can suffuse behaviour, derail morale and cohesion, and ultimately undermine combat effectiveness.

A common point in all these chapters is their relevance to the problems faced by the CAF today. Even the primarily historical chapters raise fundamental questions about behaviour that we can use to interrogate contemporary issues. In Cookson-Hills's work on the prevalence of rape during the Second World War, for example, we may see shades of the CAF's distressingly unsuccessful attempts to combat sexual violence and harassment by changing a heavily masculinized and gendered military culture as part of Operation Honour (2015–20). These problems, it turns out, may form part of an observable pattern seventy-five years old or more. They also go together with the CAF's hypermasculine warrior culture criticized by Breede and Davis, who conclude that not only is the warrior identity not necessary to combat motivation, it may indeed be toxic to combat effectiveness, retention, and recruiting in the modern CAF.

Why We Fight is a compilation of works that push the boundaries of the study of the human being in war – and particularly of the Canadian soldier in war. Many of them confront uncomfortable topics: the limits of communication, sexual violence, the failings of the warrior culture, and radicalization. Others are perspectives from scholars and military practitioners, who offer new insights arising out of long years of experience. All the chapters focus on contemporary or historical Canada wholly or in part, or are written by Canadian authors.

Chapter 1 of *Why We Fight* is by Allan English, who offers reflections on a quarter-century of teaching officer cadets, civilians, and senior service personnel at the Royal Military College of Canada, Queen's University, and the Canadian Forces College. Much of the book's historiographical background is provided in this chapter, and English offers special insights about the role of the regiment in shaping the teaching, study, and practice of combat motivation in Canada.

Chapter 2, "The Marshall Paradigm," is an essay published posthumously on behalf of Roger Spiller, who attended the CIDP workshop a few months before he passed away, and asked that the editors expand his presentation notes into a full chapter on his behalf. Spiller's chapter is an update upon his classic *RUSI Journal* essay "S.L.A. Marshall and the Ratio of Fire," which marked the beginning of a new literature critical of traditional perspectives on combat motivation.[16] While the editors have expanded upon some details and added some context, particularly the Canadian content, the heart and soul of the chapter remains Roger's.

Chapter 3, "Different Language, Common Intent," by Robert Williams, is a historical account of the breakdown in communications between the First Canadian Army and a formation under its command, the Polish Armoured Division, during the crucial attack on the Falaise Gap during the summer of 1944. Williams's study of Canadian-Polish relations is not only an illuminating new perspective on an old historiographical debate about the Second World War; it is a lesson on the perils of operating without shared understanding and a critique of the ad hoc assumptions underlying many modern coalition operations. Williams draws upon his experience as a senior intelligence officer to frame the difficulties faced in maintaining alliance connections when personal interactions are functioning at cross-purposes.

Chapter 4, "Sexual Violence as Combat Motivation," by Claire Cookson-Hills, discusses the highly controversial – but timely – topic of sexual violence perpetrated by soldiers of the Canadian Army during the Second World War. Her analysis of violence by Canadian soldiers against German women in the war's final days raises troubling questions about the place of sexualized violence in our understanding of the human side of warfare. There are few baser impulses than sexual violence, and ignoring its place in the history of war – and, ominously, the future of war – would be a grievous omission.

Chapter 5, "Strangers in Arms," by Robert C. Engen, is derived from the keynote address given at the CIDP workshop in November 2016. It lays out the case for understanding "swift trust" and rapidly formed bonds as central to the experience of high-intensity combat, using the Canadian experience of the Second World War as a case study.

Chapter 6, "Combat Motivation in the Contemporary Canadian Army," is by Ian Hope, a former battle group commander in Canada's first combat deployment to Afghanistan in 2006. Hope's take on the topic of how soldiers are motivated draws from his academic knowledge, long military career, and combat experience in several theatres. This chapter offers a vital updating of this topic, one which accounts for Canada's most recent combat deployments as seen through the eyes of a tactical unit commander.

Chapter 7, jointly written by H. Christian Breede and Karen D. Davis, is a critical dissection of warrior culture and the toxicity that hypermasculinized warrior expectations can cultivate in the behaviour of soldiers that subscribe to them. Written by a former junior leader in Afghanistan and one of the most respected voices on gender in today's Canadian Armed Forces, this chapter explores the drawbacks of "the warrior" as an idealized human archetype and contrasts it with the imperatives of the professional soldier.

Chapter 8, "Beliefs: What Motivates Insurgents," by Robert Martyn, explores the underlying motivations and behaviours of adversaries and insurgents that CAF personnel may well find themselves confronting in the near future. Martyn focuses upon what underwrites radicalization – of individuals and of groups – and how this phenomenon needs to be understood by those preparing to fight it.

Chapter 9, "Women, Social Networks, and Radicalization," by Victoria Tait, Joshua Clark, and Lena Saleh, complements Martyn's chapter with a rigorous social science examination of women operating in terrorist "dark networks" on social media platforms. This chapter examines both the process of radicalization in the information age and the methods by which we can observe it happening. The radicalization process and the creation of new adversaries in non-traditional spaces are vital topics for the security of Canadian society.

Why We Fight concludes in a manner similar to the earlier CIDP workshop: with a roundtable discussion between experts and practitioners in the field. Somewhat abridged and edited from an hour-long session, this conversation – which includes Hope, Breede, Engen, English, Williams, and Dr Lee Windsor, from the University of New Brunswick, presents some concluding thoughts on the human dimension of war.

The essays in this volume exist in conversation with one another, one happy result (among several) of the vigorous CIDP workshop that served as prelude to this book. The discussion on sexual violence in the Second World War begun by Cookson-Hills has clear echoes in the chapter on modern-day "warrior" culture by Breede and Davis. Not all of our authors are in agreement. The idea of "swift trust," for example, does not sit easily with Ian Hope, who provides a critique based on his own scholarship and experiences in Afghanistan, and a warning against reliance on swift trust over the more traditional bonds of the regimental system. Others, however – particularly Williams and Tait – see utility in the concept and in the "strength of weak bonds." One of the most important conclusions that we can draw from these studies is that views on human behaviour in war vary widely – even within the same army, during the same war, and discussing the same events. There is no universally true statement that can be made about what motivates soldiers to fight and compels them to keep fighting; this is the central thesis of *Why We Fight*. From S.L.A. Marshall on, many writers have made totalizing, universalizing statements about the human dimension of war, as though a human being is a "black box" (to borrow a term from the field of machine learning) for which one singular "truth" exists. Even on this point, however, there is no full consensus in these pages. Ian Hope's chapter on Afghanistan pushes back against the historical and social science studies elsewhere in the volume. His emphasis upon the timeless aspects of human beings in combat sets his work apart theoretically and draws it closer to S.L.A. Marshall's vision of continuity, rather than disruption, in human behaviour. Disagreement is a valued part of the ongoing conversation and debate on combat motivation, and on human beings in war more broadly. *Why We Fight* offers challenges to many assumptions about the human dimension of warfare, and the editors hope that it will provide fuel for even more debates.

Why now? Recent developments – even in the short time since the CIDP workshop in 2016 – have leant a special urgency to the discussion of the human dimension. Scholars, futurists, prognosticators, and even some military professionals have begun to suggest that the human dimension of warfare is nearing an end, and that, due to technological breakthroughs in artificial intelligence, we are standing on the cusp of a "post-human" age of war.[17] The idea that war is heading toward complete automation becomes a dangerous nonsense when potent interests and cultural forces proclaim its inevitability. There is considerable antihuman rhetoric emerging from the tech community, elements of which anticipate, evangelically, the eclipse of the human being in war, as well as in every other field.[18] Given that technological fetishism is strong in military circles – understandable given the nature of the profession – we must take special precautions to ensure that the study of the human dimension of warfare does not atrophy. Considering the profound gaps in our understanding of the human animal at war, now seems like an excellent moment to reassert the fundamental importance of the human dimension in military affairs.

NOTES

1 This definition is informed by: Anthony Kellett, *Combat Motivation: The Behavior of Soldiers in Battle* (Boston: Kluwer-Nijhoff, 1984), 6; Ben Shalit, *The Psychology of Conflict and Combat* (New York: Praeger, 1988), 6–7; and Peter Watson, *War on the Mind: The Military Uses and Abuses of Psychology* (New York: Basic Books, 1978), 53.

2 Ardant du Picq, *Études sur le combat: Combat antique et combat modern* (1880; Paris: Éditions Champ Libre, 1978), 82–3; Ardant du Picq, *Battle Studies: Ancient and Modern*, trans. John Greely and Robert Cotton (1880; Harrisburg, PA: The Military Service Publishing Company, 1947).

3 Samuel A. Stouffer, et al., *Studies in Social Psychology in World War II: The American Soldier, Volume 2: Combat and Its Aftermath* (Princeton, NJ: Princeton University Press, 1949); Edgar Shils and Morris Janowitz, "Cohesion and Disintegration in the Wehrmacht in World War II," *Public Opinion Quarterly* 12 (1948): 280–315; S.L.A. Marshall, *Men Against Fire: The Problem of Battle Command in Future War* (New York: William Morrow, 1947).

4 Dave Grossman, *On Killing: The Psychological Cost of Learning to Kill in War and Society* (New York: Back Bay Books, 1996).

5 Christopher Coker, *Warrior Geeks: How 21st Century Technology Is Changing the Way We Fight and Think About War* (Oxford: Oxford University Press, 2013), 84.

6 Anthony King, *The Combat Soldier: Infantry Tactics and Cohesion in the Twentieth and Twenty-First Centuries* (Oxford, UK: Oxford University Press, 2013); Jonathan Fennell, *Combat and Morale in the North African Campaign: The Eighth Army and the Path to El Alamein* (Cambridge, UK: Cambridge University Press, 2011).

7 For reference, see n1, above.

8 Terry Copp and William McAndrew, *Battle Exhaustion: Soldiers and Psychiatrists in the Canadian Army, 1939–1945* (Montreal: McGill-Queen's University Press, 1990).

9 Robert C. Engen, *Canadians Under Fire: Infantry Effectiveness in the Second World War* (Montreal: McGill-Queen's University Press, 2009); Robert C. Engen, *Strangers in Arms: Combat Motivation in the Canadian Army* (Montreal: McGill-Queen's University Press).

10 Geoffrey Hayes, *Crerar's Lieutenants: Inventing the Canadian Junior Army Officer, 1939–1945* (Vancouver: UBC Press, 2017).

11 Caroline D'Amours, "Reassessment of a Crisis: Canadian Infantry Reinforcements during the Second World War," *Canadian Army Journal* 14, no. 2 (2012): 72–89.

12 Douglas Delaney, *The Soldiers' General: Bert Hoffmeister at War* (Vancouver: UBC Press, 2006); Douglas Delaney, *The Imperial Army Project: Britain and the Land Forces of the Dominions and India, 1902–1945* (Oxford, UK: Oxford University Press, 2018).

13 Jonathan Fennell, *Fighting the People's War: The British and Commonwealth Armies and the Second World War* (Cambridge, UK: Cambridge University Press, 2019).

14 Meghan Fitzpatrick, *Invisible Scars: Mental Trauma and the Korean War* (Vancouver: UBC Press, 2017); Adam Montgomery, *The Invisible Injured: Psychological Trauma in the Canadian Military from the First World War to Afghanistan* (Montreal: McGill-Queen's University Press, 2017).

15 H. Christian Breede, Stéphanie A.H. Bélanger, and Stéfanie von Hlaky, eds., *Transhumanizing War: Performance Enhancement and the Implications for Policy, Society, and the Soldier* (McGill-Queen's University Press, 2019).

16 Roger Spiller, "S.L.A. Marshall and the Ratio of Fire," *Journal of the Royal United Services Institute* 133, no. 4 (December 1988): 63–71.

17 Christopher Coker, *Future War* (London: Polity, 2015); John R. Allen and Amir Husain, "On Hyperwar," *Proceedings of the U.S. Naval Institute* 143, no. 7 (July 2017): 30–7; Paul Scharre and Michael C. Horowitz, *Artificial Intelligence: What Every Policymaker Needs to Know* (Washington, DC: Center for a New American Security, 2018); Robert H. Latiff, *Future War: Preparing for the New Global Battlefield* (New York: Vintage, 2017).

18 Jaron Lanier, *You Are Not a Gadget: A Manifesto* (New York: Vintage, 2011), 26.

1

Traditional Paradigms of Combat Motivation in the Canadian Military: Teaching Combat Motivation, 1985–2010

Allan English

Foreign models of combat motivation, based on the historical experiences of other militaries, are often applied to the Canadian experience. However, Canadian military culture and historical experience are unique; therefore, if we are to understand combat motivation in the Canadian context, it must be based on Canadian experience. Canada's distinctive military culture and historical experience have shaped approaches to combat motivation that are unique to this country, and part of that experience is reflected in how the topic of combat motivation has been taught in our professional military education (PME) courses.

I shall explore some of that teaching experience by examining key themes and the context in which combat motivation was taught in officer PME from 1985 to 2010, especially at the Royal Military College of Canada (RMCC) and the Canadian Forces College (CFC). For this, I draw on my experience of more than thirty years studying these issues, first as a graduate student and then as an instructor and researcher in the field of combat motivation. My analysis is based, in part, on the content of the curricula during the period of my involvement, as well as my notes and recollections. I argue that the Canadian context in which combat motivation was taught during those years shaped the curricula of certain PME courses and is critical to understanding how motivating military personnel to fight was conceptualized in the Canadian Armed Forces (CAF) in that era. Furthermore, what was taught then continues to influence the culture of the CAF today and, unfortunately, that influence has contributed to resistance to cultural change, particularly toward current initiatives to eliminate sexual misconduct in the Canadian military.[1] Therefore, an understanding of traditional paradigms of combat motivation from that era is essential if CAF culture change is to be successful today and in the future.

BASIC DEFINITIONS AND ASSUMPTIONS

To begin, I shall discuss the definition of three key terms related to combat motivation that I used in my teaching. I state them here because a knowledge of the precise meaning of these terms as we used them at the time is critical to understanding not only their meaning but how the definitions created certain assumptions about human behaviour that influenced how the topic of combat motivation was taught. It is important to note in this discussion that when we taught combat motivation, we focused on the CAF's combat arms, especially the infantry because it was the most studied branch of the Canadian military. There was little in the literature on combat motivation in the other army branches, let alone the Navy or Air Force. The definitions below reflect this combat arms focus.

Morale has often been defined as "the enthusiasm and persistence with which a member of a group engages in the prescribed activity of that group."[2] In this definition, morale is a characteristic of individuals, not groups. When units are described as having high morale, they are simply groups in which a large proportion of their members has high morale.

Cohesion was thought of as group solidarity, or a bonding together of soldiers in a unit. We believed, based on the literature at the time, that cohesion was based on the primary group, i.e., those people with whom one had intimate, face-to-face association and cooperation. Such a group was, and still is, thought to have a minimum size of two people and an upper limit of ten to twelve.

Esprit de corps was characterized as the bonds between soldiers and their secondary group (e.g., the regiment), a bond made possible by that unit's leaders. The purpose of fostering esprit de corps was to help individuals identify with and accept unit leaders' goals as their own. This was considered to be a higher-order concept operating in parallel with cohesion at the primary group level.[3]

These definitions were frequently linked in ways that created certain assumptions about how military personnel were motivated to fight. Four key assumptions in the Canadian context were that: 1) the more cohesive a unit, the higher the morale of its members; 2) cohesive units have good discipline and therefore high combat motivation; 3) the regiment is essential to establishing esprit de corps; and 4) regiments are the key to fostering high combat motivation, which contributes to effectiveness in battle.[4]

In this context, the regiment was deemed to be an essential component of Canadian Army organization because it was assumed that the regimental system was indispensable to generating the highest possible combat motivation and, therefore, combat effectiveness. In addition, it was acknowledged that regimental associations, consisting of active and retired senior members of the regiment, were an important, if unofficial, component of Army governance and culture.[5]

HISTORICAL AND CULTURAL CONTEXT

While many today view the Cold War as a time of relative stability, for Canadian military personnel it was an era of turmoil and what seemed to be constant challenges to the culture and basic assumptions of the CAF.[6] This was especially true for the Army and the regimental system, which to its critics was the main cause of what they saw as a dysfunctional Army culture based on antiquated customs and traditions that were out of step with modern culture. During the Cold War era, some of the events and issues that affected the perceptions of those dealing with these issues were the integration and unification of the Canadian military, the Army's role in ensuring "national survival" in nuclear war scenario, a military ethos crisis, the perceived "civilization" of the military, the professionalization versus regimental "mafias" debate, the "decade of darkness," budget cuts, reforms resulting from the Somalia scandal, and changes in policies following the Croatia Board of Inquiry.[7]

One of the Army's responses to some of these challenges was to commission a series of internal Department of National Defence (DND) studies and reports, most of which, due to the cultural factors suggested here, confirmed the key role of the regimental system in producing and maintaining the combat effectiveness of the Army. Critics of these studies point out that since culture affects what questions can be asked, what research is considered "appropriate," how evidence is gathered and interpreted, and what conclusions are acceptable within a given culture, these internal studies were bound to arrive at conclusions that were compatible with the Army's belief system.[8] However, while these studies were used to supplement curricula addressing combat motivation, the foundation of many such courses was often Anthony Kellett's 1982 classic *Combat Motivation: The Behavior of Soldiers in Battle*. Kellett was a DND scientist and his book was based on a major report, published in 1980, which he had written for DND on the topic. I chose his book as a course text because he was one of the few published authors who included the Canadian experience in his discussion of combat motivation. In his book, he synthesized much of the extensive literature on combat motivation that he had examined during his earlier work and reached conclusions that were often more nuanced than the basic assumptions described above.[9]

Kellett's two main conclusions related to this discussion were that 1) combat motivation of long-service soldiers reflects self-selection, socialization, formal discipline, long service, professional pride, and adherence to institutional values and symbols, whereas 2) combat motivation of short-service soldiers is influenced by self-discipline, short-term group affiliation, ideology, and home-front attitudes. He elaborated on these conclusions in his last chapter, stating that institutional values in the Canadian Army were nurtured by the regimental system, whereas short-service conscript armies, like the US Army, which did not use the regimental system, had weak institutional values. Without strong institutional values, conscript armies were more likely to suffer from low combat motivation than professional armies.[10]

In a cultural context, we know that institutional cultures reflect important assumptions, values, activities, and aims, which generate organizationally acceptable behaviours. We also know that how armed forces fight may be "more a function of their culture than their doctrine."[11] Similarly, national cultures affect military cultures and, while the CAF can be said to have a culture as an organization, it also consists of many subcultures, e.g., Army, Navy, Air Force, and "purple" cultures,[12] as well as unit subcultures (for example, each regiment has its own subculture).[13] Despite this cultural diversity in the CAF, as noted above, most of what we taught about combat motivation reflected the behaviour in battle of the combat arms, particularly the infantry.

Another factor that influenced what we taught was, as alluded to earlier, the intense debate over the role of the regimental system in the Army's structure and governance. Critics claimed that the regimental system was archaic and promoted the parochial interests of the regiment over the needs of the Army and the CAF, while its defenders argued that the regiment was the key to cohesion, high morale, esprit de corps, and effectiveness in combat.[14] Therefore, while it seemed appropriate at the time for us to focus on these issues in our teaching, it did not reflect the complexity of cohesion, morale, and esprit de corps as they existed among the various parts of the CAF. Nevertheless, our teaching reflected the context and debates of the day, and contributed to and reinforced certain beliefs that were part of the Canadian military culture, particularly the Army culture.[15]

BELIEFS EMBEDDED
IN CANADIAN ARMY CULTURE

At the time, there were four beliefs embedded in Canadian Army culture which influenced combat motivation research, doctrine, and behaviours, all of which in turn supported these beliefs. The first was that strong cohesion was essential to good combat motivation. This belief overlooked the fact that highly cohesive groups are not always effective and could, in fact, be dysfunctional, e.g., the Canadian Airborne Regiment and units that had mutinied or disobeyed orders.[16] The second belief was that homogeneous groups are more cohesive than heterogeneous groups, and this led to the third belief: that individuals in homogeneous groups have higher morale than those in heterogeneous groups. Together, these three beliefs led many to conclude that "others," however they might be defined at any particular time, had to be excluded, especially from combat arms units, to create cohesive groups with high morale. The fourth belief was that long service together in a unit – the regiment, for example – was important for building high morale and cohesive groups.[17] Looking back on this now, it seems odd to me that in parts of our readings and curriculum we acknowledged that high casualty rates among combat units in high-intensity battles led to units being reconstituted into effective fighting forces by adding those once considered "others."[18] But we did not reflect on how these historical facts might impact on contemporary beliefs about combat motivation.

We might think that these four beliefs have been consigned to history and been replaced by evidence-based approaches to combat motivation. However, a modern encapsulation of these beliefs can be seen in these comments by a retired US Marine Corps general, Gregory Newbold, in response to a September 2015 report on the Marines' experimental mixed-gender task force, which was used to support the Corps' request for exceptions to the Department of Defense's mandate for the full integration of females in combat units: "combat is a savage pursuit that should remain the sole domain of men ... fighting in combat is something only men can understand ... [t]he characteristics that produce uncommon valor as a common virtue are not physical at all, but are derived from the mysterious chemistry that forms in an infantry unit that revels in the most crude and profane existence so that they may be more effective killers than their foe."

This "mysterious chemistry," according to Newbold, is based on "having shared the duties of cleaning the urinals, the pleasures of a several nights of hilarious debauchery, and multiple near-death experiences."[19] I tell my students that this is an example of "magical thinking" used to defend long-held beliefs that are no longer supported by evidence, as, despite the general's invocation of traditional beliefs about combat, the Marine Corps report was rejected by the US Secretary of the Navy because of "flawed methodology" and "prejudicial thinking."[20]

Before we become too critical of the beliefs held by some of our American colleagues, we should recall that examples of this type of thinking can still be found in the CAF, as General Jonathan Vance, the Chief of the Defence Staff (CDS), in accepting Justice Marie Deschamps's report on "Sexual Misconduct and Sexual Harassment in the Canadian Armed Forces,"[21] acknowledged in August 2015 that a "sexualized culture" exists in the CAF, which "is wrong and runs contrary to the values of the profession of arms and ethical principles of DND/CAF."[22] He also admitted subsequently that his attempts to change the CAF's culture to address these issues are "already generating high levels of skepticism" in the Canadian military.[23]

THE S.L.A. MARSHALL PARADIGM

The S.L.A. Marshall paradigm played a prominent part in the debate in the United States about combat motivation in the second half of the twentieth century, and it continues to do so today.[24] Parts of it are summarized here, as it is still used by some Canadian military officers to justify clinging to some of the beliefs that support the sexualized culture in the CAF that the CDS is trying to extinguish. These are three parts of the paradigm that I emphasized in my lectures at CFC, and which persists in some parts of the CAF today: 1) no more than 15 to 20 per cent of riflemen would ever take an active role in combat; 2) the low ratio of fire is due to an inborn "fear of aggression ... part of the normal man's emotion make-up,"; and 3) "active firers" are an elite group of warriors, superior to the rest of the humanity, who are the "sheep."[25] These points are used today by some of those in the CAF who wish to justify defining the Canadian warrior ethos in terms of homogeneous groups consisting of elite male warriors.[26]

However, this paradigm was largely peripheral to the Canadian discussion on combat motivation prior to our involvement in Afghanistan, because the non-firing behaviour described by Marshall was usually attributed in our teaching to a problem of conscript "hordes" that were not as cohesive or as well-motivated as the Canadian Army. More often than not, when applied to Canadian experience, the Marshall paradigm was used to validate the idea that elite "active firers" were produced in large numbers by the regimental system and this ensured that Canadian combat troops would not perform in the way Marshall described.[27] However, Marshall's work, particularly as interpreted by his disciple David Grossman, became more influential in discussions of combat motivation in the Canadian Army in the first decade of the twenty-first century. Grossman's interpretations gained greater prominence during General Rick Hillier's tenure in senior positions (e.g., Chief of Land Staff, 2003–05; and CDS, 2005–08) when he contributed to the "Americanization" of certain aspects of CAF and Army culture.[28] The growth in Marshall's influence on the CAF was brought home to me when I attended a briefing at CFB Petawawa in May 2007, where a senior officer said that all officers about to be deployed with a battle group to Afghanistan were told to read Grossman's *On Killing*, which relies heavily on Marshall's work, because senior battle group leaders believed that this book reflected the best available reference on combat motivation.[29]

CHALLENGES TO PREVAILING BELIEFS

Two challenges to our assumptions and beliefs about combat motivation that I incorporated into my teaching came from outside of

Canada. One of the most influential works, for me, was Ben Shalit's 1988 study, *The Psychology of Conflict and Combat.* Shalit was an Israel Defense Forces (IDF) psychologist and his studies of the IDF in combat reinforced the idea that each military culture has its own characteristics requiring different ways of approaching combat motivation. Based on his detailed observations and research, Shalit reached conclusions that were quite different both from ours and from Marshall's. Five of his conclusions that influenced my teaching of combat motivation were as follows: 1) "active firers" comprise 75–80 per cent of most units; 2) "green" units often have a 100 per cent firing rate, most of it ineffective but used as a relief from the tension of combat; 3) good morale leads to good discipline, not vice versa; 4) effectiveness in action causes cohesion; and 5) strong cohesion does not necessarily result in combat effectiveness.[30] Nevertheless, when discussing the topic of combat motivation in our courses at CFC and RMCC, Marshall's views were better known than Shalit's among staff and students.[31]

Another challenge to our assumptions and beliefs came from the United States, where Roger Spiller's work challenged the Marshall paradigm directly. I referred to Spiller's work when I started teaching aspects of combat motivation at CFC in 1998. A detailed examination of his critique will be the topic of the next chapter.

CONCLUSIONS

The Canadian historical and cultural context has produced unique interpretations of how military personnel are motivated to fight. These interpretations were reflected in what was taught on this subject in officer PME from 1985 to 2010, especially at RMCC and CFC. This PME, in turn, influenced how many in the CAF thought about combat motivation. In that era, the focus of our teaching was on combat motivation in the combat arms, especially the infantry, because of the existing scholarship on the topic as well as the heated debate over the role of the regimental system in the Canadian Army. In this context, the definitions we used for morale, cohesion, and esprit de corps contributed to certain assumptions about why military personnel were motivated to fight. These assumptions supported traditionalists' beliefs that the highly cohesive, homogeneous groups fostered by the regimental system were the most highly motivated to prevail in combat. In turn, these assumptions supported the view that the regimental system was indispensable to generating combat-effective units. Portions of studies by Canadian researchers, especially Anthony Kellett, were used to buttress these assumptions based on the widely held Canadian view that the long-service Canadian soldiers sustained by the regimental system were superior to the conscript "hordes" of some of our NATO allies, especially the US Army.

The S.L.A. Marshall paradigm, that most soldiers were passive "sheep" who would not actively engage in combat, was less influential in our teaching than it was in the US Army's pedagogy. From the Canadian Army's perspective, the regimental system contributed to producing a high proportion of "active firers" in our combat units. Consequently, it was understood that Marshall's work applied more to short-service conscript armies than long-service volunteer armies like Canada's. Despite these views, and Shalit's and Spiller's challenges to Marshall's work, the Americanization of the Canadian Army, especially under General Hillier, led to Marshall's paradigm assuming greater prominence in the Canadian context. This phenomenon, as well as the infusion of the hypermasculine American-style warrior culture into the CAF at the beginning of the twenty-first century, magnified an already sexualized institutional culture and exacerbated problems with sexual misconduct. Attempts to modify this warrior culture has generated "high levels of skepticism" in parts of the CAF as well as resistance to change, which continues to frustrate the CDS's efforts to eliminate such misconduct.[32]

We can see that what was taught about combat motivation in officer PME from 1985 to 2010, with its emphasis on homogeneous groups of elite male warriors, helped to create a military culture that the CDS declared was "contrary to the values of the profession of arms and ethical principles of DND/CAF." Yet there are those in the CAF today who continue to embrace this culture.[33] A lesson to take from the experience described here is that our PME, especially those aspects related to combat motivation, must evolve to reflect the profession of arms in this country; otherwise it may contribute to a dysfunctional culture that does not reflect Canada's military in the twenty-first century.

NOTES

1 Allan English, "Sexual Harassment and Sexual Assault in the Canadian Armed Forces: Systemic Obstacles to Comprehensive Culture Change,"

paper presented at the IUS Canada Conference, Ottawa, 21–23 October 2016.

2 Frederick J. Manning, "Morale, Cohesion, and Esprit de Corps," in *Handbook of Military Psychology*, ed. Reuven Gal and A. David Mangelsdorff (New York: Wiley, 1991), 455.

3 Ibid., 453–69; Allan English, "Lecture Outline and Notes, War Studies 530 – Behavioural Science Applications to Warfare: Interpreting Human Behaviour in War, Royal Military College of Canada" (n.d., [1996]).

4 See, for example: Anthony Kellett, *Combat Motivation: The Behavior of Soldiers in Battle* (Boston: Kluwer, 1982), 97–117, 319–24.

5 Peter Kasurak, *A National Force: The Evolution of Canada's Army* (Vancouver: UBC Press, 2013), 151–2, 243, 248.

6 Randall Wakelam, "Dealing with Complexity and Ambiguity: Learning to Solve Problems Which Defy Solution," Strathrobyn Papers, Canadian Forces College, no. 4 (Toronto: Centre for National Security Studies, 2010): 3–4, http://www.cfc.forces.gc.ca/237/251/wakelam-eng.pdf.

7 For details on these issues and events, see: Kasurak, *A National Force*, 1–75, 150–70, 252–93.

8 Allan English, *Understanding Military Culture: A Canadian Perspective* (Montreal: McGill-Queen's University Press, 2004), 36, 89–90, 103–10.

9 Kellett, *Combat Motivation*, xv–xvi, 319–36. Another influential reference used in my courses was Darryl Henderson, *Cohesion: The Human Element in Combat* (Washington, DC: National Defense University Press, 1985).

10 Kellett, *Combat Motivation*, 334–6.

11 Paul Johnston, "Doctrine Is Not Enough: The Effect of Doctrine on the Behaviour of Armies," *Parameters* 30, no. 3 (Autumn 1996): 30.

12 A "purple" organization is one that does not have a specific environmental designation or affiliation, and is present in all services. Organizations specific to a service are often referred to, respectively, as "dark blue" (navy), "green" (army), and "light blue" (air force).

13 Allan English and John Westrop, *Canadian Air Force Leadership and Command: The Human Dimension of Expeditionary Air Force Operations* (Trenton, ON: Canadian Forces Aerospace Warfare Centre, 2007), 159–60, http://airforceapp.forces.gc.ca/cfawc/eLibrary/pubs/Leadership_and_Command-2007-01-19.pdf. For a more detailed analysis, see: Donna Winslow, "Canadian Society and its Army," *Canadian Military Journal* 4, no. 4 (Winter 2003–04): 11–24.

14 English, *Understanding Military Culture*, 36, 52, 89–90, 103–4; Kasurak, *A National Force*, 150–7, 163–70, 206, 235–7, 243, 248, 268.

15 English, "Lecture Outline and Notes."

16 Howard G. Coombs, ed., *The Insubordinate and the Noncompliant: Case Studies of Canadian Mutiny and Disobedience, 1920 to Present* (Toronto: Dundurn Group, 2007).

17 Kellett, *Combat Motivation*, 319–35.

18 Ibid., 123–4.

19 Gregory Newbold, "What Tempers the Steel of an Infantry Unit," *War on the Rocks* (9 September 2015), https://warontherocks.com/2015/09/ what-tempers-the-steel-of-an-infantry-unit/.

20 Gretel C. Kovach, "Marine Corps study says units with women fall short on combat skills," *Los Angeles Times*, 12 September 2015, http://www. latimes.com/nation/la-na-marines-women-20150912-story.html.

21 Marie Deschamps, "External Review into Sexual Misconduct and Sexual Harassment in the Canadian Armed Forces," External Review Authority, Department of National Defence, 27 March 2015, https://www.canada.ca/ en/department-national-defence/corporate/reports-publications/sexual-misbehaviour/external-review-2015.html.

22 Canada, Department of National Defence, "CDS Op Order – Op HONOUR," 14 August 2015, https://www.canada.ca/content/dam/dnd-mdn/migration/assets/FORCES_Internet/docs/en/caf-community-support-services-harassment/cds-op-order-op-honour.pdf.

23 Jonathan Vance, "The Chief of the Defence Staff, General Jonathan Vance, Addresses Sexual Misconduct in the Canadian Armed Forces," *Canadian Military Journal* 16, no. 3 (Summer 2016).

24 See, for example: Frederick J. Manning, "Cohesion and Readiness," *Air University Review* (January-February 1981): 69–70; Robert Engen, "Killing for their Country: A New Look at 'Killology,'" *Canadian Military Journal* 9, no. 2 (Summer 2008).

25 English, "Lecture Outline and Notes"; and Allan English, "Professional Studies – Military Staff Skills Programme – Workshop: Critical Thinking and Effective Writing C/PS/MSS/J/MSS/W-1," extracts from Canadian Forces College curriculum packages, 1998–2002.

26 English, "Sexual Harassment and Sexual Assault"; Karen D. Davis and Brian McKee, "Women in the Military: Facing the Warrior Framework," in *Challenge and Change in the Military: Gender and Diversity Issues*, ed. Franklin C. Pinch, Allister T. MacIntyre, Phyllis Browne, and Alan C. Okros (Kingston, ON: Canadian Defence Academy Press, 2004), 52–75.

27 English, "Lecture Outline and Notes"; English, "Professional Studies – Military Staff Skills Programme"; Kellett, *Combat Motivation*, 71, 322, 335.

28 Engen, "Killing for their Country"; Canada, Department of National Defence, *A Guide to Reading on Professionalism and Leadership* (Kingston, ON: Canadian Forces Leadership Institute, Canadian Defence Academy, 2006), 26; Allan English, "Outside Canadian Forces Transformation Looking In," *Canadian Military Journal* 11, no. 2 (2011): 12–20.

29 Dave Grossman, *On Killing: The Psychological Cost of Learning to Kill in War and Society* (New York: Back Bay Books, 1996).

30 Ben Shalit, *The Psychology of Conflict and Combat* (New York: Praeger, 1988), 135–41.

31 English, "Professional Studies – Military Staff Skills Programme"; and Allan English, "Some Effective Writing and Critical Thinking Exercises – DS Notes for Annex A, C/PS/MSS/J/MSS/W-1," Canadian Forces College, n.d. [2001].

32 Vance, "The Chief of the Defence Staff."

33 Ibid.

2

The Marshall Paradigm: American and Canadian Perspectives

Roger Spiller with Robert C. Engen and Allan English

In 1947, Samuel Lyman Atwood Marshall – better known to the world as S.L.A. or "Slam" Marshall – published a book titled *Men Against Fire*, which would come to dominate discussions of combat motivation in the United States and other Western armies since the Second World War. As we saw in the previous chapter, the influence of Marshall's work on the Canadian understanding of combat motivation in the late twentieth century was more limited due to assumptions that his conclusions applied to conscript armies, not to long-service, all-volunteer forces like Canada's. However, at the beginning of the twenty-first century, an increasing Americanization of the Canadian Armed Forces, particularly the Army, has led to the paradigm Marshall established in *Men Against Fire* becoming more influential in Canadian debates. It is important for us to understand the origins and classic critiques of this paradigm and of Marshall's understanding of combat motivation, which this essay revisits.

Marshall was an American journalist and sometime military writer who served as a US Army combat historian during the Second World War. The title of his book was a bold one, suggesting a universal, comprehensive study of a subject that had defied scholarly investigation for centuries: the behaviour of soldiers in the extremities of mortal combat. This had long been war's *terra incognita*. The high drama of war, the great personalities, the intricacies of strategy and operations, the evolution of military technologies, even the great social movements which wars reflected or set afoot – these subjects were well-documented and accessible. But the sources through which scholars entered the world of war disappeared at the threshold of combat. After the

Enlightenment, those who actually did the fighting began to write, but offered only impressionistic, fleeting glimpses of combat by way of letters, journals, and memoirs. In *Men Against Fire*, S.L.A. Marshall claimed that he had found a different, scientific way into the world of combat. This book cemented the man's reputation and created a paradigm for understanding combat motivation in the US and other Western armies since the Second World War.

The centrepiece of Marshall's book, the thesis around which the rest of it spun, was his assertion that in the Second World War only 25 per cent of American infantrymen fired their weapons in combat. This "ratio of fire," as he called this equation, applied in the *best* case – in infantry companies that were well-trained, experienced, and well-led. In less well-prepared companies, the ratio dropped as low as 15 per cent. The "ratio of fire" was neither guess nor mere impression, Marshall claimed. The assertion, he wrote, had its basis in his systematic collection of data from 600 after-action interviews with men from US Army rifle companies fresh off the line. He further insisted that this ratio held true regardless of the tactical context in which these rifle companies fought: it was a *tactical constant*. Unless deliberate steps were taken to correct it, Marshall's "ratio of fire" was the behavioural default for the American GI: at best, only a quarter would actively fire in combat.[1]

The "ratio of fire" was not only the centerpiece of *Men Against Fire*; it became the crux of Marshall's considerable postwar reputation. For forty years after his book appeared, S.L.A. Marshall stood unchallenged as *the* authority on an aspect of war about which military historians knew so little – the behaviour of soldiers in combat. For them, and for many professional soldiers, Marshall's ratio served as their paradigm for understanding the US Army's combat performance in the Second World War.

Except that it was not true. As is quite widely known now, Marshall collected no such data. Neither his papers, letters, notebooks, nor his wartime colleagues record him ever addressing such an issue in his post-combat interviews with rifle companies (the number of interviews he claimed to have conducted also being untrue). In fact, no one, including Marshall, knew what the "ratio of fire" really was. That is because there was no such thing.[2]

The academic and military debate over Marshall's credibility is now almost thirty years old, but one of the central questions behind it has never been fully addressed: why did Marshall's assertion seem so plausible when he first made it? Why was it possible for Marshall's readers to accept his "ratio of fire"? How could it be that between 75 and 85 per cent of American infantrymen never fired their weapons, even to protect their own lives – or even to protect the lives of their comrades? Was there an underlying reason for this reluctance to fight, or this reluctance to kill?

Marshall's answer was widely accepted because it was based on a belief so commonly held in the 1940s that readers found it easy to accept. That belief was simply this: modern man, educated, cosseted, and dissipated by the ease of urban life, never tested physically, was unequal to the demands of modern war. Just as modern warfare imposed an ever-greater burden on the individual, that individual was less able than ever to meet the challenge. Echoes of this refrain were heard from all the leading nations from the middle of the nineteenth century onward. Professional soldiers voiced little confidence in the raw human material from which they were to build their armies. For example, historian Michael Howard points out that before the First World War, many people believed that improved standards of living had increased the instinct of self-preservation and diminished the spirit of self-sacrifice among the youth of the industrialized nations. A view common among members of older generations was that the physical powers of the human species, as displayed by younger generations, were diminishing and that the "religious and national enthusiasm of a bygone age [was] lacking." Most European armies attempted to instill what they saw as the proper values into new conscripts, thereby infusing those values into the nation itself as the conscripts returned to civil society after their military service. Some factions of the French Army, led by officers like Ferdinand Foch and in the tradition of Charles Ardant du Picq, called for a moral crusade by the army to re-establish military virtues in a degenerate civil society.[3] The problem became ever more pressing as leading armies reached numerical and material parity, which forced them to seek victory elsewhere – not in numerical or material advantage, but in the ineffable spirit of their troops. If victory were no longer a matter of numbers or materiel, then morale, elan, fighting spirit, would have to win the day.[4] But what if the fighting spirit had been bred out of men by modern life even before they put on a uniform? The fear was, as British Major General Sir Walter Knox put it so succinctly on the eve of the Great War, that "the physically-deteriorated race of town-bred humanity" is getting "dangerously low on the scale of virility."[5] The experience of the First World War should have put a definitive end to such blimpish beliefs, which were social prejudices masquerading as military wisdom. But it did not. In 1943, no less a figure than General George C. Marshall, Chief of Staff of the US Army, complained: "While our enemies were teaching their youths to endure hardships, contribute to the national welfare, and to prepare for war, our young people were led to expect luxuries, to depend upon a paternal government for assistance in making a livelihood and to look upon soldiers and war as unnecessary and hateful."[6] Some Canadian sources likewise lamented how modern urban civilization "has set as its highest ideal the prolongation, amelioration, and preservation of human life. From his mother's knee the citizen is taught 'safety first' and respect for the welfare of his fellow man."[7]

The Allied armies have been accused of forgetting the lessons of the First World War by 1940, but that is not quite true. Senior officers remembered well enough the epidemic of shell shock which plagued all the combatant armies in that war; and if they somehow forgot, the 68,000 shell-shock patients from the First World War still being treated in America's VA hospitals in 1942 – 58 per cent of all VA patients – were enough to remind them, as were the ongoing bills.[8] In Canada, by the end of fiscal year 1938, the government had spent $750 million on active pensions since the war's end, and during the interwar years the annual cost of veterans' programs and pensions was the second-largest government expense, next to servicing the national debt.[9] Furthermore, by 1939, in trying economic times, those outwardly uninjured veterans pensioned in Canada for "shellshock" represented 50 per cent of the more than 70,000 veterans receiving pensions[10] – all this despite the fact that a ruthless Board of Neurologists and Psychiatrists disqualified many pension applications based on shell shock as being the fault of "a constitutional predisposition which may be either inborn or acquired in later life," rather than the army's fault.[11] As one American VA psychiatrist wrote at the time, the problem of neuropsychiatric cases "reaches from war to war."

By 1940, this epidemic of "weakness" was thought to be preventable. As the wartime draft began in the United States, the Selective Service set itself to reject any inductee judged physically or mentally deficient, confident it could identify traits of personality or character that predestined a man to fail as a soldier. To say that the state of knowledge of human behaviour at the time was less than crude is an understatement. In all the United States, there were less than

3,000 trained psychiatrists[12] and American medical schools, for the most part, did not carry psychiatry courses in their curricula. Psychiatric medical education in the English-speaking world was in "a dismal state" until at least the end of the Second World War,[13] with a prominent British psychiatrist declaring that "to most medical men psychological medicine is a closed book."[14] US Selective Service examinations were therefore conducted by general practitioners, whose knowledge of psychiatry was rudimentary if it existed at all. Many of those rejected simply gave the wrong answer to their favourite question: "Do you like girls?" It was therefore possible for the psychiatric assistant to the Army's surgeon general to write in 1941, without fear of disapproval: "There is no place in the Army for the physical or mental weakling. The Army should not be regarded as a gymnasium for the training and developing of the undernourished and underdeveloped, nor as a psychiatric clinic for the proper adjustment of adolescents who need emotional support."[15]

Fifteen million men were examined under this policy and 4.6 million rejected for military service; of the latter, 1.8 million were rejected on psychiatric or behavioural grounds. So purified, the Army took to the field. In 1940, the US Army counted thirty-six psychiatrists in all, and each division's medical staff had one on the rolls, but the following year the Army abolished these positions. When the chief surgeon for Operation TORCH, in 1942, was asked whether a psychiatrist should accompany the landings in North Africa, he replied that he hoped one could be found *if needed*.[16] Yet in the Second World War, despite a Selective Service rejection rate fifteen times higher than that of the First World War, "neuropsychiatric" admissions to military hospitals were twice the WWI rate and separations from the military for mental and emotional reasons were nearly three times that rate. Psychiatric discharges were the largest single category of disability discharges for the US military between 1939 and 1945.[17]

The scale of the problem was different in Canada, but no less acute – perhaps even more so owing to the country's more limited pool of potential soldiers. Between April 1942 and 1945 – the end of the war – the Canadian Army examined almost 450,000 men for general service and rejected some 162,000, some 32 per cent of them on psychiatric grounds.[18]

From the first American actions in the Pacific and North Africa came reports from divisional and battalion surgeons of healthy combat soldiers behaving abnormally, some so severely they had to be

medically evacuated. On Guadalcanal, the number of psychiatric casualties who had to be evacuated equalled those evacuated for physical
wounds. On the island of New Georgia, the 43rd Infantry Division
came apart at the seams when it encountered "moderate" enemy resistance – 1,850 psychiatric casualties in its first month in action, or
15 per cent of its total strength. Over the course of the war, psychiatric
disorders were the leading cause of all medical evacuations from the
Pacific theatre of operations. And in North Africa, after the American
disasters at Kasserine Pass and Faïd Pass, these casualties rose precipi-
tously to 34 per cent of all non-battle casualties. This was the situation
when Roy Grinker, one of the few trained psychiatrists in that theatre,
wrote in one of his earliest reports: "the question is *not* why men break
down from the stresses of combat, but *why don't they?*"[19]

These disabling, traumatic stress reactions were suffered by *healthy*
soldiers, who in most cases recovered after a few days off the line,
often no farther from the fighting than their company kitchen. But
throughout the war, in every theatre of operations, nosological confusion was rampant among commanders and medical authorities alike.
Standard definitions and treatment protocols simply did not exist.
This confusion dates to the First World War and reflected the debate
among the British Commonwealth forces over how to deal with
combat-stress casualties. Early in the war, those in the British and
Canadian armies who could not cope with the mental strain of combat
were categorized as suffering from hysteria, a disease believed to be
caused by a lack of willpower, laziness, or moral depravity.[20] Later,
many labels were used to describe stress casualties, including "neuropsychiatric disabilities," "neurosis," and "shell shock." However,
many commanders felt that "the *British* soldier or 'hero' could not
possibly show 'mental' symptoms."[21] And the medical community
engaged in a lively debate over the merits of various diagnostic labels
and treatment regimes. At war's end, however, this situation was not
resolved satisfactorily, and the lack of consensus among medical
personnel and policy makers was reflected by official use of the term
"Not Yet Diagnosed – Nervous" (NYDN) among Commonwealth
forces, from about 1917 until at least the middle of the Second World
War.[22] One thing was clear enough to those on the line: fundamental
assumptions about the infantryman's life in combat had to be seriously revised.

S.L.A. Marshall, the keen journalist, seemed not to notice any of
these developments. In *Men Against Fire*, Marshall's soldier was,

above all else, a *constant* soldier. The trials of combat challenged him only once: the moment when he was first required to fire his weapon. If he was a properly trained and disciplined soldier, if he was a functioning member of a primary group, and if he was properly officered, he might triumph over his civilian weakness. He passed his baptism of fire and used his weapon, or he did not. Marshall's soldier then attained a state of soldierly grace and functioned effectively thereafter.

The picture that field reports across the Allied armies painted was not merely at variance with the vision of the soldier as depicted by Marshall, it flatly contradicted it. The picture from the field was one of unremitting physical and psychological turbulence. In contrast to Marshall's constant soldier, real infantrymen were in a race against destruction and dysfunction. In this picture, fear was ever-present on the battlefield and nothing could assuage it – and fear itself was dynamic, intensifying or relaxing often without reference to the severity of combat action.[23] This picture revealed that the psychological strain of living in fear over time ultimately led to psychological crisis, and that this crisis could be the result of an accumulation of traumatic events over time rather than a single dramatic event. That the primary group upon which Marshall counted as the bedrock of psychological solidarity and soldierly endurance could just as easily work as a source of stress, as the primary group was vulnerable to attrition as well; and that surviving soldiers were beset by an ever-greater sense of isolation. And that, in the end, there was no such thing as "getting used to combat." The US Army found in the Second World War that after thirty-five days of sustained combat, 98 per cent of soldiers exhibited "adverse psychiatric symptoms." It was concluded that given enough stress, virtually anyone would suffer a breakdown.[24]

What is most remarkable, given Marshall's time in the field, is how little he understood about the realities of combat. For much of the war he travelled in important company, observing the infantry at work and associating with battle-wise commanders in the Pacific and in Europe in the months after D-Day. Yet he seemed oblivious to the life of the fighting soldier, which, every day on the line, challenged his simplistic view of the complexities of combat.

Marshall claimed proudly that the "ratio of fire" was his discovery and his alone. He wrote that he had not done research, nor had he consulted with his colleagues or with any of the line commanders whose paths he crossed during the war. His encounters with professional historians in the field appear to have made little impact on either party.[25] (Marshall was mimicking a common theme in military doctrine at the time, as articulated in 1900, for example, by Colonel Ferdinand Foch (later Marshal of France) in lectures at the French École de Guerre: "Fire is the supreme argument ... The superiority of fire becomes the most important element of an infantry's fighting value."[26]) Armed with his personal military experience and the results of his claimed 600 interviews – it would have been physically impossible, incidentally, for him to carry out as many interviews as he claimed, as doing so would have taken him well into 1947[27] – Marshall insisted that there was no need to inquire further.

There are good reasons to suspect, if not definitively prove, that the source for Marshall's "ratio of fire" was not the battlefields of the Second World War at all, but the killing grounds of the mid-nineteenth century. A French army officer, Colonel Charles Ardant du Picq, had fought in Crimea, Syria, and Algeria before being killed, in 1870, commanding the Tenth Regiment of the Line at the Battle of Mars-la-Tour during the Franco-Prussian War.[28] Prior to his death, he penned *Études sur le combat*, a truly innovative and original study of war from the soldier's perspective. Du Picq's work had been seminal to French military thought between 1870 and 1914, permeating the army and providing the intellectual inspiration for the ascendant *offensive à outrance* (excessive offensive) that gripped the French.[29] The US Army commissioned the translation into English of du Picq's work in 1921 under the title *Battle Studies*, and during the interwar period the book was well known among American military professionals (a new translation, by this chapter's primary author, was published in 2017). This work was likely where Marshall's inspiration for the "ratio of fire" came from. In his general discussion on modern battle, du Picq wrote: "At a distance, numbers of troops without cohesion may be impressive, but close up they are reduced to fifty or twenty-five per cent who really fight" (the original French makes it clearer that du Picq is making general estimates).[30] But du Picq was a seasoned professional who had seen the worst war had to offer, and in his book he denounced any attempt to reduce what he called "the essential question" – i.e., the human question – of war down to mathematics. He knew perfectly well that the soldier's combat performance could not be reduced to simplistic formulae.

That, however, was only of several coincidences between *Men Against Fire* and *Études sur le combat*. Reading the two books side-by-side is like listening to music in an echo chamber. Almost every important observation Marshall made in his book was anticipated by du Picq. There were so many coincidences that in 1969, the historian Stephen Ambrose wrote to Marshall, inquiring that, as there were so many similarities, would Marshall consider du Picq his inspiration? Marshall curtly replied that he had not read du Picq before writing *Men Against Fire*, forgetting that he quotes du Picq by name in his book, on page 154. Earlier in the text, however, where Marshall expounds on his "ratio of fire," du Picq's name is nowhere to be seen.

In a personal conversation with the primary author of this chapter in the late 1980s, the military historian Martin Blumenson, who had worked in that capacity under Marshall in the European theatre of operations during the war, said that Marshall "could never leave a fact alone." That proved to be an understatement. There are many instances in which Marshall had played with the truth, sometimes cleverly and with effect, sometimes for no reason at all except to show himself in the best possible light. The catalogue of his prevarications is lengthy and depressing. Marshall frequently spoke of his First World War experience, claiming to be the youngest commissioned officer in the American Expeditionary Force.[31] Research by his own grandson, who sought to verify this claim and others – including stories about being in the trenches on 11 November 1918 – showed them to be quite false.[32] Perhaps worst of all, Marshall's claim to have gathered systematic, scientific data is verifiably untrue.

The 1989 RUSI *Journal* essay, which opened the floodgates of criticism on Marshall, was intended to warn historians and soldiers not to accept the man's work so uncritically. Inevitably, Marshall's supporters rose to his defence. None of his prevarications made any difference, they said. Marshall had intuitively and brilliantly deduced a profound truth about modern combat. All the rest was mere pedantry. Even today, it is not difficult to find those across academia, the military, and the popular media who write in Marshall's defence or cite his "ratio of fire" as authoritative. For example, one of Marshall's most prominent acolytes, Dave Grossman, imitates Marshall's methodology in his work.[33] Rather than engage in an evidence-based debate when challenged, he refers to existing and supposedly "authoritative" texts that support his conclusions and suggests that since Marshall is dead, his work is beyond criticism.[34]

We, however, are not among those who agree that he is beyond reproach. Marshall went about his work oblivious to the responsibility that the discipline of military history imposes on those who practice it. In this discipline, the connection between evidence, thought, and action can be direct and mortal. There is just the chance that someone may risk their life, or that of another, because of something we have written or said, some insight they have taken from our work that can be applied in battle. Such a responsibility does not much trouble the sleep of the Renaissance or literary historian. But as this present volume shows, scholarship and practice are closely entwined in military affairs, and the stakes are much higher. Marshall, with his penchant for self-promotion, never took this responsibility seriously. But all the authors of this essay have, over the years, engaged with colleagues and professionals who took Marshall at his word, and took him very seriously at that.

Fortunately, the state of knowledge about the psychodynamics of combat has advanced considerably since Marshall wrote, thanks to the work of a new generation of scholars, many of whom are represented in this present volume. We may, finally, have escaped the grip of the paradigm that Marshall has imposed upon this subject for so long.

NOTES

1 S.L.A. Marshall, *Men Against Fire: The Problem of Battle Command in Future War* (1947; Gloucester, MA: Peter Smith, 1978).

2 Roger J. Spiller, "S.L.A. Marshall and the Ratio of Fire," *Journal of the Royal United Services Institute* 133, no. 4 (December 1988): 63–71.

3 Michael Howard, "Men Against Fire: The Doctrine of the Offensive in 1914," in *Makers of Modern Strategy*, ed. Peter Paret (Princeton: Princeton University Press, 1986), 513–14, 519.

4 Robert A. Doughty, *Pyrrhic Victory: French Strategy and Operations in the Great War* (Cambridge, MS: Belknap Press, 2005), 25–6; Ardant du Picq, *Battle Studies*, trans. Roger J. Spiller (1880; Lawrence, KS: University Press of Kansas, 2017), xiii–xlix.

5 Quoted in: Tim Travers, *The Killing Ground: The British Army, the Western Front, and the Emergence of Modern Warfare, 1900–1918* (Boston: Allen and Unwin, 1987), 40.

6 George C. Marshall, "Rejections of Inductees for Military Service for Reasons Relating to Psychoneurotics," *Neuropsychiatry in World War II* (Washington, DC: Department of the Army, 1946), 133.

7 W.R. Chamberlain, "Training the Functional Rifleman," *Canadian Army Journal* 4, no. 9 (February 1951): 26.

8 Roger J. Spiller, "Shellshock," *American Heritage* 41, no. 4 (May-June 1990): 74–86. The essay is also available at: https://www.american heritage.com/shellshock.

9 Kellen Kurschinski, "State, Service, and Survival: Canada's Great War Disabled, 1914–1944," (PhD diss., McMaster University, 2014), 415.

10 Desmond Morton, "Military Medicine and State Medicine: Historical Notes on the Canadian Army Medical Corps in the First World War 1914–1919," in *Canadian Health Care and the State*, ed. David C. Naylor (Montreal: McGill-Queen's University Press, 1992), 38–66; and Desmond Morton, *A Military History of Canada*, 3rd ed. (Toronto: McClelland and Stewart, 1992), 167.

11 Canada, Department of National Defence, "Physical Standards and Instructions for the Medical Examination of Serving Soldiers and Recruits for the Canadian Army," Canadian Army Headquarters, Ottawa, 1943, 103–9.

12 Andrew Scull, "Contested Jurisdictions: Psychiatry, Psychoanalysis, and Clinical Psychology in the United States, 1940–2010," *Medical History* 55, no. 3 (July 2011): 401–6.

13 Gerald N. Grob, *Mental Illness and American Society 1875–1940* (Princeton, NJ: Princeton University Press, 1983), 270, 283, 285.

14 Emanuel Miller, preface to *The Neuroses in War*, ed. Emanuel Miller (New York: Macmillan, 1940), vii.

15 P.S. Madigan, "Military Psychiatry," *Army Medical Bullet* 56 (April 1941): 61–9.

16 Neither the Americans nor the British (who really should have known better) made sufficient plans for handling psychiatric cases during TORCH. See: Ben Shephard, *A War of Nerves: Soldiers and Psychiatrists in the Twentieth Century* (Cambridge: Harvard University Press, 2003), 210–11.

17 Richard A. Gabriel, *Military Psychiatry: A Comparative Perspective* (New York: Greenwood Press, 1986), 34.

18 W.R. Feasby, *Official History of the Canadian Medical Services 1939–1945: Volume Two, Clinical Subjects* (Ottawa: Edmond Cloutier, 1953), 416–17.

19 Roy Richard Grinker and John Paul Spiegel, *War Neuroses in North Africa: The Tunisian Campaign, January to May, 1943* (New York: Air Surgeon, Army Air Forces, 1943).

20 Michael J. Clark, "The Rejection of Psychological Approaches to Mental Disorder in Late Nineteenth-Century British Psychiatry," in *Madhouses,*

Mad-Doctors, and Madmen, ed. Andrew Scull (London: Athlone, 1981), 293–7.

21 Robert H. Ahrenfeldt, *Psychiatry in the British Army in the Second World War* (London: Routledge and Kegan Paul, 1958), 6. Emphasis in original.

22 Terry Copp and Mark Humphries, *Combat Stress in the 20th Century: The Commonwealth Perspective* (Kingston, ON: Canadian Defence Academy Press, 2010), 14–15, 126n, 129.

23 British operational research studies from the fighting in North Africa in 1942, which involved interviewing some 300 wounded men on the moral effects of the weapons used against them, found no obvious correlation between the tendency of soldiers to fear a weapon and the likelihood of being wounded by it. Army Operational Research Group, "The Moral Effect of Weapons," 1943, Laurier Centre for Military, Strategic and Disarmament Studies Archive, RG 1, File 00023. Echoes of this phenomenon can be seen in Canadian battle experience questionnaires filled out during the war.

24 Richard Gabriel, *No More Heroes: Madness and Psychiatry in War* (New York: Hill and Wang, 1987), 121.

25 Tim Cook mentions a meeting between Canadian official historian C.P. Stacey and S.L.A. Marshall in northwestern Europe. See: Tim Cook, *Clio's Warriors: Canadian Historians and the Writing of the World Wars* (Vancouver: UBC Press, 2006), 110–11.

26 Quoted in Howard, "Men Against Fire," 512.

27 Roger Spiller, "S.L.A. Marshall and the Ratio of Fire," *RUSI Journal* 133 (1988): 68.

28 Geoffrey Warwo, *The Franco-Prussian War: The German Conquest of France in 1870–71* (New York: Cambridge University Press, 2003), 154.

29 Doughty, *Pyrrhic Victory*, 25–6.

30 Ardant du Picq, *Battle Studies: Ancient and Modern*, trans. John Greely and Robert Cotton (Harrisburg, PA: The Military Service Publishing Company, 1947), 132. In the original French: "… *et les troupes sans cohésion font nombre de loin, c'est quelque chose, mais, de près, se réduisent à moitié, au quart, comme combattants réels.*" Ardant du Picq, *Études sur le combat: Combat antique et combat modern* (Paris: Éditions Champ Libre, 1978), 82–3.

31 S.L.A. Marshall, *Bringing Up the Rear: A Memoir* (San Rafael, CA: Presidio Press, 1979), 15.

32 John Marshall, *Reconciliation Road: A Family Odyssey of War and Honor* (Syracuse: Syracuse University Press, 1993), 53, 69.

33 Robert Engen, "Killing for their Country: A New Look at 'Killology,'" *Canadian Military Journal* 9, no. 2 (Summer 2008).

34 Dave Grossman, "S.L.A. Marshall Revisited ... ?", *Canadian Military Journal* 9, no. 4 [2008–09].

3

Different Language, Common Intent: Mutual Understanding between Poles and Canadians, 1944

Robert Williams

I was working late one night when a Polish officer reported to me at the International Security Assistance Force (ISAF) headquarters in Kabul. "Good evening," he said in accented English. I welcomed him and asked, in English, how he was. "Good evening," he replied. After several more questions in English went nowhere, it became clear to me that his knowledge of English (or comfort in using it) was very limited, so I switched to Polish. He and I communicated primarily in Polish for the rest of our time serving together. The problem? It was only purest (and fortuitous) coincidence that I happen to speak Polish; the major had not been assigned to me because someone in authority was aware of my language knowledge. It could just as easily have been a language impasse, which is certainly not the way for a coalition to communicate and operate effectively. My personal experience with the Poles in Afghanistan indicated that insufficient effort had been devoted to the issue of the language barrier. However, as Canada is presently contributing to and commanding a Latvia-based multinational battle group that includes Polish soldiers, the issue continues to demand attention.[1]

War is chaotic and confusion prevails despite the leaders' best-laid plans. The participants are often tired, rarely fully informed as to enemy intentions, and forced to make difficult choices, as a result of successes and failures, in order to maintain momentum or operational tempo. In the confusion that prevails, time and resources are rarely in adequate supply. If, into this mixture of competing factors, is added the additional complicating factors of strangers from different cultural backgrounds who are unfamiliar with the primary operating language of their superior headquarters and neighbouring allies, clear communication of operational intent and reporting of combat results becomes a challenge. It may border upon impossibility. Mistakes will happen as a result of misunderstandings; therefore, additional attention must be paid to minimize how linguistic and cultural differences can negatively affect communications. This paper will argue that the decision of where to deploy linguistically diverse coalition partners must not be left to chance, but should be treated as a vital part of interoperability and motivation. Informed decisions about linguistic diversity, taken after consideration and analysis of language and culture criteria, do not guarantee operational success, but will certainly assist in the more effective conduct of coalition operations. The question of basic mutual understanding is a facet of the human dimension of warfare that rarely gets the attention it requires given the complexity and heterogeneity of modern coalition operations.

My experience in Afghanistan paralleled a major problem from Canadian history and underscored how little things have changed since an earlier occasion, decades ago, when Poles and Canadians served together: the experience of General Stanisław Maczek's 1st Polish Armoured Division under Canadian command in northwest France in 1944–45. I intend to use the case of Canadian-Polish interoperability during the Second World War to demonstrate my broader point about linguistic diversity in coalitions. On 12 April 1945, soldiers of Maczek's 1st Polish Armoured Division, advancing eastward from the Netherlands into Germany after a long fight against a determined German enemy, reached Stalag VI-B, a German-run prisoner-of-war (POW) camp at Oberlangen in northern Germany. This camp held 1,728 Polish women – members of the Polish Home Army (Armia Krajowa, or AK) taken captive at the end of the ill-fated Warsaw Uprising in October 1944.[2] It was only after several minutes of misunderstandings that the two groups were finally able to identify one another's national origins and communicate. Here was a major communications challenge, even when both groups spoke the same language and in the event of a non-confrontational meeting, the prison camp guards having fled or surrendered.[3] As this chapter will show, the Oberlangen incident represents only the least of the communications friction experienced by Maczek and the Poles while under Canadian command.

Communications problems dogged the Poles and played an important role in the Northwest Europe theatre of operations. According
to Polish Captain Ted Walewicz, while trying to clarify orders on the
night of 18 August 1944, the unit's French guide misunderstood the
Polish pronunciation of their objective, Chambois: "We were given
the order to secure *Chambois*, but we were led instead to *les Champeux*.
It was unbelievable."[4] Although such a mistake could have occurred
in a Canadian unit, it would have been less likely. It would also have
been quicker for a native English speaker to have rechecked geographical coordinates if there was any confusion. As it turned out, the Poles
ended up penetrating well behind enemy lines, where they came upon
the headquarters of the German 2nd s s Panzer Division, even as the
2nd Polish Armoured Regiment commanded by Colonel Stanisław
Koszutski also arrived, unintentionally and fortuitously, in Champeux.
"The unexpected arrival of the Polish tanks in Champeux," as one
historian's account tells it, "threw the Germans into such confusion
that their counter-attack was delayed for forty-eight hours allowing
time for the British and Canadians to bring sufficient force forward
to meet the counter-attack."[5] This misunderstanding could well have
had disastrous results for the Polish 2nd Armoured Regiment – either
its loss by capture or death – as it unexpectedly faced overwhelming
enemy numbers at night. In the ensuing firefight the Poles captured
the command post, but trusting to such good fortune is not an operational method.

THEORY

How does one establish and ensure that common intent is understood
within a military coalition when communications difficulties are
exacerbated by language and culture? When building an international,
multilingual coalition, the challenges that military leaders and their
staffs face require greater effort to overcome than would be the case
in a unilingual, monocultural force. The operational goal in any coalition should be to maximize the potential to have additional allied
military personnel and equipment ready to use, when and where
required. Military commanders are needed who are comfortable in
the cultures involved, understand the importance of a culture's unique
characteristics, and are aware of how cultural differences can alter
perceptions.[6] The importance of cultural understanding cannot and

should not be overlooked by alliances in the building and deployment of coalition military forces.

Ross Pigeau and Carol McCann's essay "Establishing Common Intent: The Key to Coordinated Action" provides a perspective and precise phraseology that form a common thread throughout this chapter. According to Pigeau-McCann, "the concept of intent includes an explicit portion that contains the stated objective (as well as all of its elaborations) and an implicit portion that remains unexpressed for reasons of expediency but nonetheless is assumed to be understood."[7] The three factors they describe as influencing a commander's balance between explicit and implicit intent – knowledge, reasoning ability, and commitment – are themes employed throughout the narrative.[8] These terms need to be briefly unpacked to demonstrate their relevance to a study of Maczek's division.

The first of Pigeau and McCann's factors for establishing common intent is *shared knowledge*. In essence, if a commander is not confident that his explicit intent has been understood – i.e., if he is not confident that his subordinates have understood what he wants them to do – then he must take the time to explain his intent more fully. If a commander is not confident, however, that his subordinates share even the same principles for acceptable behaviour, this task will prove to be much more difficult.[9] Although he was able to receive, understand, and then discuss the plans he received from his superior, Maczek admitted that his lack of competency in English was a limiting factor.[10] How might his lack of English have limited him in understanding his commander's intent? How might having to work through interpreters have inhibited his complete understanding of orders and his ability to respond as to his readiness to carry them out? Despite commanding an untried unit – the 1st Polish Armoured Division was seeing only its first combat operations – Maczek had prior combat experience as a commander in both Poland (1939) and France (1940), and knew what he had to do to motivate his soldiers. On the subject of motivating troops, II Canadian Corps Commander Lieutenant-General G.G. Simonds saw, as McGilvray puts it, that "the Poles were different to the Canadian and British soldiers under his command and realized that they could not be controlled in the same ways he controlled British and Canadian troops."[11] Below, I describe how this difference in military cultures would have affected the communication of common intent and made it more difficult.

The second common intent factor is *comparable reasoning ability*. According to Pigeau and McCann, "shared knowledge of the commander's objective as well as shared knowledge of the acceptable solution space, is not sufficient for coordinated action."[12] The commander must also be aware of the reasoning abilities that exist among the diverse members in his coalition, and what he must do to accommodate them. Simonds had access to Signals Intelligence (SIGINT) ULTRA information, but Maczek did not.[13] It was unique for an Allied corps commander, let alone the members of his staff, to have enjoyed such access, since dissemination of ULTRA intelligence to the First Canadian Army and below was very restricted.[14] According to General Harold Alexander, serving in Tunisia in 1943, on the subject of ULTRA intercepts: "The knowledge not only of the enemy's precise strength and disposition but also how, when and where he intends to carry out his operations has brought a new dimension into the prosecution of the war."[15]

The last of the three common intent factors is *shared commitment and motivation*. "How much effort," ask Pigeau and McCann, "must a commander expend towards maximizing the motivation and level of commitment of his subordinates?"[16] A commander should endeavour to motivate his subordinates as he explains his intent. This is essential when soldiers are tired or hungry, and particularly when they have experienced defeat and seen comrades killed or wounded. A sense of hopelessness or despondency can result in only grudging acceptance of a task, or worse. Conveying one's intent is not simply explaining a concept of operations or a plan; it is the best opportunity to motivate and invigorate – or, depending on audience and conditions, to reinvigorate – subordinates and allies. This effort is essential to ensuring that all the members of a coalition or alliance are equally committed to working together and supporting one another in the achievement of common objective. Language and shared intent are therefore fundamental to combat motivation.

Work on this important subject is not limited to Pigeau and McCann. Recent military contributions include the US Marine Corps' *Operational Culture for the Warfighter: Principles and Applications*, a planning tool and aid for the soldier produced by the American military to explain why so-called "foundational features of culture" challenge military operations in various cultural settings.[17] Intended as a practical handbook for the US Marines, *Operational Culture for the Warfighter* was intended to fill a gap in professional military education (PME) identified (or rediscovered) during the Iraq and Afghanistan deployments post-2001. University of Kansas Professor Adrian R. Lewis has described it as, "an effort to get Marines and service members to think critically and comprehensively about the cultural aspects of American military operations in foreign countries in order to facilitate mission accomplishment."[18] Identifying key points and offering suggestions, *Operational Culture for the Warfighter* is written for soldiers to help them think about how best to address cultural issues before they are immersed in operations where unaddressed or misunderstood cultural issues are affecting military operations.

THE POLES IN NORTHWEST EUROPE, 1944

In the early stages of the Second World War, prior to the placement of Maczek's 1st Polish Armoured Division under First Canadian Army command in the summer of 1944, Polish military personnel had been under the command of the Free French and British armies in different theatres of operations. These Polish soldiers were part of various reformed, remnant, or newly created military formations and units assembled in the aftermath of the September 1939 German invasion of Poland. The military cooperation and voluntary subordination of Polish Army units began under the French Army in 1939, was followed by the Poles' control by the British Army in the Middle East from 1941 to 1943 and in Italy in 1944, and eventually led to the subordination of the 1st Polish Armoured Division under the British and Canadian armies in northwestern Europe in 1944 and 1945. The Poles were some of the most battle-experienced and highly motivated troops in any formation they belonged to, but rarely shared anything linguistically or culturally with those under whose command they operated.

The 1st Polish Armoured Division was formed, trained, and put through its paces during practical military exercises in the United Kingdom for almost two years prior to embarking for Normandy in late July 1944. To prepare for their deployment as part of the Allied coalition, the Poles were required to operate alongside non-Polish-speaking soldiers, first in training exercises and then in combat conditions. In all these scenarios, rapid communications were essential for success and, in many cases, survival. In early August 1944, the Poles were subordinated for operational purposes to the command of II Canadian Corps, a formation whose lingua franca was English, with British and English-speaking Canadian officers and soldiers making up the bulk of its manpower within the corps headquarters and divisional formations. This subordination had been planned for two years and the Poles were noted as being highly motivated during the training process. During Exercise "Link," held in September 1943, it was observed that "the Commander Polish Armoured Division was not to be deflected from his object, quite rightly continued his advance with the main mass of his division."[19] Prior to 1944, many junior and mid-level Polish army officers in the United Kingdom attended military courses where the language of instruction was English, but were given minimal actual English-language instruction.[20] French had been a more common second language among Poles up to 1939, so the overall level of English fluency, even at high levels, was low. After joining II Canadian Corps in Normandy, the Poles also had to adapt to Canadian jargon and the widespread use of acronyms. To make matters worse, Canadians and Poles had been given no opportunity to train together prior to the 1st Polish Armoured Division's placement under Canadian command.[21]

Further exacerbating these language barriers were cultural misunderstandings between the Poles and their English-speaking allies. Were these a result of impatience, ignorance, or xenophobia – i.e., the *shared knowledge* factor? Prior to the Second World War, the Polish military had cooperated extensively with the French Army, but not at all with the British Army. Pigeau and McCann's *comparable reasoning* factor can be seen here. The Poles' hatred of both Russia and Germany, the unique Polish method of waging war, and Polish pride (perhaps construed as arrogance) were all subjects whose study would have allowed the British and the Canadians to better understand the *comparable reasoning* and *motivation* of their Polish allies. Instead, they remained strangers. Canadian and British soldiers were to discover on the ground that the Poles had quite different temperaments and ways of doing things, but had not been prepared for this beforehand. The Poles, in their enthusiasm to defeat the Germans, could and did get out of step with neighbouring Allied formations, causing serious exposure of the resulting unprotected flanks. They also used up ammunition and fuel at such a rate that the Allied logistical system was unable to cope with the resultant resupply requirements.[22] The Polish Army recognized that its soldiers fought for Poland and, as such, spiritual succor was part of the Polish forces' philosophy. The importance of this spiritual dimension was amplified by the fact that the Poles were far from home, participating in combat, and facing an uncertain future (i.e., the fate of postwar Poland and their return to it). Although the Canadian and British armies had military chaplains who played a spiritual role in their respective militaries, the central importance of padres in the Polish units was never fully understood by them. Simply put, the Poles had no time to get to know their Anglo-Canadian peers (or vice versa) during the North West Europe Campaign in August 1944.

Maczek's challenge as commander of the 1st Polish Armoured Division was to ensure that he understood II Canadian Corps Commander Simonds's intent, so that he could translate his superior's direction into clear orders that his own officers and soldiers could understand and implement. This understanding would have been complicated further by the expectation, often implicit, of how to exploit operational successes and react when unable to achieve on time (or at all) the objectives assigned by his superior commander. Though multilingual and experienced in working in a second language, Maczek possessed only limited ability in English. Moreover, prior to operations in August 1944, and though he possessed some knowledge of French from his school days, Simonds had no experience commanding non-English-speaking allies.

The familiarity of commanders and staffs with their subordinates, and with one another, when combined with joint training, are vital for building effective working relationships. Unfortunately, because the 1st Polish Armoured Division joined II Canadian Corps only on 5 August 1944, just prior to the beginning of Operation Totalize, there was no time for Polish units to practice communications with their neighbouring Canadian peers, the units of Major-General George Kitching's 4th Canadian Armoured Division. The soldiers in these two divisions had never exercised together and had only met just prior to joining battle. Neither formation understood how their new allies operated. The two division commanders did not know each other; Simonds knew Kitching, but neither of them knew Maczek. Strangers may be able to work together effectively in a high-pressure combat situation (see Robert Engen's chapter in this volume), but when those strangers do not fully understand superior direction and are unable to communicate with their allies with ease, or at all, success is unlikely. Individual motivation is not sufficient without shared intent. Additionally, Kitching, who lacked armoured experience, had not exercised his forces as a whole prior to battle, so the Canadians and Poles went into battle as untried armoured divisions.[23] Thus, these two mutually supporting Allied armoured divisions, with different primary languages and an ability to communicate with one another that was limited at best, entered combat together as strangers.

Given that there had been only three days (5–8 August 1944) between the formal subordination of the 1st Polish Armoured Division under II Canadian Corps and their deployment in Operation Totalize, how clear, really, could the commander's intent have been made to the Polish soldier on the ground? Simonds's orders received by Divisional Commander Maczek would have to be translated into Polish, and tasks then assigned to subordinate brigades who would assign them in turn to the subordinate battalions, and then the companies. All of this staff work requires energy, accuracy, and time to coordinate. Translation of orders would have provided the literal – i.e., explicit – intent, provided they were rendered accurately (recall Chambois/Champeux). Inferred intent, on the other hand, would have been less clear or, in the worst case, lost entirely. While these battle procedures were being conducted, there would have been operational changes coming down from II Canadian Corps headquarters as a result of the dynamic situation on the battlefield. These amendments to orders also needed to be understood and communicated to subordinate units. More importantly, units would have to prepare for the upcoming combat and move to the location of the battle. Given the combined effects of the stress of combat, the constant flow of orders, and the effect of the terrain on radio communications, it should come as no surprise that mistakes were made. These geographical conditions, exacerbated by different languages, neighbouring units who were strangers to one another, and the fact that it was the 1st Polish Armoured Division's first time in combat as a formation, made a difficult situation untenable.

To summarize their performance during Operation Totalize, both of the untried armoured divisions (4th Canadian and 1st Polish) encountered heavy opposition, made limited progress, and were consequently unable to complete their assigned roles in the operation's second phase: "The failure of the armoured divisions (in their first major engagement) to get forward rapidly on the afternoon of the 8th of August (1944) had given the enemy time to bring back elements of the SS formations to strengthen his defences in the rear." By 11 August, the Allied offensive had ground to a halt.[24] Maczek may not have been the only commander with whom Simonds had difficulty communicating shared intent: Major-General Kitching, of the 4th Canadian Armoured Division, was sacked, perhaps unjustly, at the end of the campaign.[25]

LESSONS

Despite the passage of more than seventy years since Operation Totalize, useful lessons may still be learned from the 1st Polish Armoured Division's experiences while under Canadian command. The situation in Canada during the Second World War was not as it is today, in a country that espouses multiculturalism as opposed to cultural assimilation. The challenges, sometimes competing ones, in multinational operations consist of understanding both one's allies and the cultural environment in which one is to conduct military or humanitarian relief operations. According to Allan English, "establishing common intent can be one of the greatest challenges in joint and integrated operations where the differences in national and organizational cultures are frequently barriers to its creation."[26] The relevant question for today is: what takes priority when it comes to allocating a commander's scarce resources? Communicating common intent is not easy at the best of times. In the words of US General Stanley McChrystal: "A leader must constantly restate any message he feels is important, and do so in the clearest possible terms. It serves to inform new members and remind veterans."[27] Even when there is a common language of operation, unstated nuances and implied inferences may be missed without sufficient attention being paid to overcoming linguistic and cultural barriers. Identification of such barriers between coalition allies should be undertaken early in the planning process, prior to the beginning of operations. As much time as possible should be devoted to efforts aimed at reducing or eliminating the barriers of language or culture. Such efforts may include the identification of qualified liaison personnel, specific language training, and the translation and practice of existing operational procedures. Time spent on these efforts is never wasted when it comes to creating the bedrock for coalition operations. On the battlefield, commanders cannot always be physically present or available via radio or telephone to confirm or reconfirm what they require of their subordinate commanders. To that end, the clarity of the commander's intent should be ensured at every possible opportunity. Barriers that prevent or hinder this understanding, such as differences of language and cultural background, need to be overcome as far in advance as possible, and well before the chaos of active operations renders them insurmountable. How to achieve this goal, and how much effort must be applied toward it, remain command decisions – and, as such, may be informed by the lessons of history.

Pairing forces from nations that can already communicate with one another via a common language, or have previous experience working together in training or operations, are important options to consider in partner selection and deployment, particularly when time for coalition building is unavailable or limited. Commanders can aid in communicating implicit intent by creating opportunities to increase familiarity, promote mutual understanding, and build trust. Comprehensive joint training exercises and familiarity-building events need to be planned and executed. Operational training must not be ignored, either intentionally or inadvertently, as is too often the case; and must consist of more than ad hoc events with lessons identified in training incorporated into standard operating procedures. Coalition partners meeting for the first time while deployed on operations should be the exception, not the norm. As much effort as possible should be applied toward reducing the barriers to working with strangers. In retrospect, more effort should have been devoted to reducing the language barrier that the Poles of Maczek's division encountered under Allied command in the period prior to their first deployment in the Normandy campaign. Had this been achieved, the Polish and Canadian armoured divisions might have met with greater success during Operation Totalize.

NOTES

1 Lee Berthiaume, "Canadian-led NATO force in Latvia taking shape," *Toronto Star*, 17 September 2016.
2 Róza Bednorz, *Jeńcy Wojenni w Niewoli Wehrmacht* (Opole: Centralne Muzeum Jeńców Wojennych w Łambinowicach Opolu, 1985), 41.
3 Library and Archives Canada (hereafter LAC) RG-24-G-3-1-a, vol. 10942, file 245 P1.013 (D5), HQ 4 Liaison HQ SITREP 131131B APR 1945, 13 April 1945. The summary in the operations log for the unit was somewhat less than emotional when it factually stated that "elements of 2 Polish Armoured Regiment freed a camp of approx. 1,700 Polish

women in area 6173 providing protection for the camp and taking about 30 guards PW."

4 W. Denis Whitaker, *Victory at Falaise: The Soldiers' Story* (Toronto: HarperCollins, 2000), 216.

5 Henry Maule, *Caen: The Brutal Battle and Breakout from Normandy* (Trowridge, Wiltshire, UK: David and Charles, 1988), 162.

6 James C. Bradford, *The Military and Conflict between Cultures: Soldiers at the Interface* (College Station: Texas A&M Press, 1997), 231–2.

7 Ross Pigeau and Carol McCann, "Establishing Common Intent: The Key to Co-ordinated Military Action," in *Leadership and Command: The Operational Art*, ed. Allan English (Kingston, ON: Canadian Defence Academy Press, 2006), 91.

8 Ibid., 97.

9 Ibid.

10 Piotr Potomski, *Generał broni Stanisław Władysław Maczek* (Warsaw: Wydawnictwo Uniwersytetu Warszawskiego, 2008), 208.

11 Evan McGilvray, *The Black Devils' March – A Doomed Odyssey: The 1st Polish Armoured Division 1939–45* (Trowbridge, Wiltshire, UK: Helion, 2005), 15.

12 Pigeau and McCann, "Establishing Common Intent," 98.

13 Frederick W. Winterbottom, *The Ultra Secret* (Toronto: Harper and Row, 1974), 124. General Simonds was put in the picture at General Crerar's request. He was an enthusiastic ULTRA customer.

14 First Canadian Army recipients of ULTRA intelligence: LGen H.D.G. Crerar, GOC; LGen G.G. Simonds, GOC; Brig C.C. Mann, COS; Col G.E. Beament, CIGS; LCol W.B.T. Reynolds, GSO 1 Air; LCol E.D. Danby, GSO 1 Ops; LCol McDougall, GSO (1B); LCol P. Wright, GSO 1; Maj J.A. Apis, GSO 2. G2 SHAEF Internal Memo, "List of Recipients of Ultra," Richard Collins Papers (G2 SHAEF), August 1944, US Army Military History Institute (hereafter MHI), Carlisle, PA. Also: "Reports by US Army ULTRA Representatives with Field Army Commands in the European Theatre of operations 1945," SRH-023, MHI. Quoted from Roman Jarymowycz, "Canadian Armour in Normandy: Operation Totalize and the Quest for Operational Manouevre," *Canadian Military History* 7, no. 2 (1998): 36.

15 Winterbottom, *The Ultra Secret*, 187.

16 Pigeau and McCann, "Establishing Common Intent," 100.

17 Barak A. Salmoni and Paula Holmes-Eber, *Operational Culture for the Warfighter: Principles and Applications* (Quantico, VA: Marine Corps University Press, 2011).

18 Ibid., inside cover promo blurb.

19 Eastern Command, "Exercise 'Link,' Director's Notes, Part II – Points of
   General Interest Arising from the EXERCISE," undated, p. 6, para. 7(a),
   LAC RG 24, vol. 10, p. 728.

20 Potomski, *Generał broni Stanisław Władysław Maczek*, 219.

21 Robert Williams, "Poles Apart: Language and Cultural Barriers Pertaining
   to the Polish Army's 1st Armoured Division in Normandy, August 1944"
   (PhD diss., Queen's University, 2017), 204.

22 Williams, "Poles Apart," 205.

23 John English, *Failure in High Command: The Canadian Army in the
   Normandy Campaign* (Ottawa: Golden Dog Press, 1995), 185.

24 Williams, "Poles Apart," 224–48.

25 Angelo Caravaggio, "A Re-Evaluation of Generalship: Lieutenant-General
   Guy Simonds and Major-General George Kitching in Normandy 1944,"
   Canadian Military History 11, no. 4 (2002): 5–19.

26 Allan English, ed., *Leadership and Command: The Operational Art*
   (Kingston, ON: Canadian Defence Academy Press, 2006), 230.

27 General Stanley McChrystal, *My Share of the Task: A Memoir* (New York:
   Penguin, 2013), 213.

4

Sexual Violence as Motivation

Claire Cookson-Hills

INTRODUCTION

Rape is an uncomfortable topic for academic study. When it comes to discussing the rape of women by Canadian soldiers in Europe toward the end of the Second World War, the problems and discomforts multiply. This is not a topic that has received any public attention, but it is a pressing one with wide ramifications.

There are many stories about women as the "trophies" of war, both ancient and modern. The Roman rape of the Sabine women is the mythic archetype for present-day occurrences such as the Islamic State of Iraq and the Levant (ISIL) giving its soldiers Yazidi women from their slave markets, or Boko Haram kidnapping Nigerian schoolgirls and forcing them into marriages with their soldiers. The Sabine women became the mothers of Rome and their violation was a military and civil necessity, however unpalatable to contemporary sensibilities. As described in such narratives, women were "stolen," "captured," and used to reward faithful soldiers; their bodies themselves became implements of revenge or the "spoils of war."

Echoes of these narratives are sometimes evident in twenty-first-century Western democracies and the history of the British Empire. United Nations peacekeepers have become embroiled in multiple scandals involving sexual exploitation and rape. In Haiti, revelations of a child-sex ring of Sri Lankan soldiers resulted in 114 of the approximately 900 Sri Lankan peacekeepers being sent home (but not charged).[1] UN peacekeepers, from Burundi and Gabon, operating in the Central African Republic (CAR) have also been investigated for sexual exploitation of children, and twice the UN has outlined policy directives about how its peacekeepers are to proceed in their interactions with civilian populations in war-torn or unstable economic circumstances.[2] Despite the UN banner, Sri Lanka, Burundi, and Gabon have poor human rights records and are not close Canadian allies (although at the time this chapter was written, Sri Lankans and Burundians were serving with Canadian peacekeepers in Mali in the United Nations Multidimensional Integrated Stabilization Mission in Mali, or MINUSMA) and the behaviour of those countries' soldiers does not seem comparable to those of Western democracies.[3] Another example of such attitudes toward women in war contexts took place in 2012, when the Israel Defense Forces' chief rabbi, Eyal Karim, argued publicly that Jewish soldiers "lying with attractive Gentile women against their will" was permitted under Torah law. He argued that rape would "satisfy the evil inclination" of male soldiers when on campaign in a religiously acceptable fashion.[4] In effect, the IDF's top religious authority was arguing for rape to be considered a legitimate form of "sexual comfort" – an outlet for soldiers not unlike the "comfort women" that the Japanese Army provided for its soldiers during the Second World War.[5] The British Empire, too, had a long history of providing prostitutes for military personnel as one of the "necessaries" of overseas service. In the nineteenth century, the British imperial armies organized military brothels as a way of regulating and thus curbing rampant sexually transmitted infections (STIs).[6] In 1885, for example, one Indian Army military surgeon promoted "the comparative respectability and safety [of intercourse] with a recognized registered [prostitute]." By the Second World War, British troops in the Far East were able to obtain "Hong Kong wives," a practice which traded on the desperation and hunger of Chinese refugee families and the old policies of permissible prostitution. It allowed the most attractive women to become the "common-law wives" of British soldiers in exchange for their family being given food and money. Medical and military authorities tacitly supported the "Hong Kong wives" arrangement, viewing an illicit monogamous relationship as much preferable to troops frequenting brothels and putting themselves at risk for venereal disease. When they arrived in 1941, Canadian soldiers were unofficially offered their choice of Chinese women.[7] Historian Philippa Levine argues that by speaking openly of army brothels and prostitution as if the sexual intercourse were consensual, the army obscured the power differential between the soldiers and the prostitutes, and, indeed, the colonizer and colonized.[8] Today, in the judgment of the

International Criminal Court (ICC), these women would have been subject to a "coercive environment," which sees all consent as "irrelevant when that consent is obtained as a male soldier."[9] Historically, and more recently, some of Canada's international partners, close allies, and the United Kingdom (the progenitor of our military traditions) have condoned sexual violence or offered sexual slavery to soldiers to trade in desperate and vulnerable women and children.

The complex issues of consent, sex, and rape in war are inseparable from conquest, power, and authority. Indeed, as mentioned above, there is no line between sex and rape in war according to the ICC. More realistically, in the minds of survivors, perpetrators, witnesses, and society, sex and rape are distinct, even if the distinction can be hazy. This chapter assumes that rape is about one actor asserting (his) power and that sex is about two people sharing pleasure. Although sexual violence occurs against individuals of all genders and ages, this article will focus on sexual violence directed toward women and girls by men; my primary source data concern sexual violence against European women and girls. When the lines between rape and consensual sex are blurry, I will explain how and why.[10] Canadian soldiers of the Second World War are at the heart of this chapter – their beliefs, values, and behaviours. The soldiers named are neither a "few bad apples" (a few individuals committing all the rapes) nor "boys being boys" (rape as unavoidably, stereotypically male behaviour). Even though only a minority of Canadian soldiers raped European women and girls, I argue that the Canadian Army hierarchy did not prevent rape and willfully ignored the suffering of civilian populations – up to a point. Rape was not treated the same in all times and places during the Second World War, and the Canadian Army accepted a certain amount of abusive behaviour toward civilian women as unproblematic. The actions of some Canadian soldiers followed from a specific hypersexualized culture of front-line soldiers, which created the conditions where sexual conquest became a part of troops' combat motivation. This chapter will discuss the rape of European women by Canadian soldiers at the end of the Second World War as an example of the Canadian Army's approach to dealing with rape and what a short "epidemic" of sexual violence against civilian women and girls suggests for the study of the human dimensions of warfare.

Sexual violence is a topic that most scholars of military history find difficult to incorporate, unless it is being discussed in the context of a specific genocidal policy or campaign of humiliation. In Bosnia, to take the best-known instance, the Serbians had a "Ram Plan" – a policy of organized genocidal rape, which used rape as a weapon of terror and the women as vessels for bearing Serbian children.[11] Historian Richard Bessel locates the Soviet army's widespread rape of German women in 1945 as mass revenge against German military crimes in Eastern Europe.[12] Canadian author Anthony Kellett's classic *Combat Motivation* (1982) makes no mention of sex (let alone sexual violence) even as a possible motivating factor for soldiers; rather, he focuses on legal combat motivations in democracies with volunteer militaries.[13] When military historians do discuss sexual violence, or rape, they downplay the prevalence of wartime rape or explain it as the degradation and humiliation of a vanquished (implicitly male) enemy.[14]

Scholars of sexual violence, by contrast, tend to assume that wartime rape is part of what soldiers are "in it" for, and these scholars often outline a complex set of motivations.[15] Jean Bethke-Elshtain argues that sexual violence in combat may stem from explicit policy, a by-product of conquest, or sheer opportunism.[16] Sociologist J. Robert Lilly, in *Taken by Force* (2007), lists nine possible reasons why soldiers might rape – but ultimately concludes that American soldiers in the Second World War mostly acted individually in what he terms "gratuitous rapes."[17] These rapes occurred without "any formal organizational support and [were] … prohibited by civil and military law, both of which provided harsh punishments."[18] Lilly emphasizes the vulnerability of European women, the opportunism of individual soldiers, and the brutalization that the soldiers had undergone since entering combat in June 1944.[19] He speculates that rape in the American army during the Second World War occurred because of "revenge, [social] bonding, and/or enhanced masculinity" associated with military identity, but felt that the documentary evidence was not conclusive.[20] By suggesting that the rapes were unconnected with formal military culture or social structures, Lilly minimizes possible systemic links between combat motivation and sexual violence in modern Western armies. Joanna Bourke, by contrast, argues that military rape may have been partially caused by "total war" – when a blurring of boundaries between home front and battle zone increased the potential for brutality against non-combatants.[21] Bourke asserts that many military cultures tolerated rape and other atrocities, "accepting them as necessary for effective combat performance."[22]

Historians of Western liberal democracies are uncomfortable with discussing why soldiers might rape in wartime. The specifics of why

Canadian soldiers in the Second World War might rape, then, are almost undiscussed in the historiography. Hugh Gordon has discussed sexual violence in Germany in his unpublished 2010 dissertation, and the forthcoming work of David Borys will be the first in-depth treatment of the interactions of Canadian soldiers and civilians in Northwest Europe.[23] In a recent *National Post* article on the anniversary of VE Day, Heidi Matthews documented stories of Canadian soldiers committing sexual violence, based on German records and oral histories, but her emphasis is on narratives of consent and victimization.[24] William John Pratt's 2015 article "Prostitutes and Prophylaxis" discusses the potential for Canadian soldiers raping prostitutes, but his focus is on venereal disease (VD), its treatment, and surveillance of soldiers, not sexual violence.[25] Generally, rapes committed by soldiers of 21 Army Group (and, by extension, the First Canadian Army) have been under-studied. German historian Miriam Gebhardt calls the British (making no distinction for the Canadians) "highly disciplined" and argues that cases of rape were probably isolated; she does not systematically deal with British military rapes.[26]

Other chapters in this volume explore the "will to fight" and the various parameters and histories of motivating soldiers for battle. In this chapter, I discuss an uncomfortable possibility: that combat motivation itself has historical connections to sexual violence, and that we ignore this truth at our peril. The prospect of rape and sexual violence was a meaningful motivator at certain times and places for some vengeful Canadian soldiers. I define combat motivation in the same way as Ian Hope ("will to fight") and Robert Engen ("the process involving a soldier's decision to fight, and to keep fighting") in their respective chapters in this volume. However, I do not accept that examining the "will to fight" need be a narrow study of the combat record. I argue that we cannot accept that a soldier's ability and readiness to fight are divorced from questions of what they are fighting for. Not every soldier fights to achieve sexual conquest, of course; as this volume's introduction suggests, there are no universal truths when it comes to fighting. That said, it is abundantly clear that many soldiers *do* fight or *have* fought, in part or in whole, for sexual spoils: to brutalize and humiliate an enemy, and because the opportunity to do so exists. Historically, some military cultures have embraced sexual violence as necessary for motivating their soldiers. If combat motivation is the will to fight, we must wrestle with some of the more distressing factors that generate that will.

To explain how sexual violence might have informed combat motivation among Canadian soldiers in the Second World War, this chapter will first outline the hypersexualized culture of the Canadian forces, then provide two parallel case studies of conquering Canadians – Sicily in summer 1943 and Germany in spring 1945 – and finally discuss a possible series of explanations for how combat motivation may have been tied up with sexual violence. Overall, a series of conflict-specific and culture-specific reasons fed into Canadian soldiers' exploitation of European women.

HYPERMASCULINITY AND MILITARY CULTURE

In April and May 1945, fifty Canadian soldiers were court martialed for rape, attempted rape, and indecent assault of German women, part of a broader wave of sexual violence by Allied soldiers. This concentration of sexual violence was not unique to the Canadians, nor were they the worst offenders – soldiers of the Soviet Red Army raped many thousands of women during their invasion of Germany in 1945. Richard Bessel contends that at least on the Eastern Front, "taking revenge against Germans was socially acceptable and widely expected."[27] Recent historical research on the final downfall of Nazi Germany suggests that the soldiers from the Western Allied nations had more in common with their Red Army counterparts than we normally presume. Thousands of German women, and some men, were apparently raped in Stuttgart when it was occupied by the French in 1945. While the Canadian Army never permitted or promoted sexual violence by its troops, and never deliberately adopted a policy where rape was used as an instrument of subjugation, there is evidence that the army turned a blind eye to it when it did not serve the military's interests to pursue rapists aggressively. Such organizational behaviour is consistent with the behaviour of other armies' military justice apparatuses in the Second World War.[28] The epidemic of rape in Germany is more visible because the Canadian Army finally used the instruments of military justice to crack down on it, when they had not done so before; there may have been similar levels of rape committed against European civilian women in other theatres of war that have never been made visible.

The parameters of masculinity – and hypermasculinity – in the Canadian Army during the war speak to an important aspect of military culture at the time. In *One of the Boys*, Paul Jackson argues that

Canadian military masculinity was defined as "aggressive, fearless, passionate, [and] indomitable," and that the front-line combat troops were supposed to be the epitome of military masculinity.[29] These ideal masculine qualities were always negotiated, both within the army's hierarchical structure and between soldiers. Aggression and passion were perceived by the army hierarchy as an inseparable part of masculinity, but too much or indiscriminate aggression could pose a threat to discipline and good order, and lead to an encounter with the army's justice system.

Military masculinity was often synonymous with getting, having, and paying for sex. Sexual innuendo formed a crucial part of barrack-room culture and even infiltrated official documents. A "short-arm inspection," for instance, was a V D inspection (as opposed to a rifle, or "long arm" inspection), which reinforced the close connections between a soldier's weapon and his penis.[30] As Jackson has argued, sexual slang formed both the insults that were hurled at other soldiers or (usually more quietly) at officers, and the ways that soldiers used to discuss feeling cheated or ill-used. Phrases like "kiss my ass," "cock-sucker," and "getting screwed/buggered/browned off" formed the day-to-day patois that soldiers used with each other.[31] To take a "golden shower" (slang: urination as sexual foreplay) was to aim a flamethrower on a high arc so that the stream of flame broke up into burning globules which fell straight down on the enemy.[32] To "feel browned off" (anally violated) was so common a metaphor for soldierly discontent that 21 Army Group censors created a "Browned Off" category for classifying the contents of the mail that they were reading through to gauge the morale of combat soldiers.[33] According to a contemporary officer, "fuck" was the most common word in a soldier's vocabulary, used as a noun, adjective, and verb.[34] In one commander's words, "fuck" was the "universal additive and adjective … a lubricant of speech."[35] In an American context, General George Patton allegedly opined that "if a soldier won't fuck, he won't fight," explicitly connecting masculinity to violence and sex.[36] The messages for the other ranks might be sex-positive or sex-negative, but sex surrounded soldiers in Europe.

Sexual contact with civilians was normal and generally outside the realm of military consideration, unless it impaired operational effectiveness. For Brigadier Christopher Vokes, his troops' frequenting prostitutes was explained by their passionate nature: "the young men I had in the brigade were vigorous, in the prime of their lives and their life expectancy, they assumed, was rather brief."[37] Canadian, British, and American soldiers were said to buy dinner first and then take Sicilian civilians to bed, according to official historian Captain A.T. Sesia, "for the most ridiculous considerations" – tinned beef or cigarettes.[38] But dinner in war-torn Europe was not an inconsequential transaction when civilians were left with nothing. Bought sex came from career prostitutes and opportunistic civilians, and issues of consent become murky when applied to populations that had few or no other choices. Vokes made this explicit: "soldiers on campaign live in the constant shadow of death and some of them adopt a philosophy of never missing an opportunity to copulate ... I hesitate to call it love-making."[39] Whether Vokes's hesitation came from issues of violence or consent is not specified.

The predominant military concern came from the VD rates (most commonly syphilis and gonorrhea) which followed sexual contact between uniformed personnel and civilians. Because of the prevalence of VD among European prostitutes, and in the understanding that treatment for VD created disease casualties, sometimes commanders placed brothels or entire towns off-limits to their troops. Other armies regulated brothels: at the controlled brothel in Tripoli, Lebanon, in 1942, 13,500 Australian soldiers recorded 11,955 attendances in twelve weeks. This brothel had military police at the door and a washing station inside.[40] However, in the Italian and Northwest European campaigns, the armies were not allowed to establish and control their own brothels. Although Brigadier Vokes attempted to set up a Canadian army-run brothel in Sicily, this plan was axed before it could be launched.[41] According to Vokes's memoir, the order from British Eighth Army Command was emphatic: "There will be no brothels. No brothels period. No brothels of any kind, opened anywhere in the Eighth Army area."[42] So, although the Canadian Army knew that its soldiers often frequented lower-class women who were not always prostitutes by choice, and that its allies were regulating brothels in other theatres of operations, sex between soldiers and prostitutes was excused with euphemisms about the "friendliness" of the population and the "vigour" of the soldiers.

Eighth Army commanders also had a sense of the complicated transactions at play – for the soldiers and the women – and disease, especially VD, was also a disciplinary problem.[43] After a thorough investigation into poor behaviour on the part of reinforcement troops in Ghent in 1944, Brigadier G.S.N. Gostling, commander of the

2nd Canadian Base Reinforcement Group, wrote, "the men on leave, for a short period, are naturally out for a good time and during that time are not overburdened with a sense of responsibility."[44] One Canadian officer thought that sex was a good indicator of overall health. He quipped, not unlike Patton, that good fighters made good lovers.[45] However, others lamented the fact that soldiers were not being uplifted by their leave, but rather "transport[ed] to an environment which encompasses and in which is heavily concentrated overcrowding, idleness and vice in all its various forms."[46] The Canadian Army's official medical history included a "brief" discussion of prostitution and VD: "despite the most emphatic directives issued at the highest levels, prostitution and the brothel flourished ... the cooperation of the Provost Corps was invaluable in imposing such limitations as were possible."[47] In a darker tone, a medical officer mentioned his fear that soldiers were not approaching the prostitutes with the "gentleness of a lover."[48] The women themselves were often demonized for their perceived low moral standards, character, and hygiene, but commanders realized that European civilians were trading sex for food or money. Complicated transactions surrounding European women and Canadian soldiers meant that the army hierarchy did not entirely discourage (or encourage) sex, a hypersexualized culture, or sexual violence. And when they went into combat, the military justice system did not always act to prosecute sexual violence against civilians.

THE CASE OF SICILY, 1943

The Sicilian campaign (Operation Husky), in which the troops of the 1st Canadian Infantry Division fought Canada's first sustained ground campaign of the Second World War, is an instructive example of sexual violence in wartime. The official historian attached to the expeditionary force headquarters to record the campaign was Captain A.T. Sesia, an unenthusiastic intelligence officer appointed by the GSO1 of the 1st Division against the wishes of the historical section, who described him as "not a writer, much less an historian."[49] Nonetheless, Sesia dutifully trod the island of Sicily, following the 1st Division headquarters, and gathered material for the official historical narrative of Canadian involvement in the campaign. He kept a personal journal as well as his field notes. On 19 July 1943, just over a week into the fighting, Sesia recorded a number of unsettling incidents involving

the Canadians, including drunkenness, the shooting of civilians, looting, and a case of gang rape at Piazza Armerina:

> [Assistant Provost Marshal Norm] Cooper seems to be pretty
> well disgusted with some of our troops who go right off the
> trolley once they have a few drinks in them. He said that at
> PIAZZA ARMERINA two Canadian soldiers entered a house at
> the point of a Tommy-gun and demanded wine and women from
> the man of the house. The frightened man supplied what little
> wine he had but tried to convey to them that he had no women
> for them. His wife, who was pregnant, was cowering with terror
> in a bedroom, but they nevertheless broke in and raped her.[50]

One incident was bad. But in his diary, Sesia also wrote about "seven
more" cases of reported rape during the fighting.[51] His skepticism,
however, quickly surfaced, and several times within the diary Sesia
tried to deny or dismiss the legitimacy of rape claims. First he wrote
that Sicilian prostitutes would make false sexual assault claims if
soldiers refused to pay: "I don't believe that [the stories of rape] are
as serious as they sound ... It is [prostitutes] ... and part-time professionals who are more likely to cry 'rape,' particularly if the troops
they are dealing with are drunk."[52] He also blamed the noxious effects
of the climate, combined with Sicilian wine, and ended by suggesting
that it was the work of a few "bad eggs" in 1st Division. Sesia was
clearly at pains to understand this behaviour on the part of Canadian
troops; he explored four different explanations, but none seemed
entirely satisfactory. No mention of the rapes made it into the official
history of the Canadians in Sicily and Italy.[53]

1st Canadian Infantry Division knew about the extent of the problems, but there does not seem to have been command consensus on
how to deal with it, and different levels of command seem to have
dealt with it differently. On 9 August 1943, the commander of
1st Canadian Division, Major-General G.G. Simonds, authorized the
release of an official circular saying, "the fact that we are operating
in a hostile country in no way diminishes the seriousness of [violent]
offences against the civilian population ... Such offences will NOT be
dealt with by Commanding Officers, but will in every instance be tried
by court martial."[54] His statement, issued during combat operations,
strongly implied that civil offences had earlier been dealt with by
internal unit discipline, without involving the Judge Advocate General

(JAG) branch. As previously mentioned, Vokes tried to set up a brothel, and, failing that, on 17 August (the last day of military operations), he ordered that VD would be dealt with as a disciplinary matter.[55] At the level of the Eighth Army, by contrast, after the fighting was over, troops were ordered to stay away from towns and cities while off-duty.[56] The direct involvement of the JAG, attempted regulation of brothels, and strictly limited contact with civilians were three methods that command employed in their bid to, in Simonds's words, avoid bringing "the Division, the Canadian Army, and our country into disrepute and dishonour."[57] There is, however, little evidence that these methods were effective: very few Canadians were prosecuted for rape charges in Sicily, the VD rate was very high,[58] and commanders eventually ordered off-duty soldiers to stay away from Sicilian towns.

More distressingly, there was almost no follow-up from the military justice apparatus. The Canadian Army only ever prosecuted three soldiers for rape in Sicily, two of them co-defendants in one trial. None of the cases that Sesia mentioned were formally charged with rape or sexual violence.[59] Indeed, the entire Italian campaign, from July 1943 to February 1945 for the Canadians, saw only twenty-two soldiers court-martialled for rape (by contrast, during the same period 102 soldiers were court martialled for drunkenness and 683 charged and found guilty of being absent without leave).[60] In Italy in April 1944, the commander of I Canadian Corps, E.L.M. Burns, reissued Simonds's warning about dealing with violent offences through the JAG, along with a statement that "Canadian soldiers [were] beginning to get a reputation for getting drunk on 'vino' and going from house to house knocking on doors and demanding 'signorinas.'"[61]

What the military authorities chose to prosecute can tell us what their priorities were with regard to maintaining discipline and control. In failing to discipline soldiers for rape, the JAG reinforced what historian Randall Wakelam has called a "culture of tolerated disobedience" – disobedience, that is, to official Army Act regulations prohibiting sexual violence against civilians.[62] The JAG branch's priority in the Italian campaign was maintaining *compliance* with order and ensuring that there was enough manpower for military necessity. Drunkenness and absence without leave were seen as more important disciplinary issues than sexual violence. A "culture of tolerated disobedience" might well have stemmed from a series of bureaucratic decisions: how and where to spend finite JAG time and resources, a need to preserve morale and manpower, and a fundamental disbelief of reported rape cases. J A G resources were especially scarce in Sicily, since during the campaign itself the J A G branch was working at arm's length out of bases in North Africa. The limited availability of transport, time, and resources needed to properly conduct Field General Courts Martial mitigated against reported civil crimes being brought to trial, and the fact that members of an "enemy" population under military occupation were the victims might have made reporting and serious investigation of rape less likely even if those resources were available. When dealing with rape charges, the officers also had to assess whether the soldier and civilian complainant should be sent to North Africa to give evidence in the midst of an ongoing campaign. Additionally, the severity of civil crimes meant that soldiers were more likely to have heavy automatic sentences, which could end their military careers. In the case of the front-line combat troops, commanders were concerned about lowered morale before battle (not to mention the hours lost investigating the crimes and escorting soldiers).

CASE STUDY: GERMANY, CANADIAN SOLDIERS, AND SEXUAL VIOLENCE

When the First Canadian Army entered Germany in 1945, however, official policy changed. The Canadian Army, in compliance with British regulations, strictly enforced a policy of non-association with German civilians for its troops, and put a non-fraternization order into effect. Official non-fraternization meant no communication with German civilians, no billeting with German civilians, and no recreational leave in Germany (troops had to travel to Belgium for leave), although in practice this was not easy to arrange.[63] Merely speaking with German women became a minor fraternization offence, but "associating with" German women and girls was a serious breach of fraternization rules and all reported instances of sexual contact with German women were to be prosecuted. Canadian Army Routine Order 443 noted: "Sexual intercourse is a flagrant breach of the non-fraternization directive and will always be dealt with by courts martial ... [when] intercourse results from fear [of violence] the crime of rape is committed."[64] Legally, the non-fraternization order was enforced with an Army Act charge under Section 40, "conduct to the prejudice of military discipline," which was punishable by imprisonment.[65] Additionally, Canadian soldiers in Germany were not given the opportunity to be ignorant of the order; all soldiers were ordered to read a pamphlet

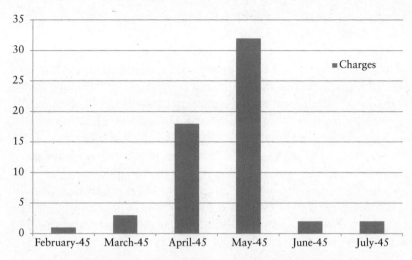

Figure 4.1 Number of rape, attempted rape, and indecent assault courts martial against Canadian soldiers involving German civilians, February–July 1945 (organized by date of incident). This figure documents charges, not convictions.

outlining what non-fraternization entailed, explained that it was forbidden, and then required to sign that they had read and understood. Their signatures were kept in unit records and brought out when charges of fraternization were levelled against individuals.[66]

Because of the non-fraternization order, for the first time, soldiers were prosecuted for sexual violence against German civilians. Figure 4.1 presents a breakdown of the numbers of rape cases in Germany and when these cases occurred. Although fifty-eight Canadians were charged in total, fifty of those courts martial were for accusations in April and May 1945. Most of the charges date from just before VE Day, between 20 April and 10 May, and occurred around the city of Oldenburg, in Lower Saxony – the Canadian area of occupation. [67] According to existing historical accounts, sexual violence perpetrated in Germany by the American and Soviet armies came from predominantly non-combat support troops in the follow-up waves of invasion and occupation.[68] In contrast, over 85 per cent of the Canadian men charged with sexual violence were from combat units (see Figure 4.2). The supporting services were not as far forward during the time period in question, so it stands to reason that the men involved would be primarily from combat units; no definitive causal link can be established here, but the results are worth investigating.

The priority of the Canadian JAG was punishing violations of the non-fraternization order by troops under combat arms, to keep soldiers disciplined in and after battle. As mentioned above, the priorities of military justice are to enforce good order and discipline and "[ensure] expected behaviour in battle."[69] For the first time in the war, the Canadian army used the military justice system systematically to punish sexual violence by its troops. The number of courts martial for rape, attempted rape, and indecent assault skyrocketed – from twenty-two in the entire seventeen months of the Italian campaign to thirty-two cases in May 1945. In this case study, rape, attempted rape, and indecent assault have been grouped together to isolate non-consensual sexual crimes, as opposed to military persecution of male soldiers pursuing consensual homosexual relationships with other male soldiers.[70]

When rape allegations were brought against Canadian soldiers in Germany, the trials tended to progress in a set manner. First, an identity parade was arranged to see if the woman (or women) could identify the soldier(s). Specific units were assigned to clearly defined occupation areas, so the rationale was that only a small number of soldiers could conceivably have carried out the acts. Women who identified their attacker quickly were more likely to be perceived as credible than those who hesitated or asked to see a few men. After the identity parade, the provosts took statements from accuser(s), witnesses, and the accused if he wished; the trial was convened one to two weeks later. The court consisted of a president and members – usually captains, majors, or lieutenant-colonels – officers assigned for both the prosecution and the defence, and a judicial advisor (JA). The judicial advisor could question witnesses, but his main job was to provide legal advice to the court, which was made up of available field-grade officers and not specialists in military law. In cases of rape, the JA gave the court standardized military legal advice: the act of rape was penetration with a woman not the soldier's wife, "without her consent, by force, fear or fraud." A conviction for rape was possible without corroborating evidence, but "it is dangerous to convict without it."[71] The courts were very interested in the precise location of the crime, whether there had been witnesses to some or all of it, whether the accused possessed and/or threatened the use of a firearm, and the presence or absence of a medical examination in the aftermath, and its findings. After hearing both the witnesses for prosecution and defence, and the accused if he decided to testify (he did not have to), and final

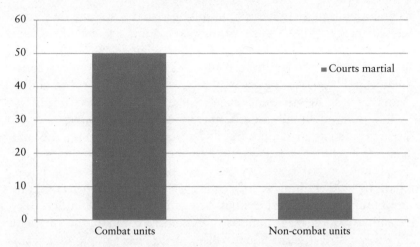

Figure 4.2 Courts martial for rape, attempted rape, or indecent assault, Canadian Army in Germany, 1945.

summations, the court decided if the soldier was innocent of all charges, guilty of rape, or guilty of fraternization. If guilt was legally established (for either charge) the soldier and his defending officer submitted a plea in mitigation, which was an argument about the soldier, his character, and why he should not be given a long sentence or discharged with ignominy.

Clear patterns emerge from the courts martial indices and records. Courts were more sympathetic to accusers who told clear, coherent stories, who quickly picked out their attackers from identity parades, and who had witnesses corroborating part or all of their stories. For either the prosecution or defence, the courts clearly believed that the most credible witnesses were other Canadian soldiers. In the trial of Acting Sergeant F. Gaspich, the word of his fellow soldier, Private Pschida, was clinching evidence for the prosecution, even though Gaspich outranked Pschida.[72] Similarly, soldiers' testimony could be used to protect those who had been "unjustly" accused; the comrades of Gunner Guay told the court that he had been on duty all evening on 24 April 1945 and could not have been involved in the rape of Aline G. or present during the rape of Kate S.[73] Guay was one of four soldiers who were acquitted of all charges; the court believed that they had not been involved.

Although fifty-eight Canadian soldiers were charged for sexual violence against Germans between February and July 1945, only fifty

German women were named, because of what J. Robert Lilly calls "buddy rapes."[74] In instances of gang rape, a few soldiers (often from the same unit) were implicated, with differentiated sentences for those whom the court perceived as the initiators and the followers. By 1945, joint trials for sexual violence were relatively rare; the JAG had clearly learned not to invest resources in joint trials if they were not likely to be successful. In the case of Gunner Guay, this JAG tactic paid off, as he was acquitted of all charges while another accused rapist of the same group of women and girls, Gunner Lefebvre, was successfully prosecuted and sentenced to ten years' penal servitude.[75] However, charging soldiers individually meant that German accusers had to testify separately against each of their rapists, and sometimes on different days. Sergeant Leddicoat and Gunner Provan, of the 4th Field Regiment, Royal Canadian Artillery, were charged and convicted separately on 13 and 14 June 1945 of the rape of Adele C. The sergeant was reduced to the ranks and sentenced to eighteen months' detention; Provan, who was convicted of raping Islamarie H. as well, was also sentenced to eighteen months' detention.

Once a soldier was convicted of rape, indecent assault, or disobeying the non-fraternization order, punishments varied widely. The longest single sentences for rape happened during the Italian campaign, when two soldiers received sentences of fifteen years. In Germany, the longest rape conviction was ten years of penal servitude, but most soldiers were given two- or five-year sentences.[76] Those soldiers convicted of indecent assault (a lesser charge than rape or fraternization) usually received somewhere between six and eighteen months' imprisonment. Often, those guilty of fraternizing received somewhere between six months' detention and two years' imprisonment with hard labour. Without a standard set of punishments, the crimes probably looked like they were being punished capriciously. What can be said, however, is that most of the soldiers charged with rape were convicted of some crime, whether that crime was rape, attempted rape, or fraternization.

SEXUAL VIOLENCE AS MOTIVATION

In *Taken by Force*, J. Robert Lilly outlines nine possible explanations for why soldiers might rape in warfare and how sexual violence could form a part of why soldiers fight. Although Lilly favours different explanations, I will broadly use his rationale as a framework for this section – and I add the possibility of an underlying masculine sexism, which is more thoroughly developed in feminist theory and scholarship.[77] Some explanations are unsuitable or unsatisfactory in the context of the Canadian Army, including explicit official strategy, cultural genocide, masculine sexism, and payment for military service, and this section explains why. In contrast, elements of informal reward, humiliation, revenge, opportunism, and military culture best fit the available evidence. As with other elements of human behaviour, the motivations of Canadian soldiers in the Second World War are complex; no single explanation is sufficient to explain how rape in warfare might be a factor in the will to fight.

Unsatisfactory Explanations

In contrast to some other twentieth-century conflicts, wartime sexual violence in the Canadian Army was not an official strategy or an attempt at genocide. During the wars in the former Yugoslavia (1992–95), for instance, sexual violence was part of an attempt by the Serbian government and military to destroy Bosnia's Muslim minority – a genocide effected by co-opting the next generation through its potential mothers.[78] The war-crimes tribunals against Serbian officials were the first to explicitly outline wartime rape as a tool of genocide.[79] In the Democratic Republic of the Congo (DRC) during the Second Congo War (1998–2003), by contrast, militias were not conducting genocide but attempting to destroy community bonds through the communal shame of rape.[80] In both of these late-twentieth-century instances, gang rape by soldiers was common and, in the DRC, usually performed in front of male family members. Fear of (or obedience to) orders might explain sexual violence as combat motivation; in the Canadian case, however, rape was illegal under the Army Act. Similarly, the non-fraternization order and the high number of Canadians court-martialled for the prohibited behaviour suggests that rape was not part of official, or even unofficial, policy. If Canadians were consciously practicing genocide through rape, it was certainly not condoned or supported in any official capacity.

When rape is not an official, genocidal policy, scholars of rape and sexual violence have sometimes pointed to an innate cultural sexism that has pervaded global societies – rape as an implicit threat held against all women by all men.[81] This scholarly tradition has been rehabilitated by Miriam Gebhardt, who points to sexual violence against German civilians being part of a wider European and North American crisis of masculinity – one that framed relations between men and women as the "battle of the sexes" wherein women were the enemy. Seeking to explain the rapes committed by Soviet, British, and American troops (no mention of the Canadians), Gebhardt turns to innate cultural and masculine sexism as a reason for why soldiers raped. She argues that wartime rape came from military bonding, which in turn came out of a shared sexism and fear of women's rights. In her words, "the dramatization of sexuality and gender roles in wartime ... [and] the subconscious insecurity with regards to identity in view of the growing women's labour force created a climate of anti-female aggression in both the West and the East."[82] Gebhardt's account is problematic for a few reasons: it does not consider the possibility of men raping other men, the cultural differences between the Soviet, American, British, and Canadian armies, or sociological differences in how rape was committed and punished by different armies in different countries. Nor does it answer the question of why only a few soldiers were (apparently) involved in sexual violence. Sexism may have been a contributing factor in some instances of rape for some soldiers, but this totalizing and simplistic explanation does not hold up to serious scrutiny.

Plunder as payment for military service was more complicated for Canadian soldiers in the Second World War, because Canadian soldiers stole and raped in the aftermath of battle. Historically, unpaid or mercenary armies would be given a set time period (usually three days) to sack a defeated city.[83] With the commanders' permission, sacking a city included pillage, destruction, and sexual violence against the defeated population. However, the soldiers of the Canadian army in the Second World War were neither unpaid nor mercenaries – nor were they encouraged to act in such a manner by their commanders or military culture. They were paid, and paid better than their British counterparts, for taking on the risks of being a soldier. As an all-volunteer force, too, they brought with them civilian Canadian norms and mores, which strongly discouraged individuals from property theft, robbery, or violence against civilians. Furthermore, military discipline in the Second World War mitigated against sacking towns and cities. In his report from Operation Husky, Sesia mentioned that some Canadian troops had been looting, and the General Officer Commanding had threatened to place all towns "off-limits" to the soldiers of a particular unit for a year to compel their good behaviour.[84] Despite these actions, official reports, censorship reports, and the courts martial files themselves point to widespread looting and theft from German civilians at the end of the war.[85] However, these actions by Canadian soldiers cannot imply "payment," because they were not sanctioned by the military; at worst, the military seems to have turned a blind eye. Looting, pillaging, and (sexual) violence seem to have happened in Germany as an unauthorized way to fulfill soldiers' wants.

Satisfactory Explanations

Therefore, plunder as a form of *informal* reward is a more plausible option for why rape could form part of the will to fight. As Anthony Kellett has discussed, historically plunder was once a common system of formal and informal reward for soldiers. In the Second World War, plunder (including both rape and looting) could be what soldiers felt entitled to take from a conquered enemy population.[86] A sense of entitlement is described in the statement of Private D. Tansley: "We ... [occupied] a new farmhouse every night or so, enjoying commandeered cattle, pigs, preserves out of cellar, and fresh milk."[87] Another Canadian soldier was quoted by the censors in a letter home as saying:

> I tried to send your parcel and my officer wouldn't pass it, as it was all loot. Anyway I'll hold on to it until I get leave. I've got a whole kit bag just packed with silver ware, etc. It's really nice stuff too. Little silver dust pans for sweeping up crumbs, also a silver handled brush to go with it. A silver tray with little silver holders for cups, with pictures of flower in the bottom. As a matter of fact I've got a gold mine.[88]

The officer in this letter is permissive of looting: although he did not allow the parcel to be sent, he did not take the treasure away. Another openly asked his correspondent: "How is the loot coming up your way? Our fellows are driving new cars, bicycles and motor bikes all the time and everybody is happy. I caught onto a pretty good watch the other day that should bring quite a couple of bucks if ever I get where the people have dough." And another: "The Germans have lots and *whatever they have belongs to us now and we mean to take everything that we can lay hands on and leave nothing behind* ... the boys are helping themselves to everything they see."[89] The soldiers in these excerpts seem almost giddy with the power to procure exclusive souvenirs. Particularly when the Canadians first entered Germany in February–March 1945, the military authorities were uninclined to enforce limits on their soldiers. A Canadian soldier quoted in the March 1945 censorship report said: "They haven't told us not to loot yet, and everybody is lifting everything in sight."[90] As with the officer mentioned above, officers were not exercising their power to stop the theft of German material possessions, although explicit orders were not issued until two weeks later on 28 March.[91]

Less innocently, the courts martial records also make frequent reference to the soldiers demanding alcohol and sex, and sometimes stealing personal items, from German civilians. Gunner P.J. Claus was charged with two counts of robbery with aggravation for stealing a radio and ring from a farmhouse and for violating the non-fraternization order by lying in bed with Fraulein Greta H. (age 13). The court was convinced that Claus could not have been part of these acts, but the adults told a story of being held hostage by four soldiers, having their possessions stolen, and being forcibly separated from Greta and her younger sister.[92] In the censorship reports, a soldier recounted how a long-time comrade and another soldier were in legal trouble for "[herding] a couple of German Frauleins 'up the stairs' ahead of a Sten Gun. While one held the Sten Gun the other gave them a painless meat injection."[93] The fact that rape was being euphemistically downplayed indicated an entitled (not to say cavalier) attitude toward the Germans and their suffering, an attitude similar to that taken toward German possessions. In this example, the German women were classified as objects to be taken advantage of – their bodies became plunder.

Humiliation of the enemy, by contrast, is an explanation favoured by military historians.[94] Wartime rape could be a message from one group of men to another group of men. By raping their women, the victors demonstrate their total power over the defeated men and utter contempt for their enemies. There were shades of this motivation in the Canadian invasion of Germany. In *Fight to the Finish*, Tim Cook mentions that once Canadian soldiers crossed the Rhine into Germany, they urinated on German soil.[95] The desire to humiliate the enemy was also present in the courts martial records that I reviewed. In her description of her rape by Gunners Lefebvre and Guay, Aline G. testified that her grandfather had been a witness to a series of rapes by

Gunner Lefebvre. Her wheelchair-bound grandfather, the only man in the house at the time, was made to watch the rape of his grand-daughter and her mother, and then two other women in the house.[96]

Revenge against the German people as a potential motivation for war crimes also fits into the narratives that surround the courts martial, even though the soldiers being court-martialled shied away from that rationale in their trials. Both Hugh Gordon and Miriam Gebhardt attribute the high number of rapes in Germany to the desire for revenge. Gordon states that the rapes were a mix of attempting to humiliate the enemy and a "victory ritual" in which "Germans were the enemy and the soldiers were acting out their conquest in a more personal manner than simple territorial occupation."[97] Gebhardt attributes the increase in rapes in April and May to the discovery of German war crimes and horror at the concentration camps.[98] In some cases, German women were explicitly blamed for falsely claiming rape. The defending officer in the trial of Acting Sergeant F. Gaspich outlined the "campaign of the German Frauleins to undermine the morale of the Allied armies by encouraging advances from our soldiers" and connected it to an alleged attempt by German women to "win the peace."[99] In fact, American Lieutenant-General E.L. Clarke investigated rumours that there was a conspiracy by German women to falsely accuse Allied soldiers of rape; in June 1945, he reported that there was no such plan.[100] Still, the rumours demonstrate an ugly mood among Canadian and American troops toward German civilians. The persistence of such rumours implies that vengeance was being taken and revisited by both sides – and German women's bodies bore the brunt of such inflammatory perceptions.

Individual opportunism played a hand in the number of soldiers who raped German women. As in the American zone, the German women were often living in precarious housing situations close to or with the Canadians.[101] Some were displaced persons, refugees from the Allied bombing campaigns, who were themselves sleeping with family or friends in farms or towns that were remote or not adequately guarded. Elizabeth B., for instance, was living in Spenge because her Hildesheim home had been destroyed by firebombing in February 1945.[102] The German police had been decommissioned to await denazification, and firearms, being strictly banned for Germans (for fear of "fifth column" activities), were actively sought out by the Canadian soldiers.[103] Most German women did not speak enough English to communicate clearly with the invaders. In the sexual fraternization court martial of Private C. Gladue, Mrs Margarete P. recalled that Gladue had come into her bedroom and she had accepted his advances even though they could not communicate verbally. In her words, "when a man comes into your room at night and walks up to your bed, you know what he wants."[104] Given poor housing conditions, inadequate social protection, and unclear communications, the Canadian soldiers had ample opportunities to sexually assault German women. Hugh Gordon has found that most rapes were carried out at night, many under the influence of alcohol.[105] Cover of darkness made it more difficult for Germans to identify their attackers and limited the ability of Canadian authorities to pursue soldiers caught in the act. Nighttime was also when soldiers were off-duty, otherwise unoccupied, bored, and looking for entertainment. Although they had been banned from fraternizing, some Canadian soldiers used their power as conquerors and access to German civilians, weapons, and alcohol to plunder, pillage, and rape.

Indeed, at some level, the choices of individual soldiers may have been determined solely by their own moral compasses. Such choices seem to have been the case with Acting Sergeant Gaspich and Private Pschida, both of the Royal Regiment of Canada. While the soldiers were searching for guns in a German home, Gaspich took Elizabeth B. into a bedroom and raped her; Pschida held the other civilians at gunpoint during the rape but was not a willing accomplice, calling out to Gaspich about the lengthy search of the bedroom. When Elizabeth B. came back into the kitchen crying, Pschida twice asked his NCO if he had "laid a hand on her." Gaspich denied any impropriety "and told [Pschida] not to ask him again," as Pschida testified for the prosecution at the court martial.[106] However, here too, the limits of Pschida's sympathy and loyalty to his unit seem to be on display: despite his clear unease with the actions of his sergeant, he did not report the incident to the military police. Instead, Elizabeth B. reported her rape to the Canadian authorities.

When seeking explanations of the behaviour of these soldiers, the confluence of informal reward, humiliation, vengeance, and sheer opportunism must be combined with a permissive military culture. As discussed above, the culture of front-line soldiers placed a premium on aggressive and passionate behaviour, and drew explicit connections between sex and violence. The inconsistent responses of officers and the military legal system also may have sent mixed messages to the soldiers about what was or was not appropriate action. Leddicoat and Provan received eighteen months' detention for their rape convictions, while privates Gagen, Fendley, Hendersen, Mitchell, and McQuaid all received two-year sentences for fraternization with Katerina V. In a more sinister instance, the rape conviction of Acting Sergeant Gaspich was not confirmed by General Harry Crerar, the First Canadian Army's General Officer Commanding-in-Chief. Gaspich's language skills (he spoke Polish, Ukrainian, and Russian) may have made him too valuable to imprison. Although he probably ordered a retrial, Crerar did not provide an explanation for his refusal to confirm a three-year penal servitude conviction; he did not have to.[107]

Crerar's silence points to another important aspect within the military culture: a command-level reluctance to document and discuss rape cases against European women. Indeed, Sesia's frank observations about the reported rapes in Sicily come closer than any other Canadian Army official records to acknowledging a problem. The censorship reports contain hints and implications, but the archival records of the military operations for the invasion of Germany (formally codenamed Operation Eclipse) do not indicate a problem with sexual assault against German women. Despite multiple files about indiscipline among its personnel in Northwest Europe, the Canadian Army only tersely discussed the problem of stealing German food and property, and, as late as September 1945, exhorted its members to conduct themselves with dignity when dealing with German civilians.[108] Although soldiers were given pamphlets, made to watch anti-fraternization movies, and prosecuted thoroughly for fraternization, the army refused to admit that it had a problem with its soldiers committing acts of sexual violence. They did not investigate systematically, nor did they leave an archival paper trail to follow. On this issue, the occupation records are silent.

To what degree is sexual violence in wartime normal, or abnormal? How does sexual violence fit into issues of combat motivation? The case of the Canadian Army's invasion of Germany shows that more was at work than a few "bad eggs." Rape is one of the most under-reported crimes; writing a decade after the Second World War, Anglo-Polish criminologist Sir Leon Radzinowicz estimated that in the 1950s only 5 per cent of rapes were reported.[109] Sociologist J. Robert Lilly, citing Radzinowicz in his study of sexual violence by American GIs during the Second World War, believed that rape in the context of an invading army and a conquered people was even less likely to be reported than in peacetime civil society, and freely uses the "5 per cent argument" to gauge rough estimates of American sexual violence in Germany.[110] The number of Canadian soldiers court-martialled for raping German women is certainly only a fraction of the number of rapes that occurred involving Canadian servicemen; hundreds of incidents must have gone unreported, or happened in a gray area of coercion in late-war Germany. The number of courts martial that did occur represents this violence becoming visible for a moment in response to the army's perceived need to punish transgressors of the non-fraternization order. A troubling question remains: how normal was sexual violence at every other point in Canada's war, and to what extent is that violence rendered invisible in the historical record? Do we see the "epidemic" of rape in Germany in 1945 because there was a genuine spike in sexual violence that was duly punished, or was that level of sexual violence fairly normal, illuminated only briefly by the JAG's interest in suppressing it? Captain Sesia's evidence from Sicily in 1943 suggests that there were other campaigns in which widespread sexual violence was being ignored by the Canadian military authorities.

CONCLUSIONS

Canadian soldiers during the Second World War were expected to aspire to a military masculinity, mixing passion and aggression. Rather than let that passion and aggression flow indiscriminately, the Canadian Army channelled its soldiers' masculinity by encouraging camaraderie with fellow soldiers, enforcing obedience to the chain of command, and criminalizing sexual violence against civilians – but discouraging sexual violence was less important than encouraging camaraderie and obedience. Before April 1945, the Canadian military justice system rarely punished sexual violence against civilians, preferring to believe that the sex the soldiers took part in was bought and consensual. The military hierarchy's main concern was VD, and most sexual violence and sex with prostitutes was either dealt with at the unit level (beneath JAG notice) or not at all. Except when a rape became a gross breach of military discipline, the Canadian Army, facing serious manpower shortages, was uninterested in prosecuting aggressive soldiers for their sexual crimes. Captain Sesia's observations from Sicily strongly suggest that the lack of courts martial for rape during the Second World War does not necessarily indicate that sexual violence was not happening; it rather reflects, perhaps, the fact that only those cases that are reported, believed, and pursued by the authorities become visible in the historical record.

When a military culture becomes one of conquest, enemy civilians (women, children, and men) become vulnerable to pillage, looting, and rape. Sexual violence was not used as a motivating factor by the Canadian army in a formal sense, but the army was lax in punishing rape. For most of the commanders, provosts, and medical officers, concern about sexual relations meant concern about visiting prostitutes and contracting v d. Prior to Germany, sexual violence was court-martialled only in rare, spectacular instances. Because the Army did not utilize its system of punishments against those who used Europeans as sexual objects, such behaviour on the part of soldiers continued. In many instances, the overt sexuality of soldiers was encouraged or even applauded. In Germany, the vulnerability of civilian populations and the opportunities to abuse and exploit them came together with a collective desire, on the part of Canadian soldiers, for revenge, humiliation of the enemy, and even the sense that Canadian soldiers were "owed" the traditional bounty of conquerors. These motivations aligned with a military bureaucracy that did not wish to admit that it had a problem: the values-in-use did not line up with the espoused values of the military culture.[111] What happened in Germany was not necessarily unique – but it is possible, even likely, that the non-fraternization orders in force in Germany made widespread sexual violence highly visible, if briefly so, for the first time.

For Canadian soldiers in the Second World War, the elements of informal sexual reward, humiliation of a vanquished enemy, sexual revenge against Germany and Germans, individual sexual opportunism, and a permissive, hypersexualized military culture were all elements of how sexual violence could be an aspect of combat motivation. It is unclear if the participants themselves knew or accepted their personal motivations toward German women and girls. None of the court-martialled soldiers examined for this article pled guilty to rape; they might even have denied that sexual violence was a part of their motivation for going into battle.[112] The final takeaway from this chapter, therefore, must be that soldiers fight for a multiplicity of reasons. I caution readers to avoid simple or uni-causal explanations for sexual violence and combat motivation.

NOTES

1 Paisley Dodds, "UN Peacekeepers in Haiti Implicated in Child Sex Ring," *Independent* (UK), 14 April 2017.

2 Sandra Laville, "UN Inquiry into CAR Abuse Claims Identifies 41 Troops as Suspects," *Guardian* (UK), 5 December 2016.

3 "MINUSMA: United Nations Multidimensional Integrated Stabilization Mission in Mali," United Nations, https://minusma.unmissions.org/en (accessed 12 July 2017).

4 Elisha Ben Kimon, Telem Yahav, and Kobi Nachshoni, "IDF's Chief Rabbi-to-be permits raping women in wartime," ynetnews.com, 12 July 2016; "IDF taps Chief Rabbi who once seemed to permit wartime rape," *Times of Israel*, 12 July 2016.

5 J. Robert Lilly, *Taken by Force: Rape and American GIs in Europe during World War II* (New York: Palgrave Macmillan, 2007), 27.

6 During the Second World War, sexually transmitted infections were referred to as venereal diseases, or simply "VD." For the rest of this chapter, I will refer to STIs using contemporary terminology.

7 George S. MacDonell, *One Soldier's Story, 1939–1945: From the Fall of Hong Kong to the Defeat of Japan* (Toronto: Dundurn, 2002), 53.

8 Quoted in Philippa Levine, *Prostitution, Race and Politics: Policing Venereal Disease in the British Empire* (New York: Routledge, 2003), 282.

9 Heidi Matthews, "Allied Soldiers – including Canadians – raped thousands of German women after the Second World War: research," *National Post*, 8 May 2018.

10 See: Ruth Siefert, "War and Rape: A Preliminary Analysis," in *Mass Rape: The War against Women in Bosnia-Herzegovina*, ed. Alexandra Stigmayer (Lincoln: University of Nebraska Press, 1994), 54–72.

11 Beverly Allen, *Rape Warfare: The Hidden Genocide in Bosnia-Herzegovina and Croatia* (Minneapolis: University of Minnesota Press, 1996), 62.

12 Richard Bessel, *Germany 1945: From War to Peace* (New York: HarperCollins, 2009), 149.

13 Anthony Kellett, *Combat Motivation: The Behaviour of Soldiers in Battle* (Boston: Springer Science, 1982), 8–12.

14 Joanna Bourke's chapter on military rape contains a particularly scathing rebuttal to this perspective. See: Joanna Bourke, *Rape: A History from 1860 to the Present* (London: Virago, 2007), 382–4.

15 See, for instance: Susan Brownmiller, *Against Our Will: Men, Women and Rape* (New York: Bantam Books, 1975), 23–118; Anne Llewellyn Barstow,

ed., *War's Dirty Secret: Rape, Prostitution, and Other Crimes Against Women* (Cleveland: Pilgrim Press, 2000); Allen, *Rape Warfare.*

16 Jean Bethke Elshtain, "Women and War," in *The Oxford History of Modern War,* ed. Charles Townshend (Oxford: Oxford University Press, 2005), 306.

17 Lilly, *Taken by Force,* 28.

18 Ibid.

19 Ibid., 112. For example: "German women had few meaningful sources of protection. Not only were housing conditions ... extremely difficult and compromised, the German women were the enemy's women."

20 Ibid., 28.

21 Bourke, *Rape,* 359.

22 Ibid., 366.

23 Hugh Gordon, "Cheers and Tears: Relations between Canadian Soldiers and German Civilians, 1944–1946" (PhD diss., University of Victoria, 2010), 200–37; David Borys, *Civilians at the Sharp End: First Canadian Army Civil Affairs in Belgium* (forthcoming Montreal: McGill-Queen's University Press).

24 Matthews, "Allied Soldiers."

25 William John Pratt, "Prostitutes and Prophylaxis: Venereal Disease, Surveillance, and Discipline in the Canadian Army in Europe, 1939–1945," *Journal of the Canadian Historical Association* 26, no. 2 (2015): 120–4.

26 Miriam Gebhardt, *Crimes Unspoken: The Rape of German Women at the End of the Second World War,* trans. Nick Somers (Cambridge, UK: Polity Press, 2017), 14. Part of the problem with uncovering records of rape and sexual violence in the British army was the fact that the Army Act classified rape/sexual violence charges under the same section (41) as other civil crimes, including murder and common assault.

27 Bessel, *Germany 1945,* 149.

28 See: Ben H. Shepherd, *Hitler's Soldiers: The German Army in the Third Reich* (New Haven, CT: Yale University Press, 2016), 285; Birgit Beck, "Sexual violence and its prosecution by courts martial of the *Wehrmacht,*" in *A World at Total War: Global Conflict and the Politics of Destruction, 1937–1945,* ed. Roger Chickering (Cambridge, UK: Cambridge University Press, 2004), 317–31.

29 Paul Jackson, *One of the Boys: Homosexuality in the Military during World War II* (Montreal: McGill-Queen's University Press, 2004), 8.

30 Gordon L. Rottman, *FUBAR: Soldier Slang of World War II* (Oxford: Osprey Publishing, 2007), 98.

31 Jackson, *One of the Boys*, 32–3.
32 Robert Engen, *Strangers in Arms: Combat Motivation in the Canadian Army* (Montreal: McGill-Queen's University Press), 171–3.
33 Censorship Reports from 21 Army Group – Canadian Army Overseas, Library and Archives Canada (hereafter LAC), microfilm reel T-17925, 4/CENSOR REPS/2/1.
34 Peter Schrijvers, forward to Lilly, *Taken by Force*, xxix.
35 Chris Vokes, *My Story* (Ottawa: Gallery Books, 1985), 121.
36 Lilly, *Taken by Force*, 29.
37 Vokes, *My Story*, 123.
38 Major A.T. Sesia, "Personal Notes and Observations, Part 1 – Sicily, 24 April–2 September 1943," 45, LAC, RG 24, vol. 10878, 21 July 1943.
39 Vokes, *My Story*, 123.
40 "The Problem of VD in 7th Aust Div during Fifteen Months in the Middle East, by ADMS 7th Aust Div," 1942, 54 267/6/7 pt 6, Australian War Memorial. Thanks to Robert C. Engen for the archival information.
41 Vokes, *My Story*, 127.
42 Ibid.
43 Section 18 of the Army Act had two subsections on disease control: 18.1: "malinger[ing] or [feigning] or [producing] disease or injury"; and 18.3: "delaying cure of disease." War Office, *Manual of Military Law 1914* (London: His Majesty's Stationary Office, 1914), 396–7.
44 "Policy – Discipline," LAC RG 24 10507, file 215a21.009 (D47), 54.
45 Pratt, "Prostitutes and Prophylaxis," 127.
46 Ibid., 123.
47 W.R. Feasby, *Official History of the Canadian Medical Services 1939–1945, Volume Two: Clinical Subjects* (Ottawa: Ministry of National Defence, 1953), 113.
48 Pratt, "Prostitutes and Prophylaxis," 118.
49 Tim Cook, *Clio's Warriors: Canadian Historians and the Writing of the World Wars* (Vancouver: UBC Press, 2006), 101.
50 Major A.T. Sesia, "Personal Notes and Observations, Part 1 – Sicily, 24 April–2 September 1943," 41, LAC, RG 24 10878, 19 July 1943.
51 Ibid., 21 July 1943, 45.
52 Ibid., 45.
53 G.W.L. Nicholson, *Official History of the Canadian Army in the Second World War, Vol 2: The Canadians in Italy, 1943–1945* (Ottawa: Queen's Printer, 1956).
54 G.G. Simonds, "Special Order – Civil Relations, 9 August 1943," 70, LAC, RG 24, vol. 15657 – War Diary ADMS 1st Canadian Infantry Division. Emphasis in original.

55 G. Christopher Case, "'The "Fightin'est" Canadian General': Brigadier Christopher Vokes and His Approach to Military Command" (MA thesis, University of Ottawa, 2009), 143.

56 Ibid.

57 Simonds, "Special Order."

58 Vokes, My Story, 128.

59 Sesia was writing on 21 July 1943. The first case in the courts martial indices appears to have started on 10 August. The co-defendants had been awaiting trial for eleven days, so the report would have been made to the military police around 29 July 1945. Compiled Courts Martial Data, from Extracts of Courts Martial (Army), 1943–45, 111.6 (D3), Judge Advocate General Fonds, Directorate of History and Heritage, Ottawa.

60 Ibid.

61 E.L.M. Burns, "Behaviour of Canadian Troops to Civilians," 61, LAC, RG 24, vol. 15657 – War Diary ADMS 1st Canadian Infantry Division.

62 Randall Wakelam, "The Air Force and Flight Safety: A Culture of Tolerated Disobedience," in The Insubordinate and the Noncompliant: Case Studies of Canadian Mutiny and Disobedience, 1920 to Present, ed. Howard Coombs (Toronto: Dundurn, 2007), 345.

63 "Memorandum: Occupation of Germany," 19 September 1944, 1–5, LAC RG 24_10507, file 215a21.009 D51.

64 Order 443, 23 February 1945, LAC microfilm reel T-15813, image 759.

65 War Office, Manual of Military Law, 412.

66 "Trial of Pte. C. Gladue – Witness for the Prosecution," LAC microfilm reel T-15809, image 239.

67 Gordon, "Cheers and Tears," 200.

68 Ibid.; Brownmiller, Against Our Will, 23–118.

69 Chris Madsen, Another Kind of Justice: Canadian Military Law from Confederation to Somalia (Vancouver: UBC Press, 1999), 1.

70 For the definitive account of the Canadian military's persecution of its soldiers' consensual homosexual relationships during the Second World War, see: Jackson, One of the Boys.

71 "Court Martial of Pte B.J. Clynch – JA Sums Up," LAC microfilm reel T-15792, image 3580.

72 "Court Martial of A/Sgt F. Gaspich – Witness for the Prosecution Pte Pschida," LAC microfilm reel T-15807, images 3556–60.

73 "Court Martial of Gunner L. Guay – Witnesses for the Defence," LAC microfilm reel T-15810, images 2194–97.

74 Lilly, Taken by Force, 127–32.

75 Compiled Courts Martial Data.

76 Steven R. Welch, "Military Justice," in *International Encyclopedia of the First World War*, ed. Ute Daniel, et al. (Berlin: Freie Universität Berlin, 2014).

77 Lilly includes two other reasons which seem to have no bearing on the case study at hand: an imperial right (*droit de seigneur*) and sexual comfort rape. As mentioned above, the Canadians were prevented from opening brothels in Sicily, although regulated prostitution as a form of sexual comfort rape could describe the practices of other Allied armies. Lilly, *Taken by Force*, 28, 27.

78 Allen, *Rape Warfare*, 41–86.

79 Ian Black, "Serbs 'enslaved Muslim women at rape camps,'" *Guardian* (UK), 21 March 2000.

80 Mariam M. Kurle and Mwamini Thambwe Diggs, "Wartime Rape: A Case Study of the Democratic Republic of the Congo," in *Women, War and Weapons: Topography, Resistance and Hope*, ed. Mariam Kurtz and Lester Kurtz (Santa Barbara: Praeger, 2015), 187.

81 For the classic text, see: Brownmiller, *Against Our Will*.

82 Gebhardt, *Crimes Unspoken*, 100–3.

83 Joshua S. Goldstein, *Winning the War on War: The Decline of Armed Conflict Worldwide* (New York: Plume, 2012), 28–31.

84 Major A.T. Sesia, "Personal Notes and Observations, Part 1 – Sicily, 24 April–2 September 1943," 45, LAC, RG 24 10878, 21 July 1943.

85 Engen, *Strangers in Arms*, 181–6.

86 Kellett, *Combat Motivation*, 202.

87 Quoted in Tim Cook, *Fight to the Finish: Canadians in the Second World War, Volume 2, 1944–1945* (Toronto: Allan Lane, 2015), 398.

88 Censorship Reports, Canadian Army Overseas, 21 Army Group, 16–30 April 1945, LAC microfilm reel T-17925.

89 Ibid. Emphasis added.

90 Censorship Reports, Canadian Army Overseas, 21 Army Group, 1–15 March 1945, LAC microfilm reel T-17925.

91 "Food stolen in Germany, 28 March 1945," 2, in "Discipline – Own Forces," LAC, RG 24 10739, file 219C1.009 (D245).

92 "Court Martial of Gunner P.J. Claus," LAC microfilm reel T-15792, images 1258–1307.

93 "Non-fraternization Order," 9, Censorship Reports, 21 Army Group, 16–30 April 1945, LAC microfilm reel T-17925.

94 Bourke, *Rape*, 383–4.

95 Cook, *Fight to the Finish*, 398.

96 "Court Martial of Gunner L. Guay – Summary of Evidence, First Witness for the Prosecution," LAC microfilm reel T-15810, image 2199.

97 Gordon, "Cheers and Tears," 200, 203.
98 Gebhardt, *Crimes Unspoken*, 113.
99 "Court Martial of A/Sgt F. Gaspich – Plea in Mitigation," LAC microfilm reel T-15807, image 3573.
100 Gebhardt, *Crimes Unspoken*, 93.
101 Lilly, *Taken by Force*, 132–3.
102 "Court Martial of A/Sgt F. Gaspich – Witness for the Prosecution, Elizabeth B.," LAC microfilm reel T-15807, image 3526.
103 "Court Martial of A/Sgt F. Gaspich – Witness for the Defence, A/Sgt Gaspich," LAC microfilm reel T-15807, images 3547–8; Gebhardt, *Crimes Unspoken*, 110.
104 "Trial of Pte. C. Gladue – Witness for the Prosecution, Mrs. Margarete P.," LAC microfilm reel T-15809, image 224.
105 Gordon, "Cheers and Tears," 203.
106 "Court Martial of A/Sgt F. Gaspich – Witness for the Prosecution Pte Pschida," LAC microfilm reel T-15807, images 3556–60.
107 The GCoC's practice of not confirming courts martial findings was the subject of a memorandum from the Assistant Deputy Judge Advocate General in July 1945. The note assures that "no one directed his mind to this point and in the meantime the accused has been released." "Memorandum: Non Confirmation New Trials, 27 July 1945," 185, LAC RG 24_10507, file 215A21.009 (D47), Policy – Discipline.
108 "Policy – German Civilians, Appendix Q," LAC RG 24 10507, file 215a21.009 (D51).
109 Leon Radzinowicz, *Sexual Offences: A Report of the Cambridge Department of Criminal Science* (London: Macmillan, 1957), xv.
110 Lilly, *Taken by Force*, 11–12.
111 Allan English, *Understanding Military Culture: A Canadian Perspective* (Montreal: McGill-Queen's University Press, 2004), 19–21.
112 Gordon, "Cheers and Tears," 211.

5

Strangers in Arms:
Swift Trust and Combat Motivation

Robert C. Engen

The city of Kingston, Ontario, has an impressive military legacy. The imposing heights of Fort Henry, the network of squat Martello towers guarding the harbour, and the Rideau waterway linking Kingston to Ottawa are only its most corporeal aspects. There are other, less obvious stories carved into stone as well. There is a solemn Edwardian staircase in Mackenzie Hall at the Royal Military College of Canada (RMC), along which stained glass windows overlook framed photographs of the college's ex-cadets killed in the line of duty. Across the La Salle Causeway, at Queen's University, there is a similarly sombre stone room in what is now the John Deutsch Student Centre (originally the Students' Memorial Union), where the Queen's war dead are commemorated. Common stories link these rarely visited memorials in Kingston's two centres of higher learning. One of them involves two men killed in action in September 1944, during the liberation of Northwest Europe.

Lieutenant Donald Trumpour Knight, RMC cadet no. 2,166, and Lieutenant Edward Lear Roberts, a graduate of Queen's University's Faculty of Arts and Sciences, both came to Kingston for their schooling from other parts of Canada, and both would go on to fight as infantrymen in the First Canadian Army during the Second World War. Knight graduated from RMC in June 1934, one of the college's distinguished rugby players.[1] He served with the Royal Hamilton Light Infantry of the 2nd Canadian Infantry Division (2nd CID) and was killed the day after Operation Market-Garden opened in September of 1944, cut down by a German machine-gun post while leading a patrol following the liberation of the Port of Antwerp.

Lieutenant Roberts served with the Algonquin Regiment of the 4th Canadian Armoured Division (4th CAD), one of the division's three infantry battalions. He died of wounds in September 1944 during the Algonquins' abortive crossing of the Leopold Canal, hot on the heels of the retreating German Army.

Both Knight and Roberts were platoon commanders leading their troops into battle from the front when they died. Both were reinforcement officers; they did not "come up" with their units and had not been attached to them for long. And both were among the 1,200 platoon commander casualties – and 300 killed – in the First Canadian Army between D-Day and the end of the war with Germany. Today, Roberts and Knight are both buried in Commonwealth War Graves cemeteries in Belgium. Their deaths lend human faces to sobering statistics: between D-Day in June 1944 and VE Day in May 1945, each infantry battalion in the First Canadian Army suffered casualties between 200 and 300 per cent to their junior and field-grade officers (lieutenants, captains, majors, and lieutenant-colonels). Leading an infantry platoon was the most dangerous job on earth during the war years, followed closely by commanding an infantry company. But while the leaders were the most exposed, the other ranks paid a dear price in blood as well. Among these other ranks, most battalions suffered casualties between 150 and 200 per cent between June 1944 and the beginning of May 1945, with a much higher percentage concentrated in the rifle companies. The scale of the punishment that these units absorbed during the fighting was staggering.

The lives and intersecting deaths of these former students from Kingston highlight an important dimension of combat motivation for Canadian forces in the Second World War. This essay examines some of the most salient motivational characteristics of the Canadian Army at war between 1943 and 1945. It is a distillation of, and elaboration upon, some of the key points presented in my recent book, *Strangers in Arms: Combat Motivation in the Canadian Army, 1943–1945*.

The experiences of Knight and Roberts, of leading into battle and dying beside men who hardly knew them, was typical of much of the fighting done by the Canadian infantry during the Second World War. In his history of the 4th CAD's Lincoln and Welland Regiment, historian Geoffrey Hayes described the phenomenon:

If one views the Regiment as so many of its former members do – as a family – then the Regiment was perpetuated by no

less than four generations of fighting troops during its time in
Northwest Europe: the casualties sustained were about equal
to the strength of its four rifle companies being fully replaced
four times over … These generations are almost (but not
completely) distinct.[2]

With over 1,570 recorded killed, wounded, or missing since going
into action at the end of July 1944, the "Lincs" suffered heavily, but,
in this sense, they were entirely typical and far from the worst-hit
among the Canadian battalions serving in Northwest Europe.[3] At key
points in the campaign – in Normandy, at the Scheldt, and in the
Rhineland – casualties to Canadian infantry units were so heavy and
reinforcement so continuous that men fighting side-by-side in rifle
companies, platoons, and sections were often near or total strangers
to one another. The same was true in the Italian theatre of operations,
where two Canadian divisions and a corps headquarters fought as
part of the British Eighth Army. On average, infantry battalions in
the 1st Canadian Infantry Division (1st CID), which landed in Sicily
in July 1943, had sustained over 150 per cent casualties to other ranks
by the time they withdrew from the theatre in early 1945, and were
getting close to having lost 250 per cent of their junior officers. The
5th Canadian Armoured Division (5th CAD) arrived in Italy later, but
nonetheless suffered casualties of nearly 100 per cent to their infantry
battalions during the campaign.[4] The combination of mobile warfare
and high-intensity firepower resulted in extraordinary casualties in a
short time period. This experience was not unique to the Canadians,
but was an obstacle that every battalion had to deal with.

The statistics for this study were prepared from infantry losses
tabulated by Canadian Military Headquarters in the form of the
Consolidated Casualty Lists (CCLs), but these lists underestimate the
dire situations facing battalions in high-intensity combat.[5] The CCLs
were compiled by battalion, and while each battalion's combat
strength was slightly less than 800, just over half of that strength was
located in the four rifle companies (120 men apiece at full strength).[6]
When assessing the casualties on rifle companies in particular – the
tactical sub-units that did most of the fighting – the rate of loss compared to the battalion's strength on paper would be significantly
higher, perhaps close to double. The CCLs also account only for battle
casualties. They exclude losses from disease and non-battle injuries
(DNBI), major sources of attrition in the field. The medical units

attached to the First Canadian Army kept separate, no less detailed records. During the period between 29 July and 30 September 1944, there were some 15,879 hospital admissions in the First Canadian Army due to injuries sustained from enemy action (a rate of 336 per 1,000 per year); the great majority of these were infantrymen.[7] During the same period, there were also 6,944 hospital admissions in the army for diseases of the digestive system (diarrhea, gastroenteritis, dysentery), 4,024 for skin diseases and infections, 2,448 admissions for neuropsychiatric conditions, 456 for venereal disease, and 3,717 for non-battle injuries and accidents.[8] From these major disease and injury groups alone, there were some 17,589 recorded hospital admissions (a rate of 372 per 1,000 per year). These DNBI casualties were not concentrated in the infantry as battle injuries were, but infantrymen were as susceptible to them as anyone, and more so in the case of neuropsychiatric conditions. Such impoverishment of the manpower pool necessitated frequent reinforcement and resulted in a near-constant "personnel turbulence" as sick, injured, and wounded soldiers recovered and returned to their units from hospital.

However, turmoil from personnel turbulence was not just a matter of casualties. Infantry units were often being taken apart, reconstituted, disassembled, and rebuilt by commanders on the ground. This was done to meet both task-specific challenges in combat and urgencies created by shortfalls in the manpower availability to the infantry. One of the most underappreciated aspects of combat in the Second World War is the degree to which sub-units had to be recombined to field an effective fighting force. The German Army's ability to rally shattered units from defeat and rebuild them into cobbled-together yet combat-effective "battle groups" (*Kampfengruppen*) has been noted by historians.[9] The same process, however, has been discussed only rarely in the case of the Allies. Rather than create new units, the Allies disbanded units and sub-units and simply fed their surviving personnel into other, existing units. The British and American armies both had to disband battalions, brigades, regiments, and even whole divisions, which were broken up for reinforcements so that a smaller number of field formations could keep fighting at a high intensity.[10]

The Canadians never had to disband and reorganize on so high a level, but within battalion sub-units they did so constantly. During contact with the enemy, most casualties were sustained at the lowest level: the infantry section of ten to twelve soldiers. These sections, commonly identified as the "primary group," were routinely devastated by casualties.[11] When the number of men in these sections dropped below a certain point, a platoon commander could recombine two or more shattered sections into one stronger unit to keep them functioning. The same thing could be done by a company commander with several seriously depleted platoons, especially when key leaders and junior officers had been lost and it was necessary to consolidate both manpower and leadership. There are also accounts of entire rifle companies being temporarily disbanded and the survivors fed into the sections and platoons of other companies, so that the battalion would have at least one rifle company somewhere close to peak fighting strength.[12]

The Canadian infantry also practiced a "Left out of Battle" (LOB) system. LOB troops were elements of each battalion left behind the lines during an attack, thereby to preserve a leadership nucleus for the unit in case the worst happened during an operation, and to serve as a training cadre. The LOB system also provided a small pool of initial reinforcements who could go forward to replace losses. The Canadians employed the LOB system in all theatres and in all major combat operations after Dieppe. But since LOB was managed on a rotating basis, it constantly pulled men from their sub-units. Although this was a key part of preserving force strength, the LOB system nonetheless contributed to personnel turbulence within battalions.

Infantry were also frequently placed into task-specific groupings and teams. It was a common experience for able soldiers to be pulled from their regular sub-units and primary groups (or, in extreme cases, from different units entirely) to become part of a team being assembled for a specific mission. Patrols were the most common task-specific grouping. Officers would grab a few soldiers from different sections, different platoons, and occasionally even different companies to stage reconnoitering patrols, fighting patrols, or standing patrols (the flexible forward defence line).[13] Particularly soft-footed soldiers from several sub-units could be grouped together to lead the way during a night attack or patrol action.[14] Exceptionally fit individuals could be put into a composite unit for a mountaintop assault, as happened during the assault on Assoro in Sicily. The fluid, changeable situations on the ground meant that many missions were not carried out by men working in their normal sub-units with their normal primary group, but instead by soldiers who were put together on the basis of who was able, who was available, and who was willing to try to accomplish a particular task.

The final source of personnel turbulence came from reinforcement and replacement soldiers, who were the inevitable consequence of casualties sustained during high-intensity combat operations. Tens of thousands of new infantrymen had to be lined up in the reinforcement stream to replace losses quickly and keep battalions fighting at full pitch as much as possible. Ideally, such a process would happen outside of combat, overseen by key leaders and facilitated by LOB personnel. However, when a fight was particularly desperate, units were reinforced on the fly, the reinforcements fed straight into fighting units while still in battle. New faces appeared in the battalions at irregular intervals. Moreover, the arrival of newcomers was frequently accompanied by a "reshuffling" of the affected units to better redistribute veterans and newcomers, so that even companies that had been nearly obliterated could still have a sprinkling of experienced soldiers in them. Even those men who knew one another before the fighting began were not guaranteed to remain in the same sub-unit after the battalion had been "rested and reorganized." Newcomers were not the only ones in the reinforcement stream; during combat operations, those who had been wounded or fallen sick were fed back into the stream rather than returning directly to their units. There was a swift trade, behind the lines, in units "poaching" experienced soldiers from other units out of the common reinforcement stream. This was not a popular practice, but there was a chance that strings would be pulled and good soldiers would end up in completely new units once they finished their convalescence. In his regimental history of the Seaforth Highlanders, historian Reginald Roy recalled how, "after the Gothic Line [in August–September 1944], reinforcements arrived. Care was taken that no one platoon received a majority of reinforcements, and consequently there was some shuffling within the battalion to strike a nice balance of veterans and recruits."[15] Thus, the arrival of reinforcements could and did spur further recombination and reorganization within battalions.

All the above sources of personnel turbulence (battle and DNBI casualties, sub-unit recombination, the LOB system, task-specific groupings, and reinforcement soldiers) would have compounded one another and created unit compositions in the Canadian infantry that were far from the idealized "band of brothers." When Canadian battalions went into battle for the first time, as in Sicily or on Juno Beach, most of their men had served together for years, with strong existing relationships and shared experiences of training and leadership. But even a short time in high-intensity combat against the German Army changed units completely, primarily because of dramatically high casualty rates but also because battalions in combat shuffled personnel to try to field the most effective force possible at any given time.

Some theories of cohesion assert that motivation stems from a unit or sub-unit's leadership, teamwork, and trust (see Ian Hope's chapter in this volume). But in high-intensity combat, leadership casualties were extremely high, "teamwork" within a unit would need to be constantly relearned with strangers, and trust could not be based upon long acquaintance and personal knowledge. Perhaps most remarkable is that the losses and turbulence suffered by the Canadian Army did not cause it to fall apart. Sub-units generally continued to operate effectively when understrength (which was all the time), when combined and recombined, and when reinforced. While orders often had to be negotiated, there were few outright combat refusals and morale, insofar as it can be measured by historians, remained at a high pitch during the intense combat operations.[16] While it is difficult to make overarching generalizations about all five fighting divisions of the Canadian Army during the war, their level of fighting proficiency is considered to have risen rather than fallen during the period 1943–45, as the formations became more battle-hardened and experienced. But at the same time, the personnel turbulence was so great among both junior leaders and other infantry ranks that "battle-hardened" and "strangers in arms" became synonymous.

The question remains: what kept so many of them going for so long?

One possible answer, in Canada, is the regiment. In Chapter 1 of this volume, Allan English discusses how the "canned" Canadian answer to this question has historically been regimental loyalty and *esprit de corps*, and, in Chapter 6, Ian Hope offers a defence of the regiment as a source of support and motivation. However, there are reasons for skepticism about the durability and efficacy of regimental connections as a source of cohesion and combat motivation, at least during the high-intensity, high-casualty operations of the Second World War. The "original" soldiers who joined up at the war's outbreak and spent years together in the same unit (or who had even been involved in the peacetime militia during the interwar years) had a strong personal connection with their regiment. But could these bonds of secondary-group cohesion survive the onset of high-intensity combat? As mentioned earlier, it did not take much exposure to high-intensity combat before the regiment's "original" members were no longer showing up in unit rolls. By the end of the war, they had been replaced by newcomers several times over. Even worse for regimental tradition, however, was the lack of regional homogeneity within battalions. The objective of the Canadian Army's centralized reinforcement stream was to try to place men from the same region of Canada in battalions associated with regiments from that region. The higher leadership espoused the importance of maintaining this regional character as a basis for regimental distinctiveness. However, the system melted down upon contact with the enemy, and reinforcements were often being fed into whichever units needed them the most. As pointed out earlier, the infantrymen in most regiments initially were highly homogeneous in their regional composition, but, after a few heavy engagements, units became jumbles of men from many different regions, who had little if any pre-existing connection to one another or to the regiment. Furthermore, a series of battle experience questionnaires, completed by more than 150 Canadian infantry officers shortly after combat in 1944–45, go into considerable detail about the structure and dynamics of morale in Canadian Army units. Not once in these questionnaires was "regimental pride," "esprit de corps," "unit spirit," or anything else that could reasonably have referred to secondary-group cohesion mentioned as a source of motivation and morale for soldiers.[17] Regimental pride certainly existed and could be an integral source of social support. But the evidence does not support regimental affiliation and uniqueness as sources of the "will to fight," particularly after high-intensity fighting had taken almost all the regiment's original members. This is not to say that identification with larger groups was impossible. As Ian Hope explains, his experience of modern combat was that the "primary group" that supported and sustained soldiers should be thought of as the company, not the section or platoon. Canada's fighting in Afghanistan, however, was of a very different character from that of the Second World War, and resulted in a much lower casualty rate. Without disputing Hope's Afghanistan experience, during the Second World War rifle companies were almost as ravaged by high casualties as were sections and platoons, and thus faced the same fundamental problem. The pool and network of acquaintances and kinship would have been larger if extended to the company, but would still have been filled with strangers owing to high losses and personnel turbulence. So, if traditional notions of cohesion and regiment are inadequate, how do we explain the processes underlying why the Canadian infantrymen continued to fight?

One of the most compelling concepts to emerge in the literature on combat motivation in the past ten years is the idea of "swift trust" as an element of cohesion. The small body of swift trust literature available today posits conditions under which the trust predicating primary-group cohesion in the standard model is not necessarily based on strong existing relationships and shared experience. An Israeli study by Uzi Ben-Shalom in 2009 first described how Israel Defense Forces (IDF) units fighting in the Al-Aqsa Intifada (2000–01) "consciously and systematically" took apart and recombined units, divided them into small components, and assigned them to other elements on short notice for tactical missions. "Primary group cohesion could not be sustained," the author argues, "since the original units were under a constant process of splitting and reintegrating."[18] These processes created uncertainty among troops, but were not accompanied by breakdowns in morale, discipline, or effectiveness. Instead, these new "instant units" worked well together; although soldiers wanted to be back with their original, peer-bonded units, combat-effective composite units could nevertheless be created on the fly. Soldiers' opinions of the strangers they were assigned to work with would at first be based upon reputations, stereotypes, and cultural assumptions, but these would be replaced by professionalism and pride as motivating factors in finding ways to collaborate. Swift trust established between strangers allowed for flexibility and resilience in morale and fighting efficiency in groups where primary-group cohesion would not normally have existed.[19]

The psychological concept of swift trust holds some explanatory power for understanding how the Canadians went into battle. "Swift trust" as it existed for the IDF in the year 2000 was not the same as what was happening in the Canadian Army during the Second World War. Ben-Shalom's seminal IDF study talks about short-term units and cooperation among strangers who worked together on the assumption that they would eventually rejoin their original units. During and after high-intensity combat, infantrymen in the Canadian Army in the Second World War were thrown together in ad hoc sub-units on a much longer-term or even permanent basis, and reshuffled freely. Nonetheless, even if "swift trust" was not being deliberately relied upon in the 1940s, and was never called by that name, the process that Ben-Shalom describes may have been similar to what

Canadians experienced. Soldiers did not need the bonds of long-term friendship, knowledge, and shared experience, or of a stable primary group, so much as they needed to know that those beside them were professionals, were dependable, were trained, and could be trusted. Battle questionnaires dating from the time of the fighting in Northwest Europe in 1944–45 revealed that a major source of discontent among Canadian infantrymen was not that soldiers did not know one another; it was the impression (usually erroneous) that the strangers who were reinforcing a unit lacked training and could not be counted on. However, a much greater threat to morale came from the lack of any reinforcements at all. "Lack of reinforcements was a constant topic with the men," wrote Captain W. Parker of the Royal Hamilton Light Infantry in his questionnaire. "They felt the risk of becoming a casualty was greater, because the strength of a platoon was less. Even poorly trained reinforcements were better for morale than no reinforcements at all."[20] After the war, Lieutenant-General Charles Foulkes (who had commanded 2nd CID and I Canadian Corps) submitted an opinion on Canadian effectiveness and motivation at the Battle of Hong Kong which echoed the idea of swift trust between soldiers. "As a result of operations," Foulkes wrote, "units are required to absorb varying percentages of officers and other ranks who on occasions may have to join the unit in the middle of an operation. So long as the reinforce-personnel are adequately trained and know their jobs, mutual understanding within sub-units quickly develops."[21] Foulkes's experience – that trust developed in extremis, even between fighters who were complete strangers – meshes well with an understanding of swift trust between soldiers in the Canadian Army.

The shared training and knowledge of Canadian soldiers allowed bonds of trust and professionalism to form rapidly under fire. While not always triumphant in every action, there were few instances of the Canadians breaking and running, surrendering, or retreating en masse, and they fought the Italians and Germans in a wide variety of circumstances, usually side-by-side with strangers. At the sharp end, their training and skill with weapons was usually sufficient to glue them together and allow them to carry on as small cogs in the larger war machine. It would not have been pleasant. The psychological toll of such losses and personnel turbulence would have been extremely high. But the tactical effectiveness of the Canadian soldiers did not follow a declining trajectory during the fighting. The army's official historian, C.P. Stacey, believed that in Northwest Europe, the

Canadians moved on from an uncertain performance in Normandy to become "battle-hardened soldiers," who had "mastered every aspect of their task" and become "an exceptionally efficient fighting machine" by the end of the campaign.[22] More recent updates to the historiography, particularly by Terry Copp, have portrayed the Canadian Army as experiencing both success and failure at the command, staff, and combat levels throughout the campaign against Germany, but certainly not a degradation of fighting power.[23] Copp's book, *Cinderella Army*, quotes Lieutenant Walter Keith, a replacement infantry platoon commander, who wrote about the high casualties and the bonds that held replacements, reinforcements, and veteran soldiers together in the Regina Rifles. When Lieutenant Keith joined the Rifles' 16th Platoon in March 1945, there were only two out of thirty-two men left in the platoon who had fought in Normandy, with an additional one who had fought at the Leopold Canal in September 1944. Nonetheless, Keith was highly impressed with how his platoon functioned: "Looking back now I realize that I never once had to cajole or threaten or even encourage them to do the job they were given, they automatically did it. The section commanders unhesitatingly led their small group of riflemen where they were told to go and the section followed them, stupid though the order may have seemed to be."[24]

Bonds of cohesion and "swift trust" were not the only things that kept Canadian soldiers going, of course. Evidence from morale studies, censorship reports, and battle questionnaires provide a unique portrait of the factors central to motivation in the Canadian Army. Not surprisingly, at the top of the list were the prosaic comforts of Army life: good food, prompt mail, regular leave and, overall, the sense that in return for their sacrifices they were being looked after by the military institution. Notwithstanding complaints about the "teeth to tail" ratio of fighting to non-fighting services in the Canadian Army,[25] censorship report data strongly suggests that the soldiers' material and prosaic needs were being well met, particularly in the long Northwest Europe campaign of 1944–45.[26] Confidence in training, weapons, and support services, and in themselves, was a cornerstone of morale and motivation. Success in battle was also a key indicator of morale: the spirits of the Canadians were rarely higher than when they were achieving conspicuous success in combat, even if that success was paid for in frightfully high casualties.[27]

Aside from being a matter of historical interest, Canada's Second World War experience raises questions for modern combat motivation.

Was, for instance, the Canadian situation in the Second World War unique? Was this experience of "swift trust" and successful rapid bonding between strangers mirrored in other armies – of friend or of foe – or is this something that the Canadians were particularly or uniquely good at? What were (as Claire Cookson-Hills explores in her chapter in this volume) the potential costs associated with developing an aggressive, warfighting army that continually lost its junior leadership? Of the many Canadian Army courts martial for sexual violence against German women at the end of the Second World War, 85 per cent of offenders were from the combat arms, half of them from infantry units.[28] It is difficult to correlate motivation and discipline, or to make absolute statements about what rises in disciplinary offences may mean, but there are troubling implications nonetheless.[29] Finally, there is one of the most important questions: is cohesion a source of effectiveness, or is it perhaps more useful to think of effectiveness as a source of cohesion? It was in part the Canadian Army's conspicuous success in operations that bound strangers-in-arms together. The Canadian Army has not faced sustained high-intensity operations of this nature since the end of 1945, though there were many incidents in Korea, the former Yugoslavia, and Afghanistan where Canadians encountered heightened levels of violence. Such high losses represent a "worst-case" or "nightmare" scenario – militarily and politically. But analyzing motivation and the human dimension of war in extremis may help us to understand the art of the possible when it comes to our joint military capabilities. In the past year, the Canadian Joint Operations Command (CJOC) has been articulating a vision of "How We Fight" to the Canadian Armed Forces. This vision stresses the need to invest in the CAF's human and intellectual capital as part of a wider requirement for nuance in our use of force when facing threats that do not hold to our traditional ideas of war. As part of the process of re-evaluating how the CAF fights, it should be helpful to understand how motivation and cohesion persist even in situations of the highest intensity. The importance of swift bonds formed between team members with little or no previous knowledge of one another has even wider applicability for modern operations.

Swift trust does not explain everything about combat motivation, and is not a skeleton key to unlocking the human dimension of warfare. It does, however, offer a compelling explanation for understanding high-intensity, high-casualty combat. Swift trust provides at least a tentative explanation for how men like Lieutenants Knight and Roberts, and tens of thousands of other Canadians, existed in relation to one another and coped amid unthinkably adverse circumstances during the Second World War. As the Israel Defense Forces have found, swift trust can be developed and relied upon as a deliberate measure, but the Canadian example suggests it may also emerge organically from the needs-must situations created and aggravated by high-intensity and high-casualty combat.

NOTES

This chapter is adapted from the keynote address given at the 2016 CIDP Combat Motivation Workshop held at Fort Frontenac, Kingston, Ontario.

1 W.R.P. Bridger, *Royal Military College of Canada Review and Log of H.M.S. Stone Frigate* XV, no. 29 (June 1934): 30.

2 Geoffrey Hayes, *The Lincs: A History of the Lincoln and Welland Regiment at War* (Alma, ON: Maple Leaf Route, 1986), 4.

3 CMHQ [Canadian Military Headquarters] Records Office – Consolidated Casualty Statistics – AEF, LAC, RG 24, vols. 12695–6, RG 24 vol. 18576, file 133.065(D18D).

4 CMHQ Records Office – Consolidated Casualty Statistics – CMF, LAC RG v24, vols. 12697–8, RG 24, vol. 18576, file 133.065(D18D).

5 For a full explanation of methods and sources, see: Robert C. Engen, *Strangers in Arms: Combat Motivation in the Canadian Army, 1943–45* (Montreal: McGill-Queen's University Press, 2016), 211–18.

6 Serge Bernier, *The Royal 22e Regiment, 1914–1999*, trans. Charles Phillips (Montreal: Art Global, 2000), 117.

7 These numbers also would not have included those killed in action, who never made it to hospital.

8 Quarterly Medical Report, First Canadian Army, 1 July–30 Sept 1944, War Diary ADMS First Canadian Army, October 1944, LAC, RG 24, vol. 15647.

9 Max Hastings, *Overlord: D-Day and the Battle for Normandy* (New York: Macmillan, 1993), 183.

10 William Jackson, *The Mediterranean and Middle East, Vol. VI, Part 3 – Victory in the Mediterranean, November 1944 to May 1945* (London: Her Majesty's Stationery Office, 1987), 207.

11 Robert C. Engen, *Canadians Under Fire: Infantry Effectiveness in the Second World War* (Montreal: McGill-Queen's University Press, 2009), 175.

12 Farley Mowat, *The Regiment* (Toronto: McClelland and Stewart, 1955), 286; Reginald Roy, *The Seaforth Highlanders of Canada, 1919–1965* (Vancouver: Evergreen Press, 1969), 349.

13 For more, see: War Office, *Infantry Section Leading 1938* (London, 1938), 52–3; Engen, *Canadians Under Fire*, 111–16.

14 Engen, *Canadians Under Fire*, 117–21.

15 Roy, *Seaforth Highlanders*, 349.

16 Engen, *Strangers in Arms*, 110–15.

17 Ibid., 236–9.

18 Uzi Ben-Shalom, Zeev Lehrer, and Eyal Ben-Ari, "Cohesion During Military Operations: A Field Study on Combat Units in the Al-Aqsa Intifada," *Armed Forces and Society* 32, no. 1 (October 2005): 66–70.

19 For further discussion and literature review of swift trust, see: Engen, *Strangers in Arms*, 15–17.

20 Captain W. Parker, Royal Hamilton Light Infantry, LAC, RG 24, vol. 10450, BEQ 17.

21 Chief of the General Staff to Minister of National Defence, 9 February 1948, quoted in: Carl Vincent, *No Reason Why: The Canadian Hong Kong Tragedy, an Examination* (Toronto: Canada's Wings, 1981), 268.

22 C.P. Stacey, *The Official History of the Canadian Army in the Second World War, Vol. 3 – The Victory Campaign: Operations in Northwest Europe, 1944–1945* (Ottawa: Edmond Cloutier, 1960), 643.

23 Terry Copp, *Cinderella Army: The Canadians in Northwest Europe, 1944–1945* (Toronto: University of Toronto Press, 2006), 287.

24 Gordon Brown, *Look to Your Front – Regina Rifles: A Regiment at War, 1944–1945* (Waterloo, ON: Laurier Centre for Military Strategic and Disarmament Studies, 2001), 185–204. This account also appears in: Copp, *Cinderella Army*, 294–6.

25 E.L.M. Burns, *Manpower in the Canadian Army, 1939–1945* (Toronto: Clarke Irwin, 1956).

26 Censorship Reports – First Canadian Army, 1 Sept 1944–30 April 1945, LAC, microfilm reel T-17925.

27 Engen, *Strangers in Arms*, 110–15.

28 Canadian Armed Forces, Directorate of History and Heritage (DHH), Courts Martial Indices, boxes 10–12.

29 For more discussion of the use of evidence on army discipline to make inferences about morale and motivation, see: Engen, *Strangers in Arms*, 214–15.

6

Combat Motivation in the Contemporary Canadian Army

Ian Hope

Othryades, the lone Spartan hoplite who held the field at the end of the Battle of Thyrea (546 BC), would have understood Captain Nichola Goddard, a forward observation officer killed in Afghanistan in 2006, and she him.[1] She would appreciate his need to hold *his place in the line*; Othryades would understand the *sense of duty* that always brought her to a forward, exposed position. Neither distance in space and time, nor distinction by class, gender, or ethnicity creates an obstacle to spiritual connection of these two strangers – a connection formed by the brutal conditions of combat, which required of each a *will to fight*. Modern researchers in the field of combat motivation would do well to remember this. Regardless of how we choose to define the combat experience or to explain individual behaviour in combat, war ultimately defines those who join in it, not the other way around. What is constant are combat's extremes of violence, excessively harsh living conditions, the act of killing over and over again, and the requirement to mentally accommodate destruction, death, and fear. In this, the crushing collision of two hoplite phalanxes is not so different than the impact of a Taliban rocket-propelled grenade against the side of a light armoured vehicle (LAV); nor does the exchange of modern weapons fire produce effects dissimilar to the push and stab of the *othismos*. Either form of combat affects the minds and souls of participants in similar ways, and creates its own requirement – a will to fight despite brutality and fear.

To believe that this will to fight is a result of the imposition of a particular society's assumptions of hypermasculinity, of class expectation or submissiveness, or any kind of exclusive ethnic or gendered right or advantage is to mistake cause and effect in war. For all humanity for all of history, combat has proven that it does not discriminate; that its conditions produce a common need – a readiness to kill.[2] This reality must remain central to the study of combat motivation theory. If the will to fight is not at the centre of any theoretical construct explaining combat, then the theory has real limits and its utility may vary from temporarily useful to disastrous.

This chapter will define combat motivation, and competing theories about it, before relating how and why I chose a particular course of action to motivate my soldiers for combat and during combat in 2006. In distinction from other chapters of this book, I will restrict my definition of combat motivation to simply the *will to fight*. This is related but different from *morale* – which to me is the sense of individual and collective well-being, and can be a simple matter of dry socks, hot food, and cigarettes. There can still be a will to fight if morale is not high. Combat motivation is also distinguished from *cohesion*, which is a degree of teamwork and team spirit that may exist with or without the will to fight. These distinctions may seem to be mere nuances, but they are important nonetheless.

The will to fight is not about simply resisting the traumatic effects of war, of surviving the ordeal by fostering mental, physical, and spiritual resilience. The will to fight requires of the soldier a readiness, indeed a desire, to fight an enemy, and to prevail by killing or capturing that enemy. This is why research in combat motivation should be restricted to combat operations, where killing is essential. It is impossible to transpose the will to fight to other operational environments (such as stability or peace support operations), where killing is not the sine qua non and where soldiers are motivated more by monetary allowances, tax benefits, and the opportunity to earn a medal or advance a career.

Combat motivation is measured by fighting. There is no other true measurement. Yet measuring fighting ability objectively is very difficult. Martin van Creveld made a bold attempt to quantify how much better was the will to fight in the Wehrmacht than in the American Army during the Second World War, regardless of the fact that the German Army was obliterated by Allied forces.[3] Quantitative analysis of this type is useful but rare. Useful, as well, is evidence of a fighting reputation awarded to a foe by an enemy, as subjective as that might seem. Regardless of inexactitude of measurement, fighting remains the only test of combat motivation. Trying to determine the same by use of statistics of disciplinary infractions, muster, sick parade, and AWOL rates, and surveys regarding cohesion and morale, can add valuable context to research (see Robert Engen's chapter in this volume), but only a thorough analysis of fighting itself can reveal levels of combat motivation.

Some military historians and a legion of psychiatrists, psychologists, and social scientists have for the past century attempted to approach combat motivation outside of analysis of fighting, by examining the closely related question of why soldiers break down in combat, why there is degradation in the will to fight. This field of study is appealing because it is broader, not reliant upon measuring fighting ability, and accessible through records of psychiatric casualties in war. The historiography of the field of combat motivation over the past century shows that the preponderance of work deals with issues of "combat stress, fatigue, or exhaustion," and trauma syndromes of a wide variety of names. In the absence of studies related directly to measures of fighting effectiveness, a synopsis of the major theories of combat stress may be useful to a subsequent discussion of current Canadian practices to instill and maintain the will to fight.

Combat motivation and war trauma are evident in Homer and Herodotus, in plays by Sophocles, Euripides, Aeschylus, and Shakespeare.[4] It is the central theme of Stephen Crane's remarkable *The Red Badge of Courage* (1895). But it was not until the First World War, when large-scale industrial warfare revealed its destructive hand, that science began to examine these issues. The Great War occurred in an era when psychoanalysis gained significant social traction, and provided theorists and practitioners alike with cases aplenty. Theories on combat motivation and trauma grew. As with most theory, these were heavily shaped by the political and social realities of the time. The dominant theory of the interwar period, derived from both Lord Southborough's War Office Commission of Inquiry into Shell-Shock (1922), and consistent with the *Kriegneurosen* debate in the Weimar Republic, concluded that "fighting spirit" depended upon the moral makeup of the individual soldier, the moral fibre of a person. Both British and German military establishments refused to recognize symptoms such as "shell shock" as a medical condition. To do so might provide every soldier an easy way out, a "malingerers' charter."[5] The central idea of the official findings was that a soldier's constitutional inheritance, hereditary predisposition, and upbringing determined his performance in battle and whether he would crack under pressure.

Reliance upon "character" reinforced notions that proper breeding and schooling, and a sense of duty to "King and country," were immunizing tonics to the strains of battle. Pre-selection of soldiers based on character traits became a key factor in mobilization planning (see Roger Spiller's chapter in this volume). This construct cast a very dark shadow over a rival theory, which suggested industrial warfare brought forth conditions that guarantee that all soldiers will eventually degrade and breakdown in prolonged combat, in what would much later be referred to as "universal trauma reaction," regardless of patriotism or ingrained character.[6]

The Second World War gave us plenty more experience regarding combat motivation and trauma. In its aftermath, two theoretical constructs emerged in the American Armed Services that held long-term consequences. The first was the belief that soldier performance followed a curve, rising in effectiveness after first blooding, sustained effectiveness for a period of weeks or months, then drastic reduction in effectiveness as fatigue diminished the fighting ability of soldier and unit alike.[7] This supposition led to subsequent "tours of duty" of specific lengths for individuals and units on American military operations, such as the "Vietnam year."[8] The second theoretical construct to gain traction stemmed from an attempt to explain Wehrmacht combat effectiveness without attributing credit to Nazi ideology. Sociologists Edgar Shils and Morris Janowitz proposed that a soldier fights not because of a strength of moral fibre or notions of patriotism, but because of the pre-eminence of the "primary group" (a squad or section of eight to ten persons) which within his daily life "met his basic organic needs, offered him affection and esteem … supplied him with a sense of power and adequately regulated his relations with authority."[9] Both the "Marchand curve" and Shils/Janowitz "primary group·cohesion" theories related directly to the will to fight.

Primary group theory was widely accepted in America, but received further definition when scholars, seeking to explain soldier performance in Vietnam, concluded that even though soldiers might have strong primary group cohesion in war, their collective performance might be mediocre if they failed to have a collective commitment to achieve the missions assigned to the unit.[10] In the 1980s, Guy Siebold attempted a synthesis and formulated the "standard model" of military group cohesion comprised of four equally important components: *horizontal bonding* reinforced primary-group cohesion theory, emphasizing bonding at the small group (squad) level; *vertical bonding* and *organizational bonding* linked the squad to its leaders at the company or battalion level; and *institutional bonding* had soldiers identify with the army.[11] The Siebold construct effectively connected many theories of cohesion and combat motivation into a neat package, which is still used in American circles. In addressing the complex issues of integrating gay soldiers into Army units, or females into combat units, Robert MacCoun later proposed another model: He distinguished "task cohesion" – "the shared commitment among members to achieving a goal that requires the collective efforts of the group" – from "social cohesion" – "the extent to which group members like each other, prefer to spend their social time together ... and feel emotionally close to one another."[12] With such models, combat motivation studies made a turn away from the analysis of history toward a narrow focus on "cohesion" and a reliance on the rather complex language and nuances of the social sciences. The will to fight and battle performance exist at the margins of such studies.

In the early twenty-first century, a group of Israeli scholars directly challenged the primary-group cohesion concept in favour of a pre-eminent requirement for task cohesion. They claimed that small groups of soldiers of various units, branches, and trades, but possessed of professional expertise that was acknowledged and respected by others, allowed the Israel Defense Forces to create effective "instant units" possessing "swift trust."[13] These observers believed that the mutual respect of expertise and a common purpose were enough to overcome any lack of primary-group or social cohesion and create effective ad hoc combat units. Some scholars have used this idea to suggest how units during intense combat in the Second World War (with over 100 per cent casualty rates) continued fighting after the depletion or elimination of the original primary group.[14]

Combat motivation theory became less accessible to practitioners the more closely associated it became with studies of group cohesion using nuanced social science theory and language (not that Anglo-Canadian armies have ever paid much heed to the theoretical studies). Indeed, the impact of American combat cohesion and stress literature upon practice in the Canadian Army has remained negligible. Few of the theories outlined above have had real impact upon combat motivation thinking among practitioners. For example: in the aftermath of the Second World War, British and Commonwealth armies accepted the assertion that "battle exhaustion" was a real and serious problem in sustained combat, which could eventually affect most if not every soldier.[15] However, military leadership in these armies still maintained that selection, training, good leadership, and proper equipment, combined with a policy of rotation of individuals and units in and out of combat, could to some extent mitigate the effects of battle. While pre-selection did not produce units immune to battle exhaustion, there remained a belief that it was still useful as an indicator of an individual's ability to recover.[16] Without dismissing any theoretical framework, the British and many Commonwealth armies continued throughout the last decades of the twentieth century to hold faith in the regimental system and unit rotation as the instrumental structure through which soldiers gain motivation and sustain resilience. The overwhelming anecdotal evidence about the continued efficacy of the regimental system served to discourage questions that might have otherwise led to healthy circumspection. But with a paucity of evidence that the regimental system was in any way failing or obsolete, there is little incentive to question its utility in promoting combat motivation and resilience.[17]

The regimental system as practiced within the Canadian Army has long made tradition of maintaining strong sections, platoons, and companies, which give each soldier added sense of identity, and remains very strong. The practice of this system differs significantly from the American and German models described by Shils and Janowitz, and Siebold and MacCoun. In Commonwealth Armies (and the United States Marine Corps) the primary group for the infantry is the company, not the section or squad. It is the company that meets all of the daily needs of the soldiers, as well as their "affection and esteem" and "sense of power." When asked, Canadian infantrymen will identify themselves with so-and-so company of a particular regiment. The company remains the centre of gravity. Soldiers will readily accept a cross-posting to another section or platoon within the company, but are resentful toward extra-company postings. If wounded, it is the company they try to return to. This is an important distinction from the primary-group concept employed by social scientists, because the infantry company is by design much more resilient than sections or platoons, and contains redundancy in leadership, combat support, and logistical functions. The Canadian infantry, for this reason, attempts to keep companies together for long periods. And while a section might see a complete change in personnel during long campaigns, historically the company has been able to sustain a core of its original membership alive.

The company (or equivalently sized squadron or battery, all of them called "sub-units") is the basic building block of combat organization. It is where special-to-arms training occurs with guaranteed expertise. But in combat, it is rare that the sub-unit fights independently. The infantry company may detach a platoon to serve with a tank squadron, and the company will receive many types of "attachments," such as tanks, artillery fire observers and air controllers, engineers, police, civil affairs personnel, mechanics, medics, communications specialists, or air defence soldiers. The attached elements – together with the host company – form into a "company group" or "combat team." The Canadian Army embraced the combined arms organizational practice of combat teams and battle groups in the 1960s, well in advance of other armies, and to this day Canada is unique in its emphasis on combined arms work starting in basic training.[18] With the host sub-unit as a primary group, all attachments (especially if they are habitually attached in training) identify socially with this host in combat, making the host company even stronger. The regimental system, embracing all-arms tactical groupings, is very flexible and resilient in this regard. It is probably for this reason that we have paid less attention to Israeli studies that claim to have discovered ways to create "instant units" built simply on respect for individual expertise. In fact, there should be great caution in the Army concerning theories of "swift trust" and "instant units" for fear that some economically inclined bureaucrat might use them to dismantle our proven system of regiments and affiliations, forcing us instead into a variation on a Vietnam-era individual DEROS (Date Estimated Return from Overseas) system, with all of its failings. When Canadian Army personnel read descriptions of the Siebold model, they see little distinction (beyond definition of the primary-group level) between it and their regimental system, and soldiers and officers remain reluctant to replace known terms and procedures for the terminology and predictions of social science theory.

Upon assuming command of the 1st Battalion Princess Patricia's Canadian Light Infantry (1 PPCLI) in August 2004, I set out to prepare the unit for combat operations in Afghanistan, and in doing so I drew upon what I had learned of combat motivation theory from such great minds as Roger Spiller, Jack English, and Allan English (some of whose works grace the pages of this very volume) as well as regimental practice. I chose to train and educate using terms and definitions accessible to all.[19] I defined combat motivation simply as the *will to fight*. Without labelling things in social science terms, such as "primary-group cohesion" or "vertical," "horizontal," "task," or "social" cohesion, I informed the officers and soldiers that the will to fight required two equally important things: *teamwork* and *leadership*. These two things are not mutually exclusive, and must be reinforcing lest they cause divisions within a unit. If a unit possesses aggressive leadership with only individual soldiers below that, or has spirited soldier teams without leadership, the unit will not perform well in battle. On the other hand, if both teamwork and leadership are developed equally well, the unit will likely fight well. The individual in such a unit will be comfortable when facing the danger of war within their team, under good leadership, for this is better than trying to face it alone.

Infantry and combined-arms teamwork is best achieved by hard, realistic training, especially training with live ammunition and in engagements with other soldiers using non-lethal, marking projectiles (such as Simunition).[20] Frequent live-fire attack ranges, ambush and counter-ambush ranges, force-on-force Simunition training, especially in urban settings, complemented by a rigorous and honest debriefing system (known as "after-action review," or AAR), builds teams quickly. It also instructs individuals and teams in "how to fight," a critical precursor to instilling a *will to fight*.

One week after assuming command of the battalion, we commenced a six-week field exercise in Wainwright, Alberta, focusing on the conduct of the live-fire attack. Very few things enable teambuilding as does the live-fire attack. This must be approached incrementally, starting with ranges that exercise the two-person team (the "fire team"), conducting fire and movement drills with live ammunition. Here the team members support each other, one firing while the other moves forward, up to a point whereat they can throw grenades into a trench or building, and "clear" it with small-arms fire and the bayonet. Once proficient in this drill, the ranges continue with the four-person "group" employing similar tactics, with one team supporting the movement of another using rifles, light machine guns, light antitank weapons, grenade launchers, and hand grenades. When this level of training was complete, we commenced ranges with the eight-person infantry rifle section, and then with that section and their light armoured vehicle (LAV). All of these attack ranges have dual purpose: to bond the various organizations together by realistic and difficult battle training, wherein each member must prove proficiency with their weapon in support of other members moving forward; and to train the junior leaders (the senior soldier in the two-person team, the master corporal of the four-person group, or the sergeant in charge of the section and LAV). Training to higher levels cannot begin until the building blocks of teamwork and small group leadership are in place.

Battle inoculation and live-fire attacks are essential in producing fighting spirit and trust. I used this method for platoon and company team-building as well. By the time the battalion deployed to Kandahar in January 2006, each section had performed two dozen group and section attack ranges, and each platoon and company a good dozen more. In between the actual ranges, soldiers within the team, group, section, platoon, and company lived and worked together in tents, or simply under pieces of canvas, in the field, in cold and wet conditions. The very act of living together under these conditions also builds teamwork. In this, we sought to create the strongest primary groups – the infantry companies – concentrating on good leadership.

Once we had begun our live-fire training exercises in Wainwright, focusing on team work, I began in parallel to assess and develop leadership throughout the battalion. I was ably assisted by Chief Warrant Officer Randy Northrup, my regimental sergeant major (RSM). Randy had been the platoon warrant officer when I was a young platoon commander with the PPCLI's 2nd Battalion in Germany in the 1980s. We made a good team back then, and it was very easy to pick up where we had left off. Together we were a *command team*.[21] We were determined to make command teams at every level of the battalion by pairing a specific officer with a senior non-commissioned officer (NCO) so that the character and style of each would complement the other. With pages of names of all of our personnel in front of us, and personal notes on performance and personality, we created command teams within each platoon and company throughout the battalion, and decided when we would shift persons from job to job in order to stabilize the sections, platoons, and companies as soon as possible. In this, we removed some people from the battalion and moved others in. No decision was made about an officer without Randy's input; likewise, he made no decision on movement of a senior NCO without mine. Once we had shuffled officers and NCOs about, we settled the organization of the infantry companies and attached subunits, the primary groups that we wanted for combat operations, five months prior to our deployment and then protected these from disruption by the Brigade and the Army, who always wanted to move our people around.[22]

We continued to use live-fire attack ranges and Simunition training to reinforce company teamwork and validate our selection of leaders and command teams. At that point, however, we needed to expand the unit to include the other components that would make up our company groups and battle group (BG). This included attachments such as an administration and logistics unit known as the Forward Support Element, an artillery battery, an engineer squadron, an unmanned aerial vehicle (UAV) squadron, a surveillance troop, a medical company, and civil affairs, military police, public affairs, intelligence, and human intelligence (HUMINT) sections.[23] All of these attachments joined us in Wainwright, but needed to be molded into one team. We did this by co-locating all of our people in one bivouac, by decentralizing combat-support assets and embedding them within combat sub-units, by providing training scenarios that concentrated on establishing broad trust between each arm and corps represented in the task force, and by forcing people away from sub-unit identifiers (flags and badges) toward acceptance of a common – neutral – identifying symbol. I chose the name Battle Group Task Force Orion, after the constellation Orion – representing the mythical Greek hunter of mountain beasts – which I knew blessed Afghan skies, so that our soldiers might look up and, seeing it, feel part of a larger entity, enduring and meaningful. We adopted the constellation as our symbol, which I used deliberately to help create cohesion within this all-arms force. It is in efforts to create and maintain cohesion that trust between two or more soldiers becomes meaningful.

Creating a sense of uniqueness is important, as are symbols, badges, and ceremonies. They help to build cohesion. But they must exist within the boundaries of acceptable discipline and practice of the Canadian Armed Forces, and not be representative of exclusive subcultures that thrive outside of the chain of command. The combat leader's job is to ensure that such devices are part of, or consistent with, the organizational and institutional identifiers and value structures.

Operations in Kandahar were going to be severely hamstrung by a luxurious Home Leave Travel Assistance (HLTA) policy, which would guarantee that 20–28 per cent of the fighting echelon was on leave at any one time, causing tremendous shortfalls in platoons and companies. I deliberately chose a leave policy rotating entire sections and platoons to take their leave together, so as to not degrade small-group cohesion while keeping primary-group (company) strength sufficient. To compensate for loss of strength within a company during such leave, we began to train to move platoons around between companies, and move attachments between normal affiliated companies, in order to allow us maximum flexibility to "cut and paste" all elements of the Task Force according to need. This proved to be essential in Kandahar, as we were ordered to cover a large area with a relatively small number of troops, and I therefore needed great articulation of the Task Force's parts to cover off all tasks.

Throughout our training, I utilized the AAR method as another means to establish points of trust between teams and leaders. After each training event, whether a range or a tactical scenario, the exercising unit would commence a structured feedback session where they affirmed the training objective and critically self-assessed how they had performed collectively against the criteria for that objective. I was not excluded from this process, and I frequently opened the sessions with thoughts on how my command performance could improve to the benefit of overall unit performance. In this way, we learned to assess ourselves without being blameful or allowing individuals to hide behind rank or appointment. This established greater trust between the different command levels of the Task Force, and the RSM and I watched closely as young officers struggled to "suck up" soldier criticism of a mistake, and then collectively brainstorm how they might avoid such problems in the future. When officers can do this in front of their soldiers and not lose confidence, trust is firm.

Thus, by late November 2005, Task Force Orion had achieved a degree of cohesion. The Task Force contained approximately 850 Canadian soldiers when it arrived on operations in Kandahar, Afghanistan, in January 2006, finishing the tour of duty on 21 August 2006.[24] During that period, Task Force Orion fought over fifty engagements with Taliban fighters. Many of these engagements lasted for days and involved artillery, mortar, helicopters, and fixed-wing aircraft support. The Task Force suffered 19 killed in action, 76 wounded in action, and 4 returned to Canada for stress-related injuries, while inflicting over 500 casualties upon the Taliban. The soldiers of Task Force Orion experienced varied pressures and stresses, some traditional to combat, some unique. While building our command teams throughout the battalion, Northrup and I also prepared a comprehensive succession plan for the inevitability of leaders becoming casualties, and thus had officers and NCOs designated to assume leadership roles as soon as casualties occurred.

One key to success was maintaining the initiative. To compensate for the lack of effective intelligence that could give us accurate information on where Taliban fighters were located, Task Force Orion dispersed across the province in company groups and lived among the villagers to develop local trust and gather intelligence through human contact. This forced the soldiers to live in the LAVs or beside the artillery gun lines, often for three or more weeks at a time without shower or proper toilet. Soldiers had three to five days at Kandahar Airfield (now Kandahar International Airport) between these deployments. We changed locations constantly, under the company commander's control and discretion. These manoeuvres began to have a disruptive effect on Taliban efforts to mass in the northern section of Kandahar. I did not want the Task Force tied to multiple small military posts, and resisted pressure to build forward operating bases that would prevent us from moving around and put us into a defensive pattern. By manoeuvring constantly, we were keeping the operational initiative, the maintenance of which became something tangible to me. The subordinate commanders and I could sense when we had the enemy confused or when they seemed ready to act. I began to trust in intuition, and our concept of operations evolved to a point where we continuously planned and executed multiple large manoeuvre operations to keep the initiative. Keeping the initiative is crucial to enhancing a *will to fight* as it gives soldiers a feeling of superiority over the enemy.[25]

It was up to Task Force Orion to establish its own operational tempo and tasks, since a lack of "actionable intelligence" on the enemy meant that few specific tasks were handed down by the Brigade. Operational tempo and effectiveness were almost entirely dependent upon the personalities of the commanders. We could have very easily hunkered down into localized routines in relatively safe areas and followed a pattern of "framework patrolling," which would make us seem "busy" but in fact achieve little (except to surrender the initiative and set ourselves up for attacks by more improvised explosive devices, or IEDs). Such a passive approach would have obstructed efforts to create a will to fight. Instead, I forced myself to encourage – and to trust – the company commanders to be perpetually proactive in hunting the enemy, forcing everyone to live "outside the wire," continuously manoeuvre, and engage locals. This was difficult for everyone, especially after casualties were incurred, when there was a natural tendency to adopt caution and reduce tempo. It was at these times, especially, that I trusted the company commanders to demonstrate an aggressive spirit and maintain operational initiative through offensive action. Not all people are equal in this regard, and a good battalion commander must tailor specific missions to the company commanders' individual personalities and their will to fight.

Most of our operations followed a similar pattern. We attempted to identify a general area where the enemy was situated (the relayed information almost always indicated a twenty-to-forty-man Taliban group hiding in the vicinity of a particular village). We then attempted to manoeuvre into that district quietly, under cover of darkness, using maximum deception (using other units to drive overtly around other parts of Kandahar province to confuse the Taliban as to which village we were interested in). We tried, as much as possible, to surround the village. Using intercepts of the enemy's communications or "chatter," we would attempt to vector in upon the enemy's locations. These were never exact, and most often we had to enter villages and search everything, discovering exactly where they were only after they fired upon us.

Once found, we would attempt to fix the enemy with artillery fire and destroy him in close-quarter combat. Neither of these things was easy. It required us to stay within 100 to 150 metres of the enemy and to coordinate fires before physically moving to clear his positions. Doing so was contrary to human nature. Like operational tempo, the degree of success we had in close-quarter combat became personality-dependent. The majority of soldiers, when fired upon for the first time, would seek to disengage back toward the last safe place they occupied, such as behind a wall or in a wadi. After several encounters, they repressed this urge but were reluctant to advance under fire (especially when separated from their LAVs). Forward movement or staying in place on the close-quarter battlefield, especially after nightfall, depended on the continued presence of battalion, company, and platoon commanders, supported by the "natural fighters" in our ranks. It became evident to me in May 2006 that the number of true fighters we had was a small minority.

I would estimate that in every platoon (around forty soldiers) there were only six or seven individuals possessed of a strong, natural will to fight. Yet, these soldiers' stalwartness almost always became the psychological pivot point for the action of a section, platoon, or company engaged in combat. I came to rely on the courage of commanders and this small number of natural fighters in each platoon or company to override the inherent fear of close-quarter battle and to ensure that we kept the enemy fixed before closing to destroy him. Trust – not authority – was the essential element.

It became silently understood that trust and cohesion required an equitable sharing of risk. I travelled everywhere by vehicle – over 9,700 kilometres – and was hit four times by IEDs and rocket-propelled grenades, resulting in the loss of two of my crew, Master Corporal Loewen and Master Corporal White, grievously injured by shrapnel on separate occasions. This demonstration of shared risk went far beyond any authority conferred by rank and appointment to promote the trust essential to the fighting spirit of Task Force Orion. The company commanders were also always seen well forward in the fighting. I trusted and relied upon these commanders to apply the determination, ferocity, and courage that this hard task required. Individual leadership was essential in sustaining the collective will to fight.

Company commanders needed a natural tenacity and robustness. I trusted that they would not succumb to their fears, but would combine their talent with the natural fighters under their command to enable the platoon or company to sustain and advance in the midst of chaos, violence, uncertainty, and fear to fix and finish the enemy. I trusted that they would learn from mistakes and successes alike, that they would handle death and loss quickly, with dignity, and then move on. I trusted that they would enforce good discipline and order, yet exercise forgiveness and compassion, without jeopardizing trust.

This is not to say that I did not expect mistakes to be made. All the commanders of Task Force Orion made mistakes in operations, mostly because the experience of sustained combat operations was new to us; we had no paradigms or experiential guides. Tactical errors were made that cost life and limb. Those of us responsible for these decisions, who gave these orders, had to deal with that knowledge immediately – in the face of continued operational pressures – without compromising the faith and trust necessary for mission command to function, and without losing the leader's will to fight. Task Force Orion instituted learning processes to capture lessons learned after each major engagement and to disseminate these throughout the area of operations. At all levels, I emphasized the use of the after-action review, sometimes running them myself, in the field, after the fighting was over. Through all of this, we did not dwell on mistakes. Sometimes we did not even speak of them. Nothing is more damaging to trust and self-confidence than to see a man who acted decisively in combat, but was the victim of bad luck, be interrogated by a commander who was not present and had not felt the pressures and complexities of that moment. While I desired that commanders determine quickly what had gone right or gone wrong, I did not want this to create an environment of blame. Dealing with loss was a powerful enough motivator for quick learning. Forgiving one another quickly went a long way to avoiding the trap of the proverbial blame game.

To sustain a unit in prolonged combat, there must be a great deal of hierarchical trust. That trust demands understanding and forgiveness, especially in situations where fear is prevalent. I did not question any request by a subordinate commander who asked for a long "water break" or who needed time to sort out "communications issues" before or during battles. Sometimes I, or one of my subordinate commanders, needed a moment to thrash the dark angel that had chosen that moment to visit, before picking up and carrying on. I knew that commanders were sometimes dealing with battles within themselves, but I never asked the embarrassing questions. To let an officer know, face-to-face, that you see fear in them is to forever compromise that officer to you. To let that officer's subordinates know that you have seen fear in their immediate leader would spread that fear farther. And fear can kill the will to fight quickly. Better to grant someone time to deal with it, and to make it clear that you expect action consistent with the maintenance of the initiative over the enemy. With time, most of us became familiar with the violence and uncertainty to a point where right-brain control (rational thinking) born of a sense of duty, combined with true readiness to fight, could win over fear. But it takes time and exposure to reach this point, and trust and understanding and patience are applicable in learning to fight. Being patient and forgiving to soldiers who possess a strong sense of duty will produce units that will not let you down.

Together with teamwork and leadership, one other element is essential to the creation and sustainment of a *will to fight*: the character of the commander. Here I should borrow from General Sir John Hackett and assert that the main characteristic of military leadership in battle is a commander's "total engagement" with the unit he commands: "A man only really gets the best out of the men he commands by something approaching complete fusion of his own identity with the corporate whole they form."[26] In this complete fusion, a commander must instil a sense of superiority and confidence, a sense of moral ascendency over the enemy. This is perhaps best described in General Bill Slim's classic *Defeat into Victory*. The will to fight must reside within the commander first, if the unit is to fully adopt a fighting spirit.

I pushed my personal philosophy upon the unit, and I reinforced it continuously in combat. Task Force Orion existed to hunt down and kill or capture Taliban fighters. Each soldier in every part of the Task Force, regardless of their individual branch of service, was expected to adopt the mindset of a hunter and contribute to the collective aim of finding, fixing, and finishing any Taliban we were to encounter. A spirit grew throughout Task Force Orion – a conviction that we truly were professionally and morally superior to our Taliban enemy.

I believe that this spirit helped soldiers cope with the stress of combat, and with loss. I observed that soldiers in the rifle companies and supporting arms were less prone to stress than those in our Transport Platoon, who were exposed to the dangers of IED strikes and ambushes without recourse to taking aggressive action against the Taliban. They were the hunted, not the hunter. All other elements of Task Force Orion maintained an aggressive hunting spirit. This spirt became pervasive, and I considered it my job to keep it strong.

I wish to dwell for a moment on the commander's injection of spirit into a unit (if it is not there already). Unit spirit has often been referred to as "soul." The ancient Greek general Xenophon famously wrote that, "whichever army goes into battle stronger in soul, their enemies generally cannot withstand them."[27] Similarly, the Union Army's commanding general during the American Civil War, William Tecumseh Sherman, added his observation that "there is a soul to an army as well as to the individual man, and no general can accomplish the full work of his army unless he commands the soul of his men, as well as their bodies and legs."[28] Combat motivation researchers would do well to focus on this phenomenon of spirit or soul and its impact upon the will to fight.

In summary, I would suggest that the combat experience has changed little over the millennia, that the impact of combat upon the human mind is more constant than not, and that combat motivation has timeless elements, but also that modern theories of combat motivation tend to serve the political and scholastic purposes of their time as much as or more than military requirements. Our definitions, and their acceptability, depend upon the times in which we live, the nature of civil-military relationships, the role of the military in society, and the contemporary nature of military service. Societies tend to define and label the combat experience according to social need. Nonetheless, I believe there is still great scope for research in the field of combat motivation. Military history – especially first-person accounts of combat from the ancients to the moderns, too often ignored as completely anecdotal – contains thoughts and sentiments on combat which remain extremely similar across years and millennia – something illustrated well in John Keegan's seminal work *Face of Battle*. Many anecdotal accounts reinforce the need to build teamwork, to develop and nurture good leadership, and the importance of personality of command. Scope exists for a grand survey of such sources to examine this thing called a *will to fight*. Such research should be carried out from the historian's perspective – an attempt to reveal, not prove, something. So, too, do we need examination of how we may measure the will to fight using historical analysis. Also unexplored is a current analysis of the relative effectiveness of Wehrmacht units in the last years of the Second World War and, perhaps, how much this was the product of the German idea of the "perfectibility of man" – and of the Germans' anti-hierarchical insistence upon individual action and individual responsibility for decision making in combat, regardless of orders. These are just a few areas ready for the researcher's hoe.

Captain Nichola Goddard and her ancient forebear-in-arms Othryades were motivated by a strong sense of duty to comrade and unit, among other things. They were proven leaders within a network of strong teams. In this they were and had the necessary elements to produce a *will to fight*. These are the same elements that can mitigate, to some degree, the stress of war. That they were possessed by two so very different individuals living in such very different societies and times must surely give credence to continuity in the combat experience – a continuity ready for so much more academic exploration.

NOTES

1 For Othryades and the Battle of Thyrea, see: P. Kohlmann, "Othryades: Eine historisch-kritische Untersuchung," *Rheinisches Museum* 29 (1874): 463–80; L. Moretti, "Sparta alla metà del VI secolo II: La guerra contro Argo per la Tireatide," *Rivista di filologia classica* 76 (1948): 204–22; and J. Dillery, "Reconfiguring the Past: Thyrea, Thermopylae and Narrative Patterns of Herodotus," *American Journal of Philology* 117 (1996): 217–54. For Nichola Goddard, see: Ian Hope, *Dancing with the Dushman: Command Imperatives for the Counter-Insurgency Fight in Afghanistan* (Kingston, ON: Canadian Defence Academy Press, 2008), 86–90; and Valerie Fortney, *Sunray: The Death and Life of Captain Nichola Goddard* (Toronto: Key Porter, 2010).

2 Donald Brown, *Human Universals* (New York: McGraw-Hill, 1991); Marco Costa, *Psicologia militaire: Elementi di psicologia per gli appartenanti alle forze armate* (Milan: Franco Angeli, 2003), 42; Steven Pinker, *The Better Angels of Our Nature* (New York: Viking, 2011), 108–43; Napoleon A. Chagnon, *Noble Savages: My Life among Two Dangerous Tribes – the Yanomamö and the Anthropologists* (New York: Simon & Schuster, 2013), 49–54.

3 Martin van Crevald, *Fighting Power: German and US Army Performance 1939–1945* (Westport, CT: Greenwood Press, 1982).

4 See: Sophocles, *Ajax*; Euripides, *Philoctetes*; Aeschylus, *Seven Against Thebes* and *Oresteia*; and William Shakespeare, *Henry IV*, act 2, scene 3 (with Hotspur's wife, Lady Percy).

5 Greg Eghigian, "The German Welfare State as a Discourse in Trauma," in *Traumatic Pasts: History, Psychiatry, and Trauma in the Modern Age, 1860–1930*, ed. Mark Micale and Paul Lerner (Cambridge, UK: Cambridge University Press, 2001), 92–112.

6 The inevitability of battle trauma was a pervasive theme in interwar literature. See: Paul Fussell, *The Great War and Modern Memory* (Oxford: Oxford University Press: 1975); and Terry Copp and Mark Osborne Humphries, *Combat Stress in the 20th Century: The Commonwealth Perspective* (Kingston, ON: Canadian Defence Academy Press, 2010).

7 Roy Swank and Walter E. Marchand, "Combat Neurosis: Development of Combat Exhaustion," *Archives of Neurology and Psychology* 55 (1946): 236–47.

8 As social scientists continued research into battle stress and trauma, Second World War findings meshed with later theory to influence United States Army policy. The finite tour of duty in a combat zone became one year during the Vietnam War, with a "DEROS" (Date Estimated Return from Overseas) that was different for every person regardless of unit.

9 Edgar Shils and Morris Janowitz, "Cohesion and Disintegration in the Wehrmacht in World War II," *Public Opinion Quarterly* 12 (1948): 281. Omar Bartov and Andreas Hillgruber have put the Shils and Janowitz thesis into question with their studies on the importance of Nazi ideology in German combat motivation during the period 1939–45. See: Omar Bartov, "Historians on the Eastern Front: Andreas Hillgruber and Germany's Tragedy," in *Murder in Our Midst: The Holocaust, Industrial Killing, and Representation*, ed. Omar Bartov (Oxford: Oxford University Press, 1996), 71–88; and Omar Bartov, *Hitler's Army: Soldiers, Nazis, and War in the Third Reich* (Oxford: Oxford University Press, 1991).

10 Charles Moskos, "The American Combat Soldier in Vietnam," *Journal of Social Issues* 31 (1975): 27.

11 Guy Siebold, "The Essence of Military Group Cohesion," *Armed Forces & Society* 33, no. 2, (January 2007): 286–95.

12 Robert MacCoun, "What Is Known about Unit Cohesion and Perfomance?", in *Sexual Orientation and Military Personnel Policy: Update of RAND's 1993 Study*, ed. Bernard Rostker (Santa Monica, CA: RAND Corporation, 2010), 137–65.

13 Uzi Ben-Shalom, Zeev Lehrer, and Eyal Ben-Ari, "Cohesion during Military Operations: A Field Study on Combat Units in the Al-Aqsa Intifada," *Armed Forces & Society* 32, no. 1 (October 2005): 63–79. These authors borrowed from extant "swift trust" literature; see: Debra Myerson, Karl Weick, and Roderick Kramer, "Swift Trust and Temporary Groups," in *Trust in Organizations: Frontiers of Theory and Research*, ed. Roderick Kramer and Tom Tyler (Thousand Oaks, CA: SAGE Publications, 1996), 16–36; and Roderick Kramer, "Trust and Distrust in Organizations: Emerging Perspectives, Enduring Questions," *Annual Review of Psychology* 50 (1999): 569–98. See also: Ann Majchrzak, Sirkaa Jarvenpaa, and Andrea Hollingshead, "Coordinating Expertise Among Emergent Groups Responding to Disasters," *Organizational Science* 18, no. 1 (2007): 147–61.

14 Robert C. Engen, *Strangers in Arms: Combat Motivation in the Canadian Army, 1943–1945* (Montreal: McGill-Queen's University Press, 2016), 15–16.

15 Copp and Humphries, *Combat Stress in the 20th Century*, 365–6, 414.

16 Ibid.

17 Frank M. Richardson, *Fighting Spirit: A Study of Psychological Factors in War* (London: Leo Cooper, 1978), 14–23, 76–93.

18 As SO2 Infantry Training and Doctrine and secretary of the Army Doctrine and Training Board (1992–94), I reviewed infantry officer training among all NATO (and other) nations. This revealed that Canada was unique in delivering combined arms training within the basic officer training curriculum (with officer cadets spending nine months at the Combined Arms Training Centre in Gagetown, New Brunswick, before commissioning). The US recruit first sees combined arms at the Advanced Courses (captain grade), and the British and Australians at the All Arms Tactics Course (captain grade), while the Germans and French rely on collective training to deliver knowledge and skill in combined arms.

19 When asked to provide a singular source to guide one through the challenges of commanding soldiers under stress, I refer people to: Lord Moran,

The Anatonmy of Courage: The Classic wwi *Study of the Psychological Effects of War* (London: Constable & Robinson, 2007).

20 Simunition is non-lethal training ammunition, which is fired from a soldier's normal weapon (at limited velocity) and which leaves an ink or dye mark upon impact. It is an excellent method to train soldiers in tactics and battlecraft. See: http://simunition.com/en/.

21 While some might observe that this borrowing from US practice is a recent one, I would qualify the observation that pairing officers and nco s has always been a hallmark of the regimental system.

22 Garrison service in Canada comes with a disruptive Annual Posting Season, which affects most units and sub-units. I was able to protect my unit – the 1st Battalion, Princess Patricia's Canadian Light Infantry – from the impact of this simply because we were marked for Afghanistan in January 2006, so we experienced only the normal disruptions the summer before.

23 An unmanned aerial vehicle (uav) is a drone. Human intelligence, or humint, refers to intelligence in which the source is a human being (as opposed to a document, camera, etc.).

24 The actual strength grew to 1,150 as we added more components throughout the tour.

25 This is fundamental in all warfare. Soldiers need to be trained to respond to ieds or ambushes rapidly and aggressively in order to immediately regain the tactical initiative.

26 Sir John Hackett, *The Profession of Arms* (New York: MacMillan, 1983), 228.

27 Xenophon, *Anabasis* (*The March Up Country*), bk 3, ch. 1, v. 42, in *Xenophon in Seven Volumes*, trans. Carleton L. Brownson, vol. 3 (London: William Heinemann, 1968), 194–5.

28 William Tecumseh Sherman, *Memoirs of General William T. Sherman* (New York: D. Appleton and Company, 1886), 387.

7

"Do You Even Pro, Bro?": Persistent Testing of Warrior Identity and the Failure of Cohesion

H. Christian Breede and Karen D. Davis

What does it mean to be a soldier? Moreover, why does it matter? This chapter will engage directly with these questions, arguing that certain identities are more conducive to inclusive – and therefore cohesive – fighting units. Indeed, this chapter makes the claim that what is held up to be the ideal Canadian soldier in the early twenty-first century, while encouraged by well-meaning leaders, does in fact contribute to many of the challenges that the institution faces today. The reinforcement of dominant masculinities, which position warriors as superior to non-warriors, are too often accepted as expressions of cohesion and inclusion, even while many are denied full insider status. This chapter, titled "Do You Even Pro, Bro?",[1] challenges the professionalism of those who fully accept the warrior ethos without critical reflection on the meaning of that ethos and its impacts upon an individual's identity. From the damning findings of the external review on sexual harassment and sexual misconduct in the Canadian military conducted in 2015[2] to the persistent framing of soldier challenges as individual weakness, the Canadian military's tacit and, at times, overt espousal of an exclusive warrior ethos is at the heart of some of its more pernicious institutional challenges. Yet, the warrior ethos can make important contributions to operational effectiveness under extremely challenging conditions. Canada's experience in Afghanistan underscored the absolute imperative of combat effectiveness derived from the skills, training, leadership and, importantly, motivation of Canadian soldiers to place themselves in harm's way – the culmination of which is the ultimate expression of the military ethos, as soldiers exercised their loyalty to Canadian values and their military subordinates, peers, and leaders.

Throughout this discussion, the warrior ethos is problematized along with a call for calibration of the identity of the professional soldier.[3] This is not to say that we are arguing for an absolute retreat from the warrior concept, but we do assert that it needs to be critically engaged and, indeed, recast into a more inclusive concept. In short, there is a role for the warrior, but we argue that adopting this role cannot be done wholesale or with rigidity. Canadian values demand nothing less than the full inclusion of motivated and capable Canadian women and men in the ranks, and inclusion has not been a strong point of warrior culture. We suggest that warrior culture must increase its capacity to effectively integrate social change to reflect the values that Canadians have come to expect from their institutions, including the military. Furthermore, we claim that aggressive inclusion of functioning ideal warriors coupled with the exclusion of those who do not meet this ideal, even though they are nominally part of the same military unit, contributes to dysfunctional realities. Indeed, even within selective organizations such as an infantry battalion (all members of which are ascribed the identity of "warrior" by society), there can be a degree of exclusion as certain members more closely resemble the perceived ideal of the warrior than others, depending upon such variables as experience, gender, age, and role within the battalion. We, the authors of this chapter, approach this problem from two perspectives, one insider and one outsider with regard to warrior culture, and have reached this same conclusion. On the one hand, Breede's direct experience in difficult combat conditions in Afghanistan yielded valuable insights and led him to conduct further exploration to understand what he had experienced. This analysis provides insights into the warrior identity and explores how that identity, together with efforts on the part of infantry personnel to remain included within it, contributes to various dysfunctional operational relationships and negative mental health outcomes. Davis's perspective is informed by the historical military resistance – characterized by very slow acceptance at best – to the inclusion of women and LGBTQ persons in ground combat roles, as well as the ongoing challenge of achieving full and effective inclusion of women and men, including the broader LGBTQ community, in all roles in the Canadian military.[4]

The chapter begins with a theoretical discussion of the concept of the warrior ethos and then presents the case for why that ethos is ill-suited to a military that serves a liberal, democratic, expeditionary state such as Canada.[5] Through a discourse analysis of selected Canadian Armed Forces (CAF) documents and policy statements, as well as media and cultural sources, the case for how and why the warrior ethos has been adopted in Canada is then laid out. The implications of this argument are very real despite their philosophical and theoretical nature. This chapter seeks to recast what it means to be a soldier in Canada in such a way that ensures operational effectiveness while optimizing the inclusion and well-being of all soldiers.

WARRIOR ETHOS AND WARRIOR IDENTITY: CONCEPTUAL FRAMEWORKS

Conceptions of the ideal warrior and their relationship to combat effectiveness have persistently shaped the training, socialization, and indoctrination of soldiers for centuries. The question of what it means to be a warrior in Canada today finds its roots within historical gender roles based on biological determinism; that is, within many cultures, the role of "warrior" has represented male identity while that of "mother" has represented female identity.[6] In more recent decades, coincident with the changing nature of warfare, a warrior ethos has gained traction within military culture which emphasizes the unique characteristics of the warrior and thereby establishes boundaries between those who are deemed to be suitable warriors and those who are not.[7] From a contemporary perspective, warrior ethos represents the important distinction between the military, on the one hand, and civilian systems characterized by modern managerial practices, on the other, as well as a distinction between leadership of people and management of things/resources.[8] According to Richard Gabriel, in reinforcing this distinction, the warrior ethos places particular emphasis on the differences between soldiers and civilians: managers manage within bureaucracies to routinize practices related to predictable outcomes; while soldiers must develop "the ability and willingness to exercise judgement in unforeseen circumstances."[9] The importance of maintaining this distinction is visceral for the warrior; in fact, according to Carol Burke in her cultural analysis of change in warrior culture, for those who seek to preserve a unique military culture, civilian culture and ardent feminists who threaten the status quo are the enemy.[10]

Although the "warrior ethos," or "warrior ethic," is defined in various ways, historically there are several shared characteristics. Warrior ethos, according to the United States Center for Strategic and International Studies, is: "a code that expects individuals to aggressively engage and defeat an armed enemy in battle, promoting and valuing traits of moral and physical courage, tactical skills, emotional and physical stamina, loyalty to comrades, and determination to accomplish the tactical mission regardless of personal risk."[11]

Concurrently, many assumptions are made about who the warrior is: male, masculine, and possessed of unique and superior moral and physical attributes including an aggressive nature and proclivity to violence. Further, the warrior has been initiated into a "brotherhood" through rites of passage marked by physical prowess, a "will to kill," and the embodiment of a particular virtue that reinforces the norms and values of the group.[12] Finally, according to the analysis conducted by Judith Youngman, the warrior is not synonymous with the professional soldier; indeed, the warrior ideal is constructed to embody only those virtues found in the combat arms, even though all those who serve, in all areas of the military, can find themselves judged against these ideals.[13]

In her analysis of change and continuity within United States military culture, military sociologist Karen Dunivin describes the "combat masculine-warrior paradigm" as a deeply entrenched "cult of masculinity" that is the essence of military culture.[14] According to Dunivin, the combat masculine warrior paradigm represents a particular view of the world characterized by a collection of "broad, often unstated, assumptions, beliefs, and attitudes" that provide a foundation for the values, attitudes, and ideas that are used to make sense of the world.[15] The combat masculine warrior paradigm thrives within a traditional model of military culture that espouses ideology through ethics and custom, which are in turn supported by laws and policies that reinforce the paradigm. Importantly, Dunivin notes that this paradigm can persist even in the presence of "others" who do not readily fit the prescribed image, such as women and LGBTQ service members. However, the presence of outside "others" challenges the dominant paradigm and, as a result, hostile interactions such as harassment frequently emerge.[16] A recent study conducted by Sabine Koeszegi,

Eva Zedlacher, and René Hudribusch, for example, confirms the relationship between systemic workplace aggression and a culture characterized by traditional masculine military norms, and reveals that not only are women in the Austrian army more vulnerable to bullying than men, but almost every second soldier claimed to have witnessed aggression toward women, and every tenth soldier reported engaging in aggression toward women.[17] Closer to home, in 2014, certain media reports,[18] as well as a subsequent external, independent review on sexual harassment and sexual misconduct in the Canadian military, claimed that sexual harassment and sexual assault presented particular challenges for the military.[19] Subsequent analyses conducted by Statistics Canada in 2016 and 2018 revealed that although both women and men in the armed forces experience sexual harassment and sexual assault, women in the Regular Force are four times more likely than men to report experiences of sexual assault,[20] and LGBTQ members of the CAF were more than three times as likely to report experience of sexual assault than non-LGBTQ members.[21] Such experience supports Dunivin's persuasive argument that even though an evolving model of military culture places emphasis on inclusion, heterogeneity, egalitarianism, and tolerance, the continuation of the combat masculine warrior paradigm, aided and abetted by a continued emphasis on moralism and combat, presents a significant challenge to culture change in the military.[22] Claire Cookson-Hills's chapter in this volume, which discusses sexual violence by Canadian soldiers during the Second World War, raises the possibility that aspects of the combat masculine warrior paradigm have deep historical roots, even if the term "warrior" itself was not widely used during the Second World War.

The assumptions embedded within the warrior paradigm have provided powerful motivators for the historical exclusion of women from combat and LGBTQ persons from the military. Cynthia Enloe asserts that masculine ideals cannot be constructed without constructing ideals of femininity that are supportive and complementary.[23] Judith Hicks Stiehm has also posited that for a warrior, there is an important distinction between protector and protected; that is, an important aspect of warrior identity is the responsibility to protect the weak and vulnerable – women and children.[24] Profoundly linked to virility and procreation, the warrior ideal also depends upon contrasting heterosexual identity. In her analysis of gender, folklore, and change in military culture, Carol Burke notes that "warrior" is a favourite word of James Webb, the former secretary of the US Navy, retired Marine, and decorated Vietnam veteran. According to Burke, if warriors included women and homosexuals, Webb's fragile conception of masculinity would be shattered.[25] Martin van Creveld, a professor of military history at the Hebrew University of Jerusalem, claims that war and combat can be so important to male identity that, "if faced with a choice, men might very well give up women before they give up war."[26] Moreover, van Creveld emphasized that the inclusion of women in war would essentially rob men of the only unique claim they have to masculinity: "with the exception of their disparate roles in the physical acts of procreation, childbearing and nursing, nothing has ever been more characteristic of the relationship between men and women than men's unwillingness to allow women to take part in war and combat."[27] Excluding women from combat and placing emphasis on the performance of masculinity within the military, even as physical combat is only one of many important activities which contribute to military effectiveness, are important strategies for creating, maintaining, and strengthening masculine military identity.

Based on her analysis of masculinity in the Canadian Armed Forces (CAF) throughout the 1990s, Marcia Kovitz concluded that as women filled a proportionally greater share of positions in the organization, masculinity was transformed into new, less transparent forms.[28] Kovitz's analysis followed closely on the heels of the 1989 Canadian Human Rights Tribunal, which directed the Canadian military to fully integrate women into all environments and roles, including ground combat.[29] Until 1989, the CAF leadership had fought to maintain distinctions between combat and non-combat roles, as well as all-male combat units. The relatively recent inclusion of women in combat and LGBTQ members in the Canadian military challenged deeply held masculine military values, and military leaders employed strategies of resistance that focused on the ways in which women would have a negative impact on combat effectiveness.[30] Furthermore, this resistance placed particular emphasis on a warrior ethos focused on combat operations and warfighting to the exclusion of other military operations and roles.[31] Masculine military dominance, according to Kovitz, was exercised through the power embedded within the rank structure. Tensions among men were obscured by the structural embeddedness of male dominance and masculine unity, and were displaced onto women and their femininity.[32] In other words, the threat of gender difference prompted reinforced claims to heterosexual male cohesion, and thus camouflaged conflicts among men based on power and class difference. Instead, tensions between women and men were constructed as a rationale for gender exclusion. The presence of women, and gender integration overall, presented a threat as it cast doubt on past practices and exposed the military to criticism.[33] Moreover, Kovitz claimed that women represented a site of resistance, as they gave voice to past silences, cast doubt on existing practices, and refused to accept internal coercion.[34] Importantly, Kovitz's analysis underscores the use of the warrior ethos to exclude women based on their potential to disrupt operational effectiveness and masculine unity, thus reinforcing claims as to the role of the warrior ethos in maintaining the cohesion of heterosexual male teams, in spite of the tensions within them.

Historically, attitudes and opinions about the employment of women in the CAF have varied considerably. The increased participation of women in the Canadian military in recent decades has been publicly supported; however, military leadership has been skeptical about women's ability and suitability to serve in ground combat roles.[35] Moreover, according to Captain Thomas St. Denis, as the participation of women in the CAF expanded throughout the 1980s and 1990s, the military increasingly emphasized that all serving military members were "warriors" – a highly gendered status that challenged the full inclusion of women.[36] While this trend mirrored similar trends in other Western nations, in particular the United States, it was also concurrent with Canadian military efforts to negotiate the presence of women in the combat arms. One of the first female soldiers to enter the combat domain in the Canadian military was artillery officer Major (now Lieutenant-Colonel) Anne Reiffenstein. Like her male counterparts, Reiffenstein argues that "one of the most important things about being a soldier in a combat arms unit is warrior spirit ... a visceral response to adrenaline, aggression, fear, pride in your unit, and confidence in your capability."[37] But she also recognizes that, in spite of the physical presence of women and different others, the warrior spirit is nurtured within an essentially masculine framework:

Strength = male; weakness = female. I had a battalion Sergeant-Major who told the guys who were falling out on a march, "You are marching like a bunch of women" as if it was a bad thing. In the training system, we have told the instructors that they can no longer promote masculine expressions that imply feminine is weak, but we have not told them what to say instead. We have not developed an inclusive strategy for promoting and developing the warrior spirit. In fact, I have adopted the warrior spirit and I have caught myself saying, "Don't be such a woman!" I believe that leadership needs to support further understanding of the warrior spirit, so that it can be developed in a way that does not denigrate gender or any other social perspective.[38]

This passage is revealing for a number of reasons. First and foremost, there is the enculturation that occurs when perceived outsiders strive to be included. Reflecting on her own experience, Reiffenstein acknowledges that she eschewed an important piece of her own identity to perform the role of warrior. More importantly, however, Reiffenstein's experience underscores the failure of the institution to provide meaningful and inclusive alternatives to skewed gendered perspectives on what constitutes weakness and strength, and how they are represented by the warrior ideal. Similar to the argument we present in this chapter, Reiffenstein calls for a refocusing of the warrior framework to enhance inclusion for all who seek warrior membership.

However, according to many analysts of militarism and masculinity, the fundamentally masculine, heterosexual, and exclusive identity of the warrior that is nurtured and reinforced within military culture presents a significant challenge to efforts to effect change. In her analysis of gender and UN peacekeeping, Sandra Whitworth claims that militaries demand "exaggerated ideals of manhood and masculinity"[39] and calls for the analysis of the military to include understandings of both "manhood" and "womanhood," masculinity and femininity.[40] Making similar claims, political theorist Zillah Eisenstein observes that "a hetero-masculinist military can absorb females, but not those who defy gender differentiation"; this absorption is represented by a "re-sexing" process in the military that "allows for female masculinity rather than male femininity,"[41] thus essentially redefining women as sex-neutral soldiers while maintaining the heterosexual male identity as essential to soldier identity. In other words, claims to the masculinity of the warrior become even more important as different others are represented within a once homogenous, heterosexual, all-male domain.[42] Indeed, the use of the term "re-sexing" (rather than "re-gendering") is deliberate on Eisenstein's part, as she is making the point that rather than focus upon the biological realities of gender, militaries have tended to focus on aspects of sexuality. Furthermore, theorists claim that the military practices hegemonic masculinity. As summarized by Claire Duncanson, the term "hegemonic masculinity" is used to explain both the existence and persistence of male dominance and privilege within the context of multiple and dynamic masculinities and, in particular, those forms of masculinity that permit little opportunity for expressions of alternative masculinities or intersections with femininity.[43] This chapter argues, however, that there is room for greater inclusion and acceptance of differently gendered identities, and for the integration and expression of multiple masculinities and femininities, while maintaining the level of warrior performance needed to achieve mission success. In her analysis of Raewynn Connell's research on masculinities, Duncanson notes how Connell's theoretical framework reveals the powerful influence of hegemonic masculinities in organizations, but also suggests that hegemonic masculinity can be altered through changes in gender relations.[44] Furthermore, Duncanson's analysis reveals the potential to calibrate the warrior ethos to facilitate greater inclusion, not only of different bodies but to create space for greater contribution and inclusion among men and women. This is the alternative that this chapter seeks. But first we will examine some consequences of adopting the warrior culture.

ADOPTION AND CONSEQUENCES
OF WARRIOR CULTURE

Having established what the warrior culture is, this framework can be applied to the Canadian case by asking to what degree Canadian soldiers are seen as warriors. We also argue that the tacit – and at times overt – assignment of the warrior identity to the Canadian soldier has created several unintended and negative consequences. This argument is conducted through a discourse analysis of selected doctrinal and policy documents from both the Canadian Armed Forces and the Department of National Defence. The adoption of a warrior culture has come not just from the military itself, but also from government and civilian society. In this section, we first examine the degree to which the concept of the warrior has been incorporated into Canadian military doctrine. Second, we examine the role of institutions in ascribing this identity to Canadian soldiers. Finally, we focus on cases where Canadian society has perpetuated the idea of Canadian soldiers as warriors. These three forces – the military, institutions, and society – have succeeded in creating a warrior identity for Canadian soldiers. The consequences of adopting this identity, and some potential solutions, form the focus of the remainder of this chapter.

Since its publication in 2003, *Duty with Honour: The Profession of Arms in Canada* has been the CAF's "cornerstone document," and the fundamental, authoritative expression of what it means to be a soldier in Canada.[45] Despite its age, it remains the first stop for any investigation into the identity of the modern Canadian solider. Although replete with concepts and references relating to the profession of arms, and messages reinforcing the idea of norms and values generally consistent with Canada, the text also makes reference to the idea of the warrior. Indeed, *Duty with Honour* takes great pains to reconcile the collectivist notions of a profession with the more individualist ideals of the warrior. *Duty with Honour* argues that "military professionals today require the abilities not only of the soldier warrior, but of the soldier diplomat and the soldier scholar"; this, together with a reference to the idea of the "warrior's honour," are the only two instances where the warrior concept is presented.[46] In this manual, the warrior and the professional are presented as mutually reinforcing concepts that shape both the individual and collective identities of units within the CAF. This guidance, though well-intentioned, falls short of being useful; rather than articulate a clear vision of what soldiers are supposed to do, it merely confuses, and presents mutually exclusive identities as though they were mutually reinforcing. More problematically, *Duty with Honour* fails to properly define what is meant by the concept of the warrior. It simply plants the seed, suggesting all soldiers should adopt this identity.

Further complicating matters, the Canadian Army Implementation Strategy (CAIPS), signed off by the commander of the Canadian Army in 2015, suggests that soldiers "embrace the idea of promoting a warrior culture."[47] Unlike *Duty with Honour*, the CAIPS spends some time explaining what is meant by the terms "warrior" and "warrior culture." According to CAIPS, a warrior identity is "not something that can be taught" but rather "a way of life and an expectation of comportment that accompanies being a soldier."[48] The document sets out three components which are held to define the warrior culture and which align with a recent CAF recruiting slogan: *Strong, Proud, Ready.* Canadian soldiers need to be *strong* mentally and physically, *proud* to be soldiers standing for Canada, and *ready* to serve Canada selflessly.[49] The strategy then enumerates a series of traits that are "nested" within these three components of the warrior culture: unity of purpose, pride, readiness and resilience, ethics, skill, confidence and, finally, spirit.[50] How these relate to the warrior culture is left undeveloped, yet these eight "building blocks" are presented as another list of qualities that all soldiers should strive to exhibit.[51] Only through pursuit of more detailed definitions, such as the code proposed by the US Center for Strategic and International Studies cited earlier, does it become clear how these notions can be operationalized. In the CAIPS strategy, however, such operationalization is left to the individual soldier to figure out.

What *Duty with Honour* and CAIPS have in common is that they invoke the concept of the warrior without any real theoretical or conceptual engagement with it. There is no acknowledgment of the word's historical context, or what being a warrior has meant to societies of the past. The texts adopt the term simply as an adjective pointing to a series of desirable individual characteristics: all members of the military should aspire to be warrior-*scholars*, warrior-*diplomats*, and warrior-*soldiers*. Yet the failure to really engage with the concept, what it means for the military, and how a soldier can achieve it, is troubling. Canadian soldiers are told to be warriors, but not how to be one or what it really means. Instead, this is left to the prevailing military subcultures across the various branches and units to sort out – with uneven and problematic results.

At a broader, institutional level, the concept of the warrior has received some acknowledgment from several corners. While perhaps just a glib turn of phrase, in 2014 Stephen Harper, then prime minister, stated that Canada was a "courageous warrior"[52] on the international stage. This comment, though generally well-meaning, betrays an ignorance of what a warrior identity actually entails. More to the point, a report on the state of the CAF released in 2013 by Pierre Daigle, then National Defence and Canadian Forces Ombudsman, makes a more deliberate reference. In his report, Daigle writes: "within a single professional generation, Canadian sailors, soldiers, and airmen and airwomen adapted … seamlessly morphing from peacekeepers to peacemakers to warriors."[53] The statement's assumption that this transition has been "seamless" is unchallenged; and, more problematically, the question as to whether or not Canadian soldiers *should* be characterized as warriors remains uninvestigated.

The warrior invocation has not been limited to Canadian military institutions; civilian society has had an influence as well. Well-meaning groups like the Wounded Warrior Project, which maintains an affiliated branch in Canada and pursues a focus on mobilizing support for Canada's veterans, have adopted the identity wholesale and mirror it within the CAF and the DND.[54] The year 2006 was the moment when the public began identifying Canadian soldiers as warriors, both because of the events on the ground in Kandahar and the public discourse that ensued thereafter. That year marked the first time that Canadians were engaged in combat in a systematic way since the Korean War. One of the CAF field commanders, Colonel Ian Hope, recounts his experiences from that time elsewhere in this volume. In a general sense, these events resonated with Canadians as the "return of the Canadian warrior."[55] However, some scholars and public intellectuals have raised concerns. Ian McKay and Jamie Swift vehemently argued against this trend in their 2012 book *Warrior Nation*,[56] and Noah Richler articulated his concerns that same year in *What We Talk About When We Talk About War*.[57] All these critiques, however, have been centred on what it means for Canadian society and Canada's place in the world. But what attention has been paid to the issues addressed in this chapter is limited to a few scholarly works.[58] The impact of this simplistic, underdeveloped ascription of the warrior ethos to the CAF (and, we note, *by* the CAF), to broader institutions, and to society in general is poorly understood but at the root, we argue, of many of the personnel problems faced by the CAF today.

The few scholarly works that have dealt with the issue of the warrior concept are worth mentioning, however; one such is Allan English's recent, brief probe into what the warrior code really means in relation to the case of Robert Semrau and the supposed "mercy killing" of an Afghan insurgent in 2008.[59] This case clearly outlines some of the dangers of adopting and accepting the warrior identity without first reflecting critically upon it. That the concept of the warrior is never fully examined in Canadian military doctrine leaves the door open to interpretations beyond those its advocates may at first have intended. Nowhere in *Duty with Honour* or in the CAIPS does it state that so-called "mercy killings" are part of being a warrior – yet neither do these documents really explain what being a warrior does mean. It is left ambiguous and is therefore problematic.

Another consequence of the warrior identity is that it is unstable and, as a result, in constant need of reaffirmation for it to persist. As Steven Gardiner recently claimed, "the warrior identity itself is, moreover, an inherently unstable construction ... demanding constant testing."[60] This means that those who espouse being warriors – or are told to – are always confronting doubt as to their credentials as warriors, always being tested, and this testing will never be sufficient.

A personal experience from Afghanistan provides a compelling example of this "persistent testing" in action. Prior to deployment, I (Breede) felt an acute sense of guilt as my peers dutifully made their way over there while I remained in Canada. Some of my peers did not return, though most did. When word arrived that my unit would deploy, I was struck with an immediate sense of relief. I thought that deployment might ease my feelings of guilt. Now it was my turn to be tested. Upon arriving in Kandahar, however, my feelings simply changed to feeling guilty that I was not out on patrol, not outside the proverbial wire often enough. My unit (part of the Canadian-led Kandahar Provincial Reconstruction Team) was not engaging in combat like the soldiers in the Battle Group were. Moreover, upon my return to Canada, my guilt transformed itself again, into a need to return a second time, as many others had. Why, I asked myself, had I thought that one rotation in Afghanistan should be sufficient? The testing – manifest in my case as guilt – never ended.

This persistent testing not only challenges the individual but can also negatively impact others and even the cohesion of the organization itself. As Gardiner points out, such self-testing may manifest itself as aggression toward others, especially those deemed as less worthy by the warrior ethos. Again, given the realities of modern military engagements, satisfying the testing imposed by the warrior identity is unrealistic. Gardiner writes that "non-combat tasks in fact make up a vastly larger portion of the labour-power requirements of the Army. These specialist, technocratic skills – from engineering to law enforcement – are not well served by the warrior identity."[61] In short, the warrior identity is ill-suited to the conflicts that our soldiers are involved in – and in fact, this may be true as well for every conflict going back to the Second World War (in this regard, see Robert Engen's chapter in this volume).

Whether termed the "contemporary operating environment" (COE) as in Canadian military doctrine, "fourth-generation war" (Hammes),[62] "wars of the third kind" (Holsti),[63] or "post-modern conflict" (Krieg),[64] war is a dynamic concept. The idea of war simply as something that governments undertake, compelling a section of a country's people to serve as soldiers, is no longer an accurate conceptual framework. The "trinitarian" view – referring to Clausewitz's classic model of society, soldiers, and government coming together to prosecute a war – applies no longer.[65] The changing nature of conflict underlines Gardiner's point about specialists not being well-served by the warrior ethos. The trinitarian view holds for conflicts where there is a direct national interest;[66] in such situations, it is desirable for soldiers to be emotionally invested in the conflict as the survival of the state itself is at stake. As Andreas Krieg notes, however, a warrior is a "public soldier who is believed to sustain hardship, commit selflessly and accept personal sacrifice in execution of his/her social contractarian duty to protect the discretionary association as an extension of his/her family."[67] Soldiers who adopt a warrior ethos become more emotionally invested in the mission. They see the interests of the mission as an extension of the interests of their own family, and personalize their role in it. Service to the nation or state is thus not what binds them. Unlike the professional soldier identity, the warrior identity makes no commitment to civil-military relations as most militaries in the West have developed them.[68]

Discourses emanating from society, from government, and from the military itself have combined to push the dominant soldier identity toward that of a warrior identity. This has implications for how soldiers are motivated, what sort of culture they embody, and how they view the application of knowledge and, subsequently, of violence.

This examination has shown that soldiers who adopt the warrior identity are both intrinsically and extrinsically motivated. They are motivated to seek honour, which is intrinsic but only valuable if recognized and, as such, includes an extrinsic component. The second factor, that of cultural "embodiment," suggests that warriors seeking honour also seek to differentiate themselves from non-warriors. This is an acutely exclusive attitude and one that permeates all aspects of the warrior's life. For a warrior, there is no acceptable identity other than that of the warrior.

In terms of the application of knowledge, the warrior identifies with the expert application of skills as governed by a set of exclusive norms which set the warrior apart from the rest of society. The warrior's central focus is on the accomplishment of a task, but also on the more personal objective of meeting and passing the test of claiming to be a warrior – a test which Gardiner has so pointedly noted is constantly happening. These attributes of the warrior will be further explored in the next section.

RETURN OF THE PROFESSIONAL

Having established that the warrior identity is problematic, what then should soldiers identify with? To be clear, soldiers bear unique responsibilities, most notably that they are asked to be willing to kill and die for their country. This requirement is not hyperbolic; rather, it is enshrined in the concept of unlimited liability, which every soldier assumes. But what sort of identity captures this unique responsibility while at the same time remaining a healthy identity, both for the individual soldier and for the military?

We argue for the need to revisit the idea of the professional soldier and, indeed, we place this identity in opposition to that of the warrior. We base this argument on the work of Don Snider in which he conceptualizes the professional as someone who is intrinsically motivated, partakes in a culture of ethics, applies judgment, and is focused on service to people.[69] Snider applies this conceptualization of the profession in his critiques of the US military – in particular the US Army – and places the professional in opposition to the bureaucrat.[70] The expanded comparison between warriors, professionals, and bureaucrats that we propose is presented as Table 7.1, which compares the competing identities of warriors, professionals, and bureaucrats against the factors of motivation, culture, application, and focus.

In crafting this table, we have juxtaposed our conceptualization of the warrior alongside an amended version of Snider's comparison of professional soldiers and bureaucrats. Where Snider argues that the US Army has become excessively bureaucratized and calls for a shift toward a professional identity, we argue that in Canada this shift has gone too far, such that the main identity for Canadian soldiers has become the warrior. We are calling for a return to the middle: the professional soldier. This identity embodies the strengths of the other two competing identities while shedding their weaknesses. Indeed, the professional is the middle ground between the exclusive, inward-focused warrior and the excessively institutional and technically oriented identity of the bureaucrat.

An identity in line with a professional soldier would eschew sexual misconduct as it would be recognized to run directly counter to the

Table 7.1
Competing military identities

Factors	Warrior	Professional	Bureaucratic
Motivation	• Extrinsic and intrinsic • Work is life • Sacrificial (for reputation)	• Intrinsic • Work is a calling • Sacrificial service	• Extrinsic • Work is a job • Competition
Culture	• Honour • Exclusivity • Autonomy • Homogeneous	• Ethical • Self-policing • Autonomy • Inclusion and diversity	• Procedural compliance • Controlled • Functional diversity
Application	• Skills through training • Adherence to norms	• Expertise through education • Use of judgment	• Skills through training • Follows procedures
Focus	• Personal • Testing • Task accomplishment	• Group • Critical thinking • Task accomplishment	• Technical • Performs tasks • Stewardship

fundamental values and best interests of the group. Indeed, such actions would be deemed the quintessential "unprofessional act." The professional, who does not contend with the constant testing and unending need to prove one's warrior-ness, harbours more inclusive attitudes toward those operating in different roles within the battlespace. Capability, not how alike or different the other person may or may not be, becomes the key variable for acceptance. Finally, an emphasis on judgment, rather than rote application of procedures, permits the flexibility that the contemporary operating environment requires; and, further, the professional's depersonalized attachment to the mission enables the soldier to disconnect from it, even when their experience and expertise demands otherwise. This recognition – that the soldier is a tool of national power employed by decision makers who are elected and represent other interests alongside those of the mission at hand – is vital to the health and well-being of the soldier upon their redeployment.

This is not to say that the warrior identity is completely flawed. Rather, elements of it are useful, but their invocation demands a more nuanced understanding of what the warrior really entails as a concept. Rather than a wholesale inscription of the military as being comprised of warriors, the focus should be on individual attributes like discipline, mindfulness, and responsibility. The research and practical application of meditation, biofeedback, and aikido through the Trojan Warrior

Project, a little-known experiment conducted on twenty-five US Army Delta operators in 1985, is an example of such responsible, informed application of the warrior idea to modern soldiering.[71] Though since abandoned, interest in the Trojan project has been rekindled as demonstrated by recent articles[72] and podcasts espousing the merits of mindfulness, personal self-discipline, and mastery, not only in military settings but in everyday life.[73] We are seeing early stages of the application of mindfulness in the CAF as well, both from well-being and competency perspectives.[74] These are examples of a personal warrior spirit that can be inculcated within a broader professional soldier identity – and, indeed, any professional soldier ought to seek it out. Simply challenging our soldiers to be "warriors," however, without any further guidance, will lead to the missteps and outright abuses we have discussed above.

SUMMARY

In the fall of 2008, after more than two years of military operations in Afghanistan which saw soldiers engaged in sustained combat, the senior leadership of the CAF announced that a once-promised award for soldiers had been withdrawn.[75] Then known as the Combat Action Badge, the device was to be awarded to those soldiers who participated in combat as a means to distinguish them from soldiers who deployed to Afghanistan but saw no combat. Setting aside the administrative challenges of determining precisely which individuals qualified – within the Battle Group, the Operational Mentor and Liaison Teams, the Provincial Reconstruction Team, the Air Wing, and the Joint Task Force Headquarters – the device further reinforced the division between warriors and not-warriors. Cancelling this initiative was, upon reflection, a wise decision. Rather than assuage the soldiers who spent most of their time away from the relative comforts and amenities of Kandahar Airfield, the device would not only have reinforced the warrior/not-warrior distinction but, more concerning, it would have encouraged some personnel to seek out combat in order to "qualify" for the badge – to engage in and pass the test that Gardiner has so astutely identified. Such "war tourism," which results in needless assumption of risk in an already dangerous operational environment, represents the opposite of the professional soldier identity.

Warrior ethos and warrior identity, though historically masculine and male-dominated, have developed to include different others, including women and LGBTQ persons. In spite of the physical inclusion of such others in military units, we argue here that contemporary conceptions of the warrior assume exclusive hegemonic masculinity, which encourages social exclusion for some and, for those who seek inclusion, the persistent testing of warrior ideals, thus begging the question of who, if anyone, ever achieves full membership. The psychological struggle to achieve and sustain the warrior ideal is concurrently elusive and damaging to both individual well-being and team cohesion. It also undermines optimal collaborative efforts involving persons perceived as outsiders, but who nonetheless have important roles to play in achieving national security and military objectives. We call for a calibration of the warrior ethos in ways that value and include the characteristics of multiple masculinities, femininities, and intersecting differences such as race, religion, occupation, and organizational status, regardless of whether soldier or civilian, man or woman, and that are conducive to operational effectiveness. The professional soldier should strive to embody such attributes of the warrior ethos that are most conducive to inclusive and healthy teams – those which imbue soldiers with the capacity to permeate and diffuse dysfunctional boundaries and collaborate across the various roles required for mission success.

An identity grounded in the idea of soldier-as-professional negates the need for the persistent self-testing that arises from the soldier-as-warrior identity. It undoes the deleterious distinction of "us" – those who ventured outside the proverbial wire – from them – the soldiers whose job it was to remain in the camps and bases – and thereby helps to reinforce the kind of cohesion that comes about with the recognition that everyone is doing a job that contributes to mission success.

NOTES

1 According to blogger Jane Solomon, for example: "'Bro' is convenient because describing a professional or social dynamic as 'overly white, straight, and male' seems both too politically charged and too general; instead, 'bro' conjures a particular type of dude who operates socially by excluding those who are different." "It's Everyday Bro," http://blog.dictionary.com/brocab/.

2 Marie Deschamps, "External Review into Sexual Harassment and Sexual Misconduct in the Canadian Armed Forces," External Review Authority,

Department of National Defence, 27 March 2015, https://www.canada.ca/
en/department-national-defence/corporate/reports-publications/sexual-
misbehaviour/external-review-2015.html.

3 Various and parallel arguments have been posited by: Karen O. Dunivin,
"Military Culture: Change and Continuity," *Armed Forces & Society* 20,
no. 4 (1994): 532–3; Judith A. Youngman, "The Warrior Ethic," in *Women
in Uniform: Perceptions and Pathways*, ed. Kathryn Spurling and Elizabeth
Greenhalgh (Canberra: Australian Defence Force Academy, 2000), 19–63;
Karen D. Davis, *Negotiating Gender in the Canadian Forces, 1970–1999*
(PhD diss., Royal Military College of Canada, 2013); Thomas St. Denis,
"The Dangerous Appeal of the Warrior," *Canadian Military Journal*
(Summer 2001): 31–8; Steven L. Gardiner, "The Warrior Ethos: Discourse
and Gender in the United States Army Since 9/11," *Journal of War &
Culture Studies* 5, no. 3 (2012): 371–83; and Don M. Snider, "Will Army
2025 Be a Military Profession?", *Parameters* 45, no. 4 (2015): 39–51.

4 See, for example: Davis, *Negotiating Gender*.

5 This is similar to the claim presented in St. Denis, *The Dangerous Appeal
of the Warrior*.

6 Linda Grant de Pauw, *Battle Cries and Lullabies: Women in War from
Prehistory to the Present* (Norman, OK: University of Oklahoma Press,
1998), 13–14.

7 The changing nature of warfare – that is, as spurred by a changing geopo-
litical context, from nuclear deterrence to increased peacekeeping and
humanitarian missions, which frequently require the forward deployment
of combat support and ground combat units. See: Youngman, "The
Warrior Ethic," 34–5.

8 Richard A. Gabriel, *The Warrior's Way: A Treatise on Military Ethics*
(Kingston, ON: Canadian Defence Academy Press, 2007), 92–3.

9 Ibid., 93.

10 Carole Burke, *Camp All-American, Hanoi Jane, and the High-and-Tight:
Gender, Folklore, and Changing Military Culture* (Boston: Beacon Press,
2004), 142.

11 Youngman, "The Warrior Ethic," 36.

12 Ibid., 49.

13 Ibid., 36.

14 Davis, *Negotiating Gender*, 53.

15 Dunivin, "Military Culture," 532.

16 Ibid., 534–7.

17 Sabine Koeszegi, Eva Zedlacher, and René Hudribusch, "The War Against
the Female Soldier? The Effects of Masculine Culture on Workplace
Aggression," *Armed Forces & Society* 40, no. 2 (2014): 226–51.

18 Noémi Mercier and Alec Castonguay, "Crimes sexuels: le cancer qui ronge l'armée canadienne," *L'Actualité*, 24 April 2014; and Noémi Mercier and Alec Castonguay, "Our Military's Disgrace," *Maclean's*, 5 May 2014.

19 Deschamps, *External Review*.

20 Of personnel in the Regular Force, 4.8 per cent of women and 1.2 per cent of men reported experiencing sexual assault in the twelve months prior to a survey conducted in 2016. Further, in a 2018 survey, 4.3 per cent of women and 1.1 per cent of men in the Regular Force reported experiencing sexual assault in the twelve previous months. Adam Cotter, *Sexual Misconduct in the Canadian Armed Forces, 2016* (Ottawa: Statistics Canada, 2017), 5; Adam Cotter, *Sexual Misconduct in the Canadian Armed Forces Regular Force, 2018* (Ottawa: Statistics Canada, 2019).

21 In the twelve months prior to a survey in 2016, 5.6 per cent of LGBTQ respondents, compared to 1.6 per cent of non-LGBTQ respondents, reported experiencing sexual assault. In 2018, 4.6 per cent of transgender and gender-diverse members of the Regular Force reported experiencing sexual assault in the twelve months prior to the survey, compared to 1.4 per cent of cisgender, heterosexual Regular Force members. Cotter, *Sexual Misconduct, 2016*; Cotter, *Sexual Misconduct, 2018*, 45.

22 Dunivin, "Military Culture," 540.

23 Cynthia Enloe, "All the Men Are in the Militias, All the Women Are Victims: The Politics of Masculinity and Femininity in Nationalist Wars," in *The Women and War Reader*, ed. Lois Ann Lorentzen and Jennifer Turpin (New York: New York University Press, 1998), 54.

24 Judith H. Stiehm, "The Protected, the Protector, the Defender," *Women's Studies International Forum* 5, nos 3–4 (1982): 367–76.

25 Burke, *Camp All-American*, 142–3.

26 Martin Van Creveld, "Why Men Fight," in *War*, ed. Lawrence Friedman (New York: Oxford University Press, 1994), 88–89.

27 Ibid.

28 Marcia Kovitz, "Mining Masculinities in the Canadian Military" (PhD diss., Concordia University, 1998), 308.

29 See: Canadian Human Rights Commission, Tribunal Decision 3/89, between: Isabelle Gauthier, Joseph G. Houlden, Marie-Claude Gauthier, Georgina Ann Brown, complainants, and Canadian Armed Forces, respondent, decision rendered 20 February 1989 (Ottawa: Canadian Human Rights Commission, 1989).

30 Karen D. Davis, "Sex, Gender and Culture Intelligence in the Canadian Forces," *Commonwealth and Comparative Politics* 47 no. 4 (2009): 438; Davis, *Negotiating Gender*.

31 Ibid.

32 Kovitz, "Mining Masculinities," 308.

33 Ibid.

34 Ibid.

35 See, for example: Davis, *Negotiating Gender.*

36 Karen D. Davis and Brian McKee, "Women in the Military: Facing the Warrior Framework," in *Challenge and Change in the Military: Gender and Diversity Issues,* ed. Franklin C. Pinch (Kingston, ON: Canadian Defence Academy Press, 2004), 52–75; and Youngman, "The Warrior Ethic."

37 Youngman, "The Warrior Ethic."

38 Anne Reiffenstein, "Gender Integration – An Asymmetric Environment," in *Women and Leadership in the Canadian Forces: Perspectives and Experience,* ed. Karen D. Davis (Kingston, ON: Canadian Defence Academy Press, 2009), 5.

39 Sandra Whitworth, *Men, Militarism and UN Peacekeeping* (Boulder, CO: Lynne Rienner Publishers, 2004), 161.

40 Ibid., 15.

41 Zillah Eisenstein, *Sexual Decoys: Gender, Race and War* (London: Zed Books, 2007), 6.

42 Claire Duncanson, "Hegemonic masculinity and the possibility of change in gender relations," *Men and Masculinities* 18, no. 2 (2015): 232.

43 Ibid.

44 Ibid.

45 *Duty with Honour: The Profession of Arms in Canada* (Kingston: Canadian Defence Academy Press, 2003).

46 Ibid., 18, 34.

47 Canada, Department of National Defence, *Canadian Army Integrated Performance Strategy,* 4500-1 (CA PD), 2015, Annex A, app. 2, para. 1.

48 Ibid., para. 2.

49 Ibid., para. 2a–c.

50 Ibid., para. 3a–g.

51 Ibid., para. 4.

52 Andrew Coyne, "Stephen Harper's Canada Day Speech the latest volley in pointless history wars," *National Post,* 2 July 2014.

53 Pierre Daigle, *On the Homefront: Assessing the Wellbeing of Canada's Military Families in the New Millennium* (Ottawa: Department of National Defence, 2013), 14.

54 Wounded Warriors Canada, http://woundedwarriors.ca/home/.

55 Tina Managhan, "Highways, Heroes, and Secular Martyrs: The Symbolics of Power and Sacrifice," *Review of International Studies* 38, no. 1 (2012): 98.

56 Jamie Swift and Ian McKay, *Warrior Nation: Rebranding Canada in an Age of Anxiety* (Toronto: Between the Lines Publishing, 2012).

57 Noah Richler, *What We Talk About When We Talk About War* (Fredericton: Goose Lane Editions, 2012).

58 Allan English, *Understanding Military Culture: A Canadian Perspective* (Montreal: McGill Queen's University Press, 2004), 61–70, but also 6, 9, 46, 109. See also: Paul Jackson, *One of the Boys: Homosexuals in the Military in World War II* (Montreal: McGill-Queen's University Press, 2004), 221–69.

59 Allan English, "What is the Warrior Code?", *Globe and Mail*, 12 October 2010.

60 Gardiner, "The Warrior Ethos," 380.

61 Ibid.

62 Colonel Thomas X. Hammes, *The Sling and the Stone: On War in the 21st Century* (St. Paul, MN: Zenith Press, 2004).

63 Kalevi Holsti, *The State, War, and the State of War* (Cambridge: Cambridge University Press, 1996).

64 Andreas Krieg, "Beyond the Trinitarian Institutionalization of the Warrior Ethos – A Normative Conceptualization of Soldier and Contractor Commitment in Post-Modern Conflict," *Defence Studies* 14, no. 1 (2014): 56–75.

65 Carl von Clausewitz, *On War*, trans. Peter Paret and Michael Howard (Princeton, NJ: Princeton University Press, 1984), 89.

66 Ibid.

67 Krieg, "Beyond the Trinitarian Institutionalization," 71.

68 Hanne A. Kraugerud, "Shields of Humanity – The Ethical Constraints of Professional Combatants," *Journal of Military Ethics* 10, no. 4 (2011): 266.

69 Snider, "Will Army 2025 Be a Military Profession?", 40.

70 Ibid.

71 Richard Strozzi-Heckler, *In Search of the Warrior Spirit: Teaching Awareness and Disciplines to the Military* (Berkeley: Blue Snake Books, 2007).

72 Brian Mockenhaupt, "A State of Military Mind," *Pacific Standard*, 18 June 2012, rev. 14 June 2017, https://psmag.com/social-justice/a-state-military-mind-42839.

73 For one example: John Gretton "Jocko" Willink, *Jocko Podcast*, 2015–present, https://jockopodcast.com/.

74 As an example, meditation is now being introduced to officer cadets at the Royal Military College, in classrooms by faculty, in drop-in sessions with chaplains, and by athletic training staff as part of the physical fitness

program. Mindfulness is also identified as an important meta-cognitive strategy that contributes to the proposed model of cultural intelligence for the Canadian Forces as presented in Karen D. Davis and Justin C. Wright, "Culture and Cultural Intelligence," in *Cultural Intelligence and Leadership: An Introduction for Canadian Forces Leaders*, ed. Karen D. Davis (Kingston, ON: Canadian Defence Academy Press, 2009), 11–12.

75 David Pugliese, "Afghanistan combat action badge withdrawn," *Winnipeg Free Press*, 17 May 2009; Andrew Chung, "Military honours in Afghanistan deserved?", *Toronto Star*, 22 July 2007.

8

Beliefs:
What Motivates Insurgents

Robert Martyn

At the gateway to understanding radicalization there is a toll booth.
Those who enter must leave behind the orderly and comfortable
world in which normal people do not do terrible things. Full
admission requires examining how we are ourselves susceptible
to radicalizing influences.

Clark McCauley and Sophia Moskalenko, *Friction:*
How Radicalization Happens to Them and Us

When considering the subject of combat motivation, many will envis-
age the twentieth century's global wars – whole communities mobilizing, parades with banners and streamers, young men (and, with less
fanfare, women) doing the right thing and going off to fight Studs
Terkel's "good war." Strategic forecasters and contemporary history
suggest, however, that such "glamorous" wars are unlikely to attend
our future.[1] Since 1945, the world has averaged eight wars ongoing
annually, with guerrilla warfare being the preferred method. These
small wars are hardly a new occurrence, as any Roman legionnaire
could have recounted from Judea, Gaul, or Germania.[2]

Currently, destitute societies face existential challenges linked to
poor governance, civil conflict, and a combination of overpopulation
and agricultural catastrophe. Unmet benefits promised by globaliza-
tion further unravel the political, social, and economic fabric within
many of these states, creating more have-nots who see their downward
spiral as a call to arms. Distinctions between war, peace, and the
sanctity of non-combatants are increasingly blurred.[3] So-called "hybrid

warfare," with its broader array of lethal and non-lethal measures, effectively merges the lethality of state conflict with the fanatical and protracted fervour of irregular warfare.[4] These trends suggest a future of increasingly costly but less decisive conflicts confronting Canada's deployed personnel.

The Canadian government has proposed an energetic foreign policy agenda, which includes deploying people into the midst of an African insurrection, in addition to anti-Daesh operations and forward deployments to the Russian border.[5] UN actions in central Africa have much more in common with our recent campaign in Afghanistan than any mythical peacekeeping of Canadian memory. Mali, for example, has seen 166 peacekeeper fatalities as of the end of April 2018 – two-thirds of them by armed rebel attacks.[6] The revolt's multifaceted nature makes analysis and operational planning more difficult than it might be in more familiar nation-state insurgencies.[7] A starting point for the process, however, will be provided in this chapter: the very population-centric nature of insurgency and violent extremism, which requires nuanced thinking, including consideration of our opponents' motivations.

To explore specific motivations will involve delving into case studies from the literature of history, psychology, and sociology. Before beginning, though, two research challenges will be highlighted. The first is the potential problem of cultural mirror-imaging – presuming that an adversary thinks as we do, placing similar values and priorities on various objects. This can lead to skewed thinking in regard to "centre of gravity" – or an adversary's critical sources of moral or physical strength – which we would focus upon targeting when building our campaign plan. Second, debriefings of captured or former rebels present difficulties because their narratives may be completely fictitious. Self-justification or embellishment may translate as more heroic and visionary, or less naïve and irrational, with the result that interpretations of the same actions could be seen equally in either light, depending on the audience.

GROUP MOTIVATIONS

Analyzing insurgent motivation is a complicated matter, involving a dynamic interplay of many factors and weighing their importance from case to case. A grouping of like-minded individuals finds its cohesion reinforced by feelings of isolation and external threat, which are apt to become more extreme as "groupthink" underpins these influences. This common threat perception magnifies leaders' powers, particularly when punishing in-group divergence or idealizing the values of a particular faction.[8] Regardless of the insurgency's form, such dynamics may leverage a group's psychological groundwork to counter perceived threats with violence. Bard O'Neill, a professor at the US National War College, posits eight distinct varieties of insurgency, five of them of a revolutionary nature in that they seek to radically change the political system: traditional, egalitarian, anarchist, apocalyptic-utopian, and pluralist. The three remaining varieties are non-revolutionary, being focused more upon changing the direction of a society while retaining the form of government: secessionist, reformist, and preservationist.[9]

Traditional insurgencies tend to be more familiar, having supplanted the Cold War's Marxist egalitarian uprisings. The insurgents' aim is to revert to a past political system. This may be a recent past, such as the 1930s Spanish Nationalists seeking to abolish the Republic, or the more widespread Jihadists' desire for a return to the (idealized) caliphates of the eighth to thirteenth centuries. Considering modern jihad as a form of traditional insurgency, we start by acknowledging that Islam is a diverse religion; its adherents' views span secularist, modernist, radical, and militant orientations. Charismatic leadership, however, plays a key role in the process of collective radicalization and the propensity for violence by delivering a convincing message of encirclement and oppression. The modern movement evolved from the late nineteenth century's Jamāl al-Dīn al-Afghānī to the better-known bin Laden and al-Zarqawi. Each compelling leader has ushered in new, greater ideological extremes to justify the bloodshed.[10] Their narrative is one of crisis within both the collective and the individual, and which envisions either social mobilization or extinction.

Before being supplanted by the Jihadists, egalitarian insurrections were the leading type throughout the latter half of the twentieth century. This was natural given the nexus between anticolonial sentiment and the theoretical appeal of Marxist or Maoist doctrine, to say nothing of the benefits of Soviet or Chinese military support. Typical examples include the Malayan National Liberation Army or the Viet Cong. Although diminished, the appeal of egalitarian insurgency continued for some destitute peoples after the Cold War, as in the case of Peru's Sendero Luminoso (Shining Path). While centralized economic control by the people may sound inherently appealing, the reality is that many of these insurgencies resulted in repressive, authoritarian political regimes. This was due, in roughly equal measure, to corrupt insurgent leadership and counterinsurgent policies backing reactionary dictators simply because they were not communist.

There are three less-common revolutionary models. Of these, anarchists, such as Chechnya's "New Revolutionary Alternative," have the most extreme goals – of destroying all political systems without instituting a replacement. Apocalyptic-utopianists, such as the Japanese religious cult Aum Shinrikyo, believe that their actions will destroy political systems and clear the way for divine intervention to create a new system.[11] Conversely, the pluralist model proclaims inclusiveness, favouring individual freedom and compromise, as represented by the African National Congress toward the end of the apartheid era.[12]

Of the non-revolutionary models, the secessionists are the most common. As implied in the name, their intent is to withdraw from their current political community and establish their own government. Sometimes there may be overlap with other models if the idea of the end-state being sought is sufficiently vague to allow confusion with another paradigm – such as in the more socialist egalitarian model, for example. However, whatever their preferred politics, their primary goal is secession and the establishment of an independent homeland. Canada has military experience with several such groups, such as the Kosovo Liberation Army and the National Liberation Front for Preševo in the former Yugoslavia.

The two least-common models are the reformists and the preservationists. Reformists are quite diverse, embracing violence to further their desired program of change regarding anything from environmental issues to animal rights to anti-abortion. Conversely, preservationists target those wanting to effect change, usually to protect the status quo and the perceived political or social advantage it affords. While preservationists may be exemplified by the Ulster Defence Association, some texts refer to such groups as counterrevolutionaries or simply vigilantes, but that is beyond the scope of this chapter.[13]

Layered across these basic types are some moderating factors. For example, ethnic insurgents who experience relative deprivation and live in distinct areas, such as the Tamil Tigers, usually have secession as their ultimate goal. Where groups are intermixed geographically, such as the Rwandan Hutu and Tutsi peoples, insurrection tends to be revolutionary.[14] Yet even the desired end-state of an independent nation is not carved in stone. Stated goals may change if the group's members realize they were too ambitious, if different factions in the group hold conflicting aspirations, or if, in an attempt to attract broader support, the group's goals simply become ambiguous. Moreover, the insurgents' intermediate and ultimate goals may differ – e.g., an initial goal of disrupting or destroying governance, but an end-state of an alternative political system. Also, analysis must contend with misleading rhetoric; as noted previously, left-wing insurgent groups like Peru's Sendero Luminoso relied upon social democratic imagery or rhetoric, but often produced a far-from-egalitarian result.[15]

Before moving on to individual stimuli, there is a final potential complication to appraising group ambitions. Assessing a group's goals becomes problematic if the analyst has a partisan interest in labelling a specific insurrection to accord with a pre-conceived government aim.[16] We can see today that because of Cold War paranoid thinking, many low-intensity conflicts were painted as communist revolutions – a polemicized view that led to costly, ill-informed decisions, creating new enemies where none may have existed, and resulting in poorly devised intervention strategies.[17] Such errors recur within today's anti-terror policies and programmes.

INDIVIDUAL TRAJECTORIES

No insurgency can survive without popular backing in one form or another. Although some insurrections succeeded even after experiencing minimal initial support, others, such as "Che" Guevara's Bolivian exploits, were doomed from the beginning, having failed to gain support from either the Bolivian Communist Party, other political opposition groups, or local civilians, who, while they disliked the government, had no desire for revolt.[18] Therefore, while assessing a group's motivations is a necessary starting point, comprehensive understanding requires consideration of demography, social groups, and economics to determine the causes for which individuals will risk their lives and livelihoods by enlisting in militant groups and taking up arms. The moral outrage engendered in group grievances must resonate with members' personal experiences and often be amplified within the group to reach their full expression. Such narratives tend to be framed by senior people, such as tribal or religious leaders, or other charismatic people. Individual paths to radicalization tend to be the stories of youth, when people are most susceptible to feelings of isolation and the desire for agitation and change. Encountering only cynical or dispirited adult voices, and seeing weak possibilities for their personal future, youth are vulnerable to opinions that promise empowerment, including those proposing a more violent path. Some youth may even see Western news coverage demonizing international insurgents and terrorists as motivational. Whether they will be perceived as fiendish or heroic is irrelevant; either is preferable to the betrayal or surrender they feel from previous generations.

In a study of European radicals, the overwhelming majority of respondents described their motivation as a search for identity and meaning; militant or insurgent groups provided a clear purpose and a sense of belonging. Recurring themes include being pushed away from family or community, or pulled toward extremist authority figures whose pronouncements respond to insecurities or a sense of injustice.[19] These themes tended to be based on grievances framed as something wrong with the world that must be changed. There are four basic rationales. The prevailing, neo-Marxist explanation is one of socio-economic marginalization, whereby people are victimized by the social or economic system. Social-identity marginalization suggests that people have trouble integrating culturally or face difficulties in having their identity accepted. Those with political grievances are unhappy with policies perceived as unjust. Finally, there are those who are drawn to religious fanaticism.[20] On this last point, religious extremists "share a moral reductionism, which ascribes simple causes, and their implicit remedies, to complex events."[21] For many, especially frustrated youth, simplistic imagery and emotions provide compelling appeal.

Among young North American radicals citing extremist Islam as their personal motivation, another predominant characteristic is a personal situation either as a second-generation immigrant or as a Westerners who has converted recently to Islam. First- or third-generation jihadists are rare. Second-generation Westerners often reject their parents' faith by adopting extreme stances or interpretations, which allow them to reconstruct themselves. The tendency of the first and third generations not to become radicalized flows from having been brought up in an Islam cultural milieu or knowing how to express themselves as Muslims in secular society thanks to their parents.[22] What we are seeing, therefore, is Islamicized radicals rather than radicalized Islam – although this problem is exacerbated by many Islamist adherents who eschew strict vertical hierarchies. Unlike some faiths, in which doctrines are decreed from above, more relaxed structures allow zealots to shop around for an agreeable religious narrative, such as obligatory violence against non-believers.[23]

Although extreme, readers may relate to personal grievance as a justification for violent radicalization. When "someone wrongs us, we want justice; often we want revenge" – justice here being the due punishment of those that mistreat us, while revenge, in which we ourselves mete out the punishment, is more particular in being more personal.[24] It is this latter sense that applies to many insurgents. Ahmed Omar Saeed Sheikh, for example, a London-born son of Pakistani immigrants convicted of kidnapping and beheading reporter Daniel Pearl, spoke of playground bullying and rejection by his peer group as starting his path to radicalization.[25]

Joining a radical group for the sake of affection is also a recurring theme. Individuals can be radicalized through an attachment to family or friends, the latter of which may be long-term and pre-existing, or more recently and deliberately cultivated.[26] This was the case in the Egyptian-Canadian Khadr family, which achieved notoriety for their links to Osama bin Laden and Al-Qaeda. Ahmed Khadr (a.k.a. "al-Kanadi") and his spouse, Maha el-Samnah, actively contributed to the radicalization of several of their children, notably: daughter Zaynab, a Jihadist proselytizer; and sons Abdullah, an accused Al-Qaeda weapons procurer; Abdulkareem, paralyzed in the attack in which his father died; and Abdurahman and Omar, enemy combatants. Similarly, there has been a significant increase in teenaged girls and young women travelling to insurgent areas seeking romance and adventure. Their fantasy world, in which the male insurgents are perceived as "some sort of Robin Hood," seldom has a romance-novel ending.[27]

For some potential insurgents, martyrdom provides an adequate justification for a path of radicalization. Youth are among the highest-risk populations for suicide. In Canada, suicide accounts for 24 per cent of all deaths among 15-to-24-year-olds and 16 per cent among 16-to-44-year-olds – in both age groups, the second leading cause.[28] Adolescence is a time of dramatic change, frustration, and high emotion; for some, martyrdom gives meaning to an otherwise futile life – and death.

Finally, fear can be a significant motivator for those living in conflict zones. Individuals may believe themselves safer within a violent group than alone on the streets of a failed state. This is an often-repeated justification within Iraqi and African sectarian groups, which increasingly include children, who number among three "outlier" groups that conclude this section: child soldiers, lone-wolf actors, and the "selfie generation" of insurgents.

INDIVIDUAL OUTLIERS

Child Soldiers

Child soldiers are included here because they present our troops with a significant threat of both combat harm and operational stress injury (O S I), particularly in the form of moral injury. Such an injury is a psychological trauma affecting an individual's ethical conscience for having contravened deeply ingrained moral beliefs, causing profound emotional shame.[29] The theatres of operation in which Canadian soldiers will be called upon to interact with, and possibly kill, child soldiers cannot help but involve such heightened risk. This could potentially be exacerbated by thoughtless condemnation of "baby killers" on the home front. While the Canadian military has recently provided guidelines for dealing with child soldiers, there is no simple solution to address such an untenable situation.[30]

Globally, between 250,000 and 300,000 children are involved in roughly 75 per cent of ongoing conflicts. Precise numbers are difficult to establish as ages may be concealed, children may perform low-visibility roles, or porous regional borders in places where Canadian troops are likely to deploy make child soldiering an unquantifiable cross-border issue.[31] Their average age is just under 13, with increasing reports of underage females being thus involved. Out of fifty-five conflicts in which girls are being actively exploited, thirty-four see them being used in combat roles.[32] Wars with child combatants have tended to be protracted insurgencies, notable for extensive casualties, wherein children having no concept of the laws of war or any codified rules of engagement tend to operate with a fearsome degree of audacity.

Despite our Western abhorrence at the concept of child soldiers, our definition of childhood often varies from that of other societies. While many children are kidnapped or otherwise forced into war, some war-torn cultures see adolescence as "a function of a literate pluralistic society, which can afford to waste half a man's life in socialisation."[33] In some situations, joining the insurgents is seen as assuming their family responsibility, particularly within societies where serving local warlords provides for greater family security. Notwithstanding various international treaties outlawing it, the practice continues because, unfortunately, children are considered cheap, malleable, and expendable fighters.[34]

"Lone Wolf" Actors

"Lone wolf" actors have drawn increased Canadian attention due to the killings carried out in 2014 by extremists Martin Couture-Rouleau and Michael Zehaf-Bibeau. Couture-Rouleau and Zehalf-Bibeau had several factors in common: each had failed at multiple financial and relationship endeavours, the planning of their attacks was unsophisticated, and both had recently experienced religious conversion.[35] Both also spent considerable time on the Internet, accumulating exposure to militant narratives from charismatic role models. Anwar al-Awlaki was one such online proselytizer who was actively linked to the radicalization of Canada's "Toronto 18," the UK's Roshonara Choudhry, and American Major Nidal Hasan, the "Fort Hood killer."[36] While those who plot and conduct these attacks are often loners in person, the Internet provides an imagined community, wherein such actors may self-categorize as part of a larger extremist network with which they may interact remotely (see the chapter by Victoria Tait, Joshua Clark, and Lena Saleh in this volume).[37] This reinforces the point that radicalization is a predominantly social process requiring affirmation and encouragement by others. A psychologically disoriented person, whose search for a better life has yielded little more than bitter disillusionment, will seldom radicalize in a vacuum; thus, "self-radicalization" is frequently a misnomer. There is no evidence to support the stereotypical lone-actor profile, a sole, potential exception being psychopathology.

Compared with other mechanisms of radicalization, there is a heightened possibility of some degree of psychopathology in cases of lone actors. Research has identified potential mental-health disorders in 35 per cent of lone-actor extremists – a figure not significantly different from the 27 per cent of the adult population that experiences some form of mental disorder. The lower figure, however, includes a broad range of non-radicalized subjects, including those with anxiety and eating disorders, for example – arguably less dangerous motivators than idealizations of martyrdom.[38] Because insurgent groups are likely sensitive to the unreliability associated with psychopathology, such radicals tend to be more employable as suicide bombers than as insurgent fighters.

The Selfie Generation

Despite media and political attention on Islamic extremism, an increasing number of studies indicate that religion is declining in significance

for radicalized youth who become fighters overseas. For them, socialization and group dynamics are more important than sacred or ideological attractions. Thrills, status, and sex are their critical motivators,
especially for young males. Their frustrations and feelings, whether
related to inequality or simply boredom, trigger a desire to join group
of like-minded people. The resultant "groupthink" provides a confirmation bias, fortifying the group members' beliefs. Today, such actors
are much younger than they used to be – typically 20–24 as opposed
to 25–35, the typical jihadi terrorist's age a decade ago.[39]

These fighters are also recruited over very short timespans. Certain
youngsters are drawn to special or extreme challenges, such as individuals known to have memorized entire socio-political publications
verbatim.[40] For example, the practice of committing the Qu'ran to
memory via recitation, a tradition dating back to Islam's founding,
is seeing resurgence among the recently radicalized. This is mirrored
within non-religious movements, such as right-wing extremists mem-
orizing *The Turner Diaries* and other such manifestos. However, the
overwhelming majority have only a superficial understanding of their
putative grievances, which leads to self-constructed accounts that lend
their actions a semblance of justification. For them, being an insurgent
is envisioned as trendy, with rebels such as André Poulin (a.k.a. "Jihadi
John"), of Timmins, Ontario, enjoying prestige and celebrity – central
aspirations of the so-called "selfie-generation."[41] Therefore, for this
group, any counterinsurgency plan based on providing alternative
religious narratives will prove ineffective.

GROUP-INDIVIDUAL LINKAGES

It is likely impossible to construct any simple, single theory to explain
individual and group motivations, as so many personal, overlapping
factors are at play. Rebel groups in a given location may emerge from
a variety of prewar structures, which explains why insurgent groups
that are otherwise similar often take dramatically different forms in
regard to organization and recruitment.[42] As with some other, non-
radicalizing patterns of motivation, grievance and anger are expressed
by an individual who identifies with a group suffering injustice, despite
the absence of any personal link to the suffering party. The Palestinian-
Israeli conflict, for instance, has been cited as the "single best recruiting
tool that the jihadists possess."[43] Such radicalization has been termed
"sudden jihad syndrome" – a contentious term linked to certain

anti-Muslim writers as well as a dearth of supporting research.[44] Nonetheless, this section identifies some key areas where group and individual motivations are linked.

Wishing to understand and to have an impact upon the world, as well as develop a sense of identity from common purpose and the sense of belonging, are completely normal human desires. Such desires are unquestioningly accepted as fundamental motivators for social change; Maslow's 1943 article "A Theory of Human Motivation," in which he first presented his classic hierarchy of needs,[45] is still cited in the field of psychology and in courses on military leadership. Behavioural science debates on violent extremism have moved from single-factor explanations, such as poverty, to multilevel pathway models that emphasize the process as opposed to the act.[46] As such, radicalization is a process, not an outcome; it occurs through a confluence of multiple, overlapping components, which are often not fully understood.[47] Mechanisms of radicalization are thus more complex than simply the promulgation of a fanatical ideology. Jihadist terror is seen, for example, as emerging from Wahhabism and Salafism, but this ignores the reality that most Wahhabists and Salafists abhor violence. In fact, many Salafists, desiring to practice a seventh-century ideal of Islam, oppose the attention being drawn to them by those more radicalized. Further, ideas do not equal actions; while a significant number of Muslims may agree with certain jihadist goals, only a statistically minute percentage will ever be motivated to commit insurgent acts.

With individual and group motivators in mind, virtually every account of violent radicalization involves the ascendency of a sense of personal identity based on group membership. Connecting with others as a member of a social group can be instrumental for positive social and personal development. However, our greater concern is those for whom the group's social identity is fundamentalist or militant, which leads members to dismiss or stray from other social contacts, such as friends, family, or other acceptable norms of social behaviour.[48] While individual grievances may initially set a person on a path of extremism, this is most often expressed in terms of a hatred based upon group identity, not personal attributes. Group-based mechanisms of radicalization therefore are especially relevant, particularly in-group biases and hatred, as we see that the more extreme the group, the more strongly the insurgents self-identify.

It is this violent self-identity that is cultivated by the insurgent recruiters. The fledgling insurgent is given simple explanations for a complex and disappointing world, together with suggested outlets to ameliorate their feelings of helplessness. The newfound sense of purpose enhances a positive sense of self – perhaps for the first time. Incorporating the group's beliefs and values into the recruit's personal social identity often breeds an arrogance in regard to their newly acquired knowledge which alienates them from previous associates. While their social circle becomes smaller as friends are cast aside, attachment to the recruit's new companions becomes more intense. The disenfranchised insurgent increasingly rejects foundational values, leading to the crossing of an "alienation threshold" of cognitive radicalization, as outlined in Figure 8.1.[49] This shift is marked by the recruit's withdrawal into a small group of like-minded people, an echo chamber of ideological reinforcement in which further, more intense indoctrination can occur.

With regard to Figure 8.1, note that the difference, in terms of numbers of people, between the "predisposed to support change" and "predisposed to accept status quo" groups varies both by community and by grievance; the fifty-fifty split is represented here as such merely to illustrate the potential insurgent's increasing alienation from contrary opinion as radicalization increases. Also note that the "virtual (online) social group" is merely representative, as radicalization via social media has grown dramatically in recent years.[50]

It is the group's overarching grievance, based upon a contrary view of society's future, which draws together the disparate individual motivations to rebel. Clear analysis requires awareness of the distinctions between each insurgent's personal and group grievances in order to develop the most nuanced counter-strategy, given the potential range of individual motivations. Nonetheless, most cases show a "near-seamless blend of personal and political grievance."[51]

With the exception of the infrequent lone actor who does self-radicalize, the final step in along the extremist's trajectory is self-persuasion in action – the slippery slope. In the psychology of self-justification, each act of pushing behavioural boundaries desensitizes the insurgent further and, in turn, permits the next, more extreme act. Through this slippery slope, insurgent groups introduce new recruits to violence gradually, allowing them to demonstrate obedience while concurrently ferreting out government agents.[52] Such tests yield an added benefit for the insurgent leader in that they cement the recruit's incrimination; even if various methods of countering violent extremism prove effective, it will be increasingly difficult for the

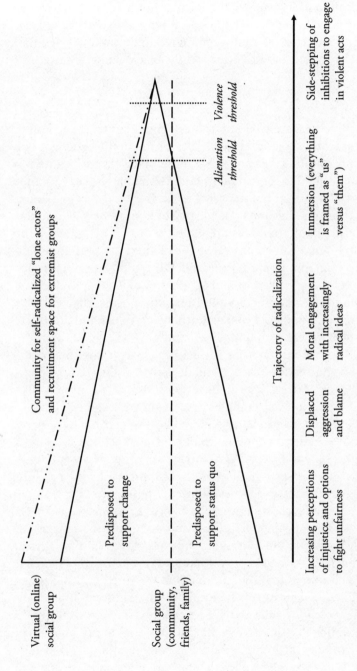

Figure 8.1 Social exclusion and the trajectory of radicalization.

now-guilty apprentice to back away. This slow escalation of assignments can lead to the crossing of a "violence threshold" of behavioural radicalization, at which point the developing adherents now self-categorize as combatants, totally committed to defending their communities in accordance with their recently articulated grievances.

CONCLUSION

Counterinsurgencies are won or lost more on the strategic and political levels than on the tactical level; judicious use of the knowledge of insurgent motivation will contribute to developing effective strategies and campaigns. In this context, a deployed Canadian force is a somewhat uniform organization, and there is a strong tendency to assume that our opponents share an equal degree of homogeneity. Given the kinds of insurgents Canadians are likely to face, however, such an assumption is false. As demonstrated above, there are near-countless potential combinations of group and individual motivations influencing enemy combatants. People and the politics of identity are central to understanding insurgencies; cultural mirror-imaging, and the assumption that we all hold similar, unchanging values and priorities, will skew operational planning, often fatally.

Although no two insurgencies are identical, many share some combination of characteristics, tactics, and objectives as they pass through similar life cycles.[53] The clear implication for our leadership is that insurgencies, due to their complex and changing natures, virtually rule out templated solutions, which are likely to prove ineffective if not outright counterproductive. Reducing nuanced concepts and unstable phenomena to catchy acronyms and applying vague pronouncements like "hearts and minds" or "exporting democracy" are at best vague, if not totally destabilizing, policy prescriptions.[54] Canada has experienced an upsurge in radicalization which is linked directly to our foreign policy – the deployment of troops to Afghanistan. Given our engagements in Iraq and in combatting extremism in Africa, this situation will undoubtedly continue. But even in acknowledging this, it must be noted that the information presented in this chapter is only a baseline assessment of insurgent motivations. Effectively combatting violent extremism requires that each be approached as a unique situation, with its own distinctive grievances and aims, informed by the combatants' group and individual motivations. An effective approach to the problem of understanding and assessing the details of insurgent motivation is offered in this volume by Tait, Clark, and Saleh, whose work charts the parameters of women's involvement in Daesh-supportive online dark networks.

This chapter began with a caution about how we in the West may be susceptible to radicalizing influences. As we engage insurgents in their various forms, we must ensure that we do not become possessed by our own demons. One can readily see antidemocratic countermeasures to radicalization which are eroding our rights and freedoms while concurrently adding to the alienation of those from whom the insurgents recruit. The vast majority in any society is not violent – even those angry at their current situation and whose grievances are expressed in vicious language. The tremendous personal cost of violent radicalization – including, at worst, death – is likely what stops most individuals from crossing that line. We must not become so extreme in our policy and military responses that we begin to convince them otherwise. It can be a slippery slope.

NOTES

1 Stéfanie von Hlatky and H. Christian Breede, eds., *Going to War? Trends in Military Intervention* (Montreal: McGill-Queen's University Press, 2016).

2 Bard E. O'Neill, *Insurgency and Terrorism: From Revolution to Apocalypse*, 2nd ed. (Washington, DC: Potomac Books, 2005), 1, 10.

3 Mathew J. Burrows, *Global Risks 2035: The Search for a New Normal* (Washington, DC: Atlantic Council, 2016), 56; *Global Trends: Paradox of Progress* (Washington, DC: National Intelligence Council, 2017), 20; von Hlatky and Breede, *Going to War.*

4 Frank G. Hoffman, "Hybrid Warfare and Challenges," *Joint Force Quarterly* 52, no. 1 (2009): 37; Williamson Murray and Peter R, Mansoor, eds., *Hybrid Warfare: Fighting Complex Opponents from the Ancient World to the Present* (Cambridge: Cambridge University Press, 2012).

5 David McDonough and Colonel Charles Davies, eds., "The Strategic Outlook for Canada," *Vimy Papers* 34 (Ottawa: Conference of Defence Associations Institute, 2017): 27.

6 United Nations, "United Nations Peacekeeping: Fatalities," https://peace keeping.un.org/en/fatalities.

7 David C. Gompert, *Heads We Win: The Cognitive Side of Counterinsurgency*, RAND Counterinsurgency Study Paper 1 (Santa Monica, CA: RAND Corporation, 2007), 33.

8 McCauley and Moskalenko, *Friction*, 32–33.

9 O'Neill, *Insurgency and Terrorism*, 20–8.

10 Haroro J. Ingram, "Tracing the Evolutionary Roots of Modern Islamic Radicalism and Militancy," *Flinders Journal of Law Reform* 10, no. 3 (2007–08): 504–6.

11 Aum Shinrikyo may have been reborn in Europe. See: "Aum Shinrikyo: The Japanese cult surfacing in Europe," *BBC News*, 6 April 2016.

12 Heidi Holland, *The Struggle: A History of the African National Congress* (New York: George Braziller, 1990).

13 See, for example: H. Jon Rosenbaum and Peter C. Sederberg, eds., *Vigilante Politics* (Philadelphia: University of Pennsylvania Press, 1976).

14 T. David Mason, "Structures of Ethnic Conflict: Revolution versus Secession in Rwanda and Sri Lanka," *Terrorism and Political Violence* 15, no. 4 (Winter 2003): 83–113.

15 Cynthia McClintock, "Why Peasants Rebel: The Case of Peru's Sendero Luminoso," *World Politics* 37, no. 1 (1984): 48–84.

16 The results of such failures of integrity may be seen in: H.R. McMaster, *Dereliction of Duty: Johnson, McNamara, the Joint Chiefs of Staff, and the Lies That Led to Vietnam* (New York: HarperCollins, 1997); Neil Sheehan, *A Bright, Shining Lie: John Paul Vann and America in Vietnam* (New York: Random House, 1988); and Colonel David H. Hackworth and Julie Sherman, *About Face: The Odyssey of an American Warrior* (New York: Simon & Shuster, 1989).

17 O'Neill, *Insurgency and Terrorism*, 32.

18 Henry Butterfield Ryan, *The Fall of Che Guevara: A Story of Soldiers, Spies, and Diplomats* (New York: Oxford University Press, 1998), 66, 157.

19 Stijn Sieckelinck and Micha de Winter, eds., *Formers & Families: Transitional Journeys in and out of Extremisms in the United Kingdom, Denmark, and The Netherlands* (The Hague: National Coordinator, Security and Counterterrorism, 2015), 13, 87–8. The author thanks Ghayda Hassan, Professor, Université du Québec à Montréal (UQAM), for recommending this excellent study.

20 Christian Leuprecht, Todd Hataley, Sophia Moskalenko, and Clark McCauley, "Winning the Battle but Losing the War? Narrative and Counter-Narratives Strategy," *Perspectives on Terrorism* 3, no. 2 (2009): 30.

21 Marc Sageman, *Leaderless Jihad: Terror Networks in the Twenty-First Century* (Philadelphia: University of Pennsylvania Press, 2008), 80.

22 Olivier Roy, "France's Oedipal Islamist Complex: The country's jihadi problem isn't about religion or politics. It's about generational revolt," *Foreign Policy*, 7 January 2016.

23 Phil Gurski, *The Threat from Within: Recognizing Al Qaeda-Inspired Radicalization and Terrorism in the West* (Lanham, MD: Rowman & Littlefield, 2016), 70.

24 McCauley and Moskalenko, *Friction*, 16.

25 Jon Stock, "Inside the Mind of a Seductive Killer," *London Times*, 21 August 2002.

26 McCauley and Moskalenko, *Friction*, 53–4.

27 Mark Silinsky, *Jihad and the West: Black Flag over Babylon* (Bloomington: Indiana University Press, 2016), 83–4.

28 Canadian Mental Health Association, "Suicide and Youth," n.d., https://toronto.cmha.ca/mental-health-2/find-help/crisis-support/ (accessed 5 March 2016).

29 Robert E. Meagher, *Killing from the Inside Out: Moral Injury and Just War* (Eugene, OR: Cascade Books, 2014), 3–5.

30 Canadian Press, "Canadian military first in world to issue guidelines on dealing with child soldiers," *National Post*, 6 February 2017.

31 Lindsay Coombs, "Are They Soldiers? Or Are They Children? Preparing the Canadian Military for the Contemporary Security Environment," *General Sir William Otter Papers* (Toronto: Royal Canadian Military Institute) 16, no. 1 (2016): 2.

32 Peter W. Singer, "Western militaries confront child soldiers threat," *Jane's Intelligence Review* 17, no. 1 (2005): 8–9.

33 Ah-Jung Lee, "Understanding and Addressing the Phenomenon of 'Child Soldiers': The Gap between the Global Humanitarian Discourse and the Local Understandings and Experiences of Young People's Military Recruitment," *Refugee Studies Centre Working Papers* (Refugee Studies Centre, University of Oxford) 52 (2009), 9, 15–6.

34 For examples, see Human Rights Watch's online resources on child soldiers: https://www.hrw.org/topic/childrens-rights/child-soldiers.

35 Note that some analysts will cite recent conversion dismissively to ignore religiosity within secular societies. See: Paul Bramadat and Lorne Dawson, *Religious Radicalization and Securitization in Canada and Beyond* (Toronto: University of Toronto Press, 2014), 308.

36 Gurski, *The Threat from Within*, 37–9.

37 Marc Sageman, *Misunderstanding Terrorism* (Philadelphia: University of Pennsylvania Press, 2007), 90–1, 124.

38 Jeanine de Roy van Zuijdewijn and Edwin Bakker, "Analysing Personal Characteristics of Lone-Actor Terrorists: Research Findings and Recommendations," *Perspectives on Terrorism* 10, no. 2 (April 2016): 44.

39 Kelvin Smith, "Non-religious radicalisation: The 'selfie' generation of terrorists," *Land Power Forum* (Australian Army), 1 November 2016, https://

www.army.gov.au/our-future/blog/strategy/non-religious-radicalisation-the-selfie-generation-of-terrorists.

40 Sieckelinck and de Winter, *Formers & Families*, 13, 87–8.

41 John McCoy and W. Andy Knight, "Homegrown Terrorism in Canada: Local Patterns, Global Trends," *Studies in Conflict & Terrorism* 38, no. 4 (2015), 268–9.

42 Paul Staniland, *Networks of Rebellion: Explaining Insurgent Cohesion and Collapse* (Ithaca, NY: Cornell University Press, 2014), 2–4.

43 Mary Habeck, *Knowing the Enemy: Jihadist Ideology and the War on Terror* (New Haven, CT: Yale University Press, 2006), 173.

44 Leuprecht et al., "Winning the Battle," 31.

45 Abraham H. Maslow, "A Theory of Human Motivation," *Psychological Review* 50, no. 4 (1943): 370–96.

46 John Horgan, *The Psychology of Terrorism* (London: Routledge, 2005). Horgan expands on these views in: John Horgan, "Deradicalization or Disengagement?", *Perspectives on Terrorism* 2, no. 4 (2008): 3–8.

47 Pete Lentini, "The Transference of Neojihadism: Towards a Process Theory of Transnational Radicalisation," in *Radicalisation Crossing Borders: New Directions in Islamist and Jihadist Political, Intellectual and Theological Thought in Practice. Refereed Proceedings from the International Conference, 26–27 November 2008, Parliament House, Melbourne, Victoria*, ed. S. Khatab, M. Bakashmar, and E. Ogru (Caulfield, Victoria, Australia: Global Terrorism Research Centre, 2009): 1–2.

48 Kate Barrelle, "Disengagement from Violent Extremism," conference paper, Summary of the GTReC ARC Linkage Project on Radicalisation Conference, Global Terrorism Research Centre (GTReC), Monash University, Clayton, Victoria, Australia, 8 November 2010, p. 2.

49 Figure 8.1 is informed by the ideas in Kate Barrelle, "Disengagement from Violent Extremism"; Leuprecht et al., "Winning the Battle"; McCauley and Moskalenko, *Friction*; Sageman, *Misunderstanding Terrorism*; and Fathali M. Moghaddam, "The Staircase to Terrorism: A Psychological Exploration," *American Psychologist* 60, no. 2 (2005): 161–9.

50 Ghayda Hassan et al., "Exposure to Extremist Online Content Could Lead to Violent Radicalization: A Systematic Review of Empirical Evidence," *International Journal of Developmental Science* 12 (2018): 71–88.

51 McCauley and Moskalenko, *Friction*, 32.

52 Ibid., 32–3, 44.

53 A commonly accepted model for such evolution consists of: emerging leadership; recruitment and building support; increasing violence and political activity; and progressively open warfare. See: United States,

Central Intelligence Agency, *Guide to the Analysis of Insurgency* (Langley, VA: CIA, 2012).

54 Douglas Porch, *Counterinsurgency: Exposing the Myths of the New Way of War* (Cambridge, UK: Cambridge University Press, 2012), 330.

9

Women in Dark Networks:
A Case Study on Daesh-Supportive
Tumblr Blogs

Victoria Tait, Joshua Clark, and Lena Saleh

Feminist scholars have confirmed that the key to advancing the goals of the women's movement is the organization of dynamic female actors into autonomous non-governmental organizations.[1] Domestic and transnational women's networks have advanced gender equality while playing central roles in the improvement of global health and welfare.[2] However, there exists a darker side to women's organization; what if powerful female networks are developed not to enable peace and stability, but to upend the current liberal democratic international order? This is the case of *dark networks* of female actors, covert communities of women loyal to illicit causes. Revolutions in social media have diversified women's involvement and untethered the reach of terrorist organizations from geo-political boundaries and constraints. It is no longer necessary for a woman to be physically present to become involved in terrorist organizations; ideological support and recruitment can now be encouraged over pre-existing Internet forums and websites. This is a new and profound form of "combat-enabling" behaviour.

While this form of organization has made terrorist networks more resilient, it also makes them accessible to scholars. By data mining these sites, scholars can now discern more about the organization of women's terrorist networks more easily than ever before, including information about these women's motivations. Accordingly, we have examined the activities of Daesh-supportive users on Tumblr, a popular blogging site where users can establish profiles and share meaningful images and quotes. Using social network analysis (SNA) methods, we have generated a social graph complete with demographic, structural, and intrapersonal network variables. Using this graph, we compare Daesh-supportive social networks with a corresponding non-supportive Tumblr baseline (see Table 9.1). We use these findings in concert with qualitative research to argue that the structure and content of Daesh-supportive blogs contain observable gendered effects that dictate their organization. From these observations, we postulate that even though women's dark networks are non-territorial entities, they augment Daesh's territorial nation-building project through the formation and dissemination of gendered narratives of support. This exploratory study illustrates the value of examining female terrorists as a collectivity, while offering qualitative and quantitative methods for scholars' future research. To contextualize the relationship between gender and terrorist activity, we first examine relevant literature on women in terrorist organizations. In this literature review, we focus explicitly on the debate surrounding women's roles in modern jihadi networks and offer a way to examine women's terrorism through a gendered network lens. This approach seeks to supplement individual-level analysis of female terrorists with a meso-level analysis of gendered networks in terrorism. We will also introduce essential concepts related to studying dark networks. From here, we introduce our case study on Daesh-supportive women's networks, with an emphasis on women in online communities. We then describe the methods we used to generate the subgraphs that form the basis of this study's quantitative analysis. We found that women's Daesh-supportive Tumblr networks are more centralized than men's networks, contain a high degree of gender homophily, and maintain weak ties to other members of the Daesh-supportive Tumblr community. Paradoxically, these weak ties, in concert with high centralization, may grant them considerable resilience. We also introduce an in-depth analysis of two selected blogs from our study to illustrate the gendered language of the network we are analyzing. Contextually, the narratives within these communities are highly gendered in accordance with the patriarchal structure of Daesh. We argue that Daesh-supportive networks on Tumblr have gendered qualities both in their structure and in their content. Furthermore, these deterritorialized entities serve an essential, discursive role in Daesh's nation-building project. In introducing the study of women's dark networks through feminist security studies and social network analysis, we also advocate for a radically cross-disciplinary approach, blurring the line between quantitative and qualitative methods.

LITERATURE

Women's jihadi terrorism presents a perfect case for the analysis of female networks, as several scholars have already discovered.[3] The authors recognize that the term *jihadi*, used in this way, is a perversion of the proper term *jihad* (to struggle/strive). Nevertheless, here we use *jihadi* to identify radical Islamic fundamentalist ideology concerned with the violent interpretation of the offensive and defensive jihad (*defensive jihad* refers to the struggle to protect observant Muslims from oppression and invasion, while *offensive jihad* refers to military conquest legitimized by a political leader).[4] This includes Wahhabi and Salafi strands of Islam as well as Islamic-nationalist organizations. The exclusionary ideology of extremist conservative organizations, such as radical Islamist groups, necessitates the gendered segregation of adherents as well as estrangement from the larger community of non-believers (*Dar al-Kufr*) where applicable. In many cases, this not only encourages members of these organizations to utilize social media to create alternative support networks, but often divides these networks by gender. Nevertheless, radical Islamic organizations vary in their stances toward female terrorists in accordance with the *fatwa* (religio-legal prohibition) they observe.[5] While Islamic-nationalist organizations like Hamas and Islamist Chechen groups employ female suicide bombers, this combative role is often prohibited for female followers of global Salafist jihad.[6] Instead, Salafi groups like Al-Qaeda have emphasized the importance of women in jihad as supporters rather than as active combatants.[7] However, this stance changed following the 2003 invasion of Iraq, when Abu Musab al-Zarqawi at least tacitly approved the involvement of women under the premise of defensive jihad in his statement that "war has broken out ... if you [Muslim men] are not going to be chivalrous knights in this war, make way for women to wage it ... Yes, by God, men have lost their manhood."[8] The invasion shifted fatwas away from *offensive* toward *defensive* jihad, which permits the inclusion of women and children in the struggle.[9] Shortly after al-Zarqawi's proclamation, Al-Qaeda's first female suicide bomber successfully completed her mission, killing herself and five military recruits near a town on the Iraqi-Syrian border (Basch-Harod 2012).[10] These details indicate a degree of ideological discord around the permissibility of women's involvement within Al-Qaeda and a softening of the organization's stance on female-perpetrated terrorism.[11] These varying positions illustrate a profound, shifting gendered ideology within jihadist terrorist organizations.

Early studies on women's online jihadi activism focused on websites like Malika El Aroud's minbar.sos. Using this website, El Aroud became notorious for encouraging terrorist recruitment and providing logistical and medical advice to attackers from the relative safety of her Belgian home.[12] This phase of online jihadism took the form of top-down website organization, whereby site administrators disseminated propaganda to viewers.[13] For online viewers, participation in this phase of online jihadism was limited to "consumption of said content and assistance in distribution through dissemination in different networks."[14] After 9/11, these sites became increasingly vulnerable to attacks by Western security forces and were frequently shut down.[15] These challenges to online jihadi activism have been overcome in the era of social media, where resilient online networks can be established with a minimum of effort. This era of communications technology has been referred to as Web 2.0, wherein "websites [are] based solely on interactive user-generated content or 'social media' as opposed to more traditional static websites where users can only view content."[16] With new social media technology, users on sites like Tumblr merely have to "fill in the blank fields" provided and, within minutes, they can connect to an entire community of jihadist sympathizers and activists.[17] Accordingly, beginning in 2004, security analysts witnessed a rapid expansion of jihadist websites using these technologies.[18] In 1997, there were only about a dozen websites dedicated to jihadist terrorism, but by 2006, there were more than 7,000.[19] Furthermore, these sites are designed to be inclusive, and many have been translated into French, English, and Russian, including popular women's sites like El Aroud's.[20] These sites are ideal for the communicative purposes of terrorist actors inasmuch as they are "decentralized ... cannot be subjected to control or restriction ... [are] not censored, and allow access to anyone who wants it."[21] The danger of female jihadi activism on social media is not simply that women can disseminate imagery or quotes, as was the case with traditional websites, but that they can use blogging to create and maintain interactive communities. Blogging sites like Tumblr have been designed for the express purpose of enabling the construction of networked communities, providing each user with their own, personalized profile. As we will illustrate, these blogs have proven to be powerful tools both of gendered communication and of gendered socialization.

Daesh has proven remarkably adept at utilizing social media tools. Daesh emerged as an offshoot of the Al-Qaeda movement in Iraq and, since its founding in the late 1990s, has grown to become an independent organization. Currently led by Abu Bakr al-Baghdadi, Daesh has become infamous for the atrocious violence of its tactics against non-compliant communities in Syria and Iraq. Like Al-Qaeda, Daesh adheres to a Salafist interpretation of Islam, but it differs in its focus on the establishment and expansion of an Islamic caliphate in the Levant rather than international attacks on the West.[22] Daesh also rejects the nationalism of Ba'athist ideology as "a means to artificially divide the Arab community."[23] Instead, Daesh seeks to establish a pan-Islamic state that transcends racial identification by uniting Muslims with "orthodox Sunnis at the pinnacle ... [while] heterodox groups such as Shi'ites, Yazidis, and Alawites are to be completely eradicated."[24] Using a variety of social media tools, Daesh has succeeded in recruiting over 2,000 Westerners to its cause in Syria and Iraq.[25] It is estimated that more than 200 of these Western members are female.[26] This skillful use of modern social media technology belies the reality that Daesh adheres to a very traditionalist gender discourse, particularly for female members. Daesh's state-building project necessitates a discourse that emphasizes the role of women as wives and mothers of the Islamic nation.[27] A pamphlet recently released by the Al-Khanssaa Brigade reveals that women are to become the wives and mothers of the Islamic State.[28] The position of women in jihad is by no means a forgone conclusion. Daesh has stated in several publications that despite its Salafi origins, it permits women to participate in jihad under certain conditions. This is significant because, although Al-Qaeda had previously used suicide bombers, women in Daesh are generally discouraged from participating in combat unless necessitated by an enemy attack that cannot be stopped by male fighters, in which case a fatwa calling for their participation will be issued.[29] Al-Khanssaa condones women's suicide attacks already perpetrated in Iraq, arguing they were necessitated by the absence of willing men.[30] At the time of writing, however, Daesh had not published any fatwas to encourage female combatants.[31]

Daesh's nation-building enterprise has been successful in targeting women through skillful usage of social media, particularly the construction of online networks. These networked communities allow jihadist-supportive women to play more active roles in terrorist movements without compromising their patriarchal foundations. Similarly, face-to-face radicalization and communication has been supplanted by online communication following the US-led invasion of Afghanistan.[32] These observations are particularly apropos when examining the online activity of Daesh-supportive women. Online communities of women have proven to be a powerful source of recruitment and support for the burgeoning Islamic State.[33] Often referring to themselves as *muhajirat* (the feminine form of *mujahid*, meaning men who journey to contribute to jihad), these online communities of Daesh-supportive women may or may not have travelled to IS-controlled territory, but nonetheless have unified to form a supportive online community.[34] Unlike earlier efforts at online jihad, the online muhajirat of Daesh have succeeded in creating expansive networks of support to recruit, educate, and train Western women to travel to Iraq and Syria, while simultaneously encouraging identity formation.[35] Using popular social networking sites like Tumblr, young women are encouraged not simply to read the Daesh information provided but to integrate it into their profiles and online identities.

Though valuable, the work conducted to date on gendered social network analysis is limited in quantity, and even less is available on women's dark networks specifically.[36] However, there have been several studies conducted on social network analysis (SNA) which, together with observations from our qualitative research, help guide the hypotheses of our study. When using SNA to examine networks of illicit activity on the Internet, the goal is to map out the system of ties (or edges) between actors (represented as nodes) in a given network.[37] While traditional social science methodologies focus on the individual characteristics of actors, such as class or ethnicity, SNA emphasizes the relational ties that connect actors.[38] By focusing on the "topology of social networks," analysts can use quantitative methods to draw conclusions about complex, interrelated systems of actors.[39] These methods can be employed to study "bright" networks – networks that are legal and visible – as well as dark networks, which are illegal and often covert.[40]

We can draw several conclusions about female participation in Daesh-supportive communities from extant research on social networks in general and dark networks in particular. First, online social networks are powerful tools for collaborative identity formation. In this regard, blogs allow women to establish identities linked to social communities that would otherwise be geographically unavailable to them.[41] Paechter (2013) argues that, "through the choice of background, the information given about the self, the individual profile picture, links to other profiles and sites, and ongoing comments about one's life and activities, a SNS [social networking site] profile allows an individual to perform their identity through their homepage."[42] Accordingly, young women who demonstrate and glamorize the Daesh lifestyle are actively incorporating the group's identity into their own, and encouraging others within the group to do the same. Further, these online social networks mark a shift away from the strong community ties of traditional collaborative action in favour of a diffuse, weak-tie network.[43] Strong ties characterize "close, solid and trusted reciprocated relationships, e.g. family and friends" whereas weak ties might describe the kind of ties formed with a co-worker.[44] This logic of *connective* action challenges Mancur Olson's thesis by eliminating membership costs,[45] and suggests that weak ties are not inimical to large-group formation when the cost of participation approaches zero.[46] We can therefore expect that weak ties will characterize online communities, though we also expect that due to the prolific use of social media, Daesh ties will be stronger than the Tumblr baseline, particularly within female networks.

We also expect a high degree of reblogging between and across bloggers of the same gender and the same ideology; this is referred to as *gender homophily*. Homophily refers to the tendency of individuals to bond with others with the same characteristics. Both gender and ideological homophily are examined in this study. This expectation is informed by knowledge of Daesh's gender-segregation policies as well as extant research on gender homophily in SNA. Females in social networks tend toward gender homophily, creating gender-exclusive networks, usually at a greater rate than men.[47] In the case of online multiplayer games, this has less to do with the biological sex of players so much as their *performance* of a gender.[48] Since researchers cannot conclusively verify the biological sex of network participants, these observations reveal only the tendencies of members that *perform* the female gender.[49] Finally, we expect a high degree of centralization in female Daesh-supportive networks. Actor centrality has proven crucial for the rapid dissemination of information and coordination of tasks.[50] There are several ways to gauge centrality, but our study measures *closeness centrality*: "actors who are closer to more actors in the network than any other actor."[51] In dark networks with high involvement costs, like a drug-smuggling ring, central positions are dangerous, and the actors who occupy them at elevated risk of arrest or murder. But in online Tumblr communities, there is little risk to occupying a central position in a network. The worst outcome an actor could expect on Tumblr would be blog deletion, in which case they can simply start a new blog page. We therefore expect that all Daesh-supportive networks will be highly centralized, regardless of gender.

Our final hypotheses can be summarized as follows:

H1. Social Networks on Tumblr will differ based on their status as supporter or non-supporter of Daesh.
H1a. Daesh-supportive communities will be centralized.
H1b. Daesh-supportive groups will post more frequently than non-supportive groups.
H1c. Daesh-supportive groups will have more mutual connections than non-supportive groups.
H1d. Daesh-supportive networks will have stronger ties than non-supportive networks.

H2. Gender will alter the structure of social networks of Daesh supporters on Tumblr.
H2a. Females are more likely to reblog other female users, while males are more likely to reblog other male users (high degree of gender homophily).
H2b. Female and male Daesh bloggers will both have a high degree of centralization.
H2c. Female bloggers will have more mutual connections than males.

METHODOLOGY

To assess these hypotheses, we drew data from the popular blogging website Tumblr, which hosts approximately 180 million blogs containing roughly 75 billion posts. Each of these posts represents a text or multimedia object. Other users can display these objects on their own blogs by "reblogging" them. Besides displaying this content, reblogging also allows a user to add commentary to the source material. This puts users in dialog with one another as they discuss or disseminate content over Tumblr.

Using this basic structure, it is possible to build a social graph representing Tumblr. Each blog becomes a node representing a person place or organization. Reblogs transform into edges (systems of ties) from the source of the material to the reblogger. This structure allows us to assess the popularity and diffusion of content on Tumblr. Well-known blogs will have a high number of reblogs, or more edges in the graph. Additionally, patterns of reblogging can expose communities of interest within the broader Tumblr network. Consider Figure 9.1, below: each dot represents a Tumblr blog, and each line represents that blog's engagement with another blog through the reblogging of its content. When combined with other descriptive statistics, these measures can help assess this examination's hypotheses.

Data Sources and Description

Constructing this social graph requires drawing data from Tumblr's application programming interface (API), which provides basic descriptive information on a user's blogging patterns. This data includes a count of a user's posts, data on who reblogged them, and summaries of the user's long-term activity. Other researchers have used API data to study topics such as terrorism or anorexia.[52] This examination uses a modified snowball sampling procedure to sample Tumblr's social graph. We began by gathering a series of "seed" blogs by known and confirmed supporters of Daesh activity on Tumblr. We then created a Python script, which iterated outward from each of these seed blogs. This script gathered data from those who reblogged one of the original seeds, and uncovered new blogs, which were added to the list of seeds. We again used the script to iterate outward from the newly discovered seed blogs, which expanded the graph and continued to add new seeds to our list of Daesh-supportive blogs. We stopped this process when the maximum diameter of the graph (the number of steps it takes to get from one blog to another) exceeded six. Six represents the outer limit of a relevant social connection between a seed blog and another site in the graph.[53]

This process results in a social graph comprised of 1,917 nodes with 11,807 edges (see Figure 9.2, below). Given this graph's high diameter, it is not feasible to consider it as a whole. As an example, consider two blogs connected by five intermediaries. Though part of the same network, they have no direct interaction with each other; to consider the two as linked is a distortion of the base reality within Tumblr. Minimizing this issue requires partitioning the graph into smaller, local communities with densely linked blogs. In this case, we

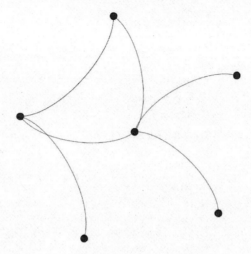

Figure 9.1 Example patterns of reblogging.

used a fast modularity algorithm to identify clusters of well-connected blogs.[54] These clusters are communities of interest wherein users engage with one another at a rate that exceeds chance. Using these communities slices the larger graph into eleven localized communities representing different discussions. These discussions include (but are not limited to) communities of Daesh supporters. By studying these extracted communities, we can compare the networks of female Daesh supporters to other bloggers.

Variables and Measures

Viewing Tumblr as a social graph allows us to extract several different variables to assess our hypotheses. These features can divide into three categories:

With two exceptions, all the above variables are straight from Tumblr's API. Gender and Daesh support need another layer of analysis to transform them into useful measures.

Assessing Daesh support required hand-coding of specific supporter blogs. Beginning with a core of well-known female Daesh supporters, we looked for other blogs using similar descriptors and tags. These potential supporters were then examined by the authors for markers of Daesh support. In situations where we reached a consensus that

Table 9.1
Variables in viewing Tumblr as a social graph

Variable	Sub-variable	Assessment method
Demographic/descriptive information	Gender	Drawn from Tumblr API
	Blog age	Drawn from Tumblr API
	Number of posts	Drawn from Tumblr API
	Content of posts	Drawn from Tumblr API
	Daesh supporter	Drawn from Tumblr API
	Uses Daesh-related language	Drawn from Tumblr API
Structural network variables	Number of times reblogged (out-degree)	Drawn from Tumblr API
	Number of times reblogged another's content (in-degree)	Drawn from Tumblr API
	Number of mutual edges (both users reblog each other)	Drawn from Tumblr API
Interpersonal network variables	Gender homophily	Hand-coding/ machine-coding
	Ideological homophily	Hand-coding/ machine-coding

the site was a Daesh supporter, we updated the seed list with the new URL. Due to the transitory nature of supporter blogs (several bloggers deleted their blogs during data collection), we were only able to establish nine supporter URLs for the seed list. However, by creating a corpus of descriptive tags that Daesh supporters used to classify their posts, we were able to find an additional twenty-six Tumblrs that used at least five tags highly correlated with Daesh supporters. As a result, the Tumblr graph includes twenty-six "tagged" users (blogs we identified through hand-coding as being ISIL-supportive) and nine "flagged" supporters (blogs identified by the Python script using our descriptive tags), with the remainder representing normal users focused on a variety of topics.

Coding gender for all users within the sample was a much more daunting task. In addition to the great number of blogs in the sample, many Tumblr users did not provide information on their gender. To achieve a coding rate high enough to model gender-related effects within the network, we turned to a machine-coding gender classification approach. First, we coded 500 blogs with identifiable gender markers. These markers included a user photograph, choice of

pronoun, and statements that established gender in the blog description. Using these coded entries as a training dataset, we trained a
logistic regression classifier, which included the number of men or
women that the Tumblr blog under examination reblogged, the number of tags used exclusively by men or by women in the training data,
the number of times these blogs reblogged someone else's content,
the number of times their content was reblogged, their total number
of posts and, finally, the proportion of connected Tumblrs that have
reblogged each other.

By splitting the coded data into a 70 per cent training dataset and
a 30 per cent test dataset, we discovered that the classifier achieved
76 per cent prediction accuracy. This equates to score of 0.79 on a
receiver operator curve (a tool for assessing the predictive power of
classification models), an acceptable level of performance given the
limited features at hand.[55] By feeding the un-coded data into the
trained model, we were able to get gender predictions for the remaining Tumblrs in the sample, providing full gender coding with an
acceptable degree of accuracy. Figure 9.2 is a visual representation of
the social network analyzed in this piece: red represents flagged Daesh-
supportive users, purple represents tagged Daesh-supportive users,
and blue represents standard Tumblr users.

FINDINGS

To assess the hypotheses advanced earlier in this examination, we
used an exponential random graph model (ERGM) to look at the
structural characteristics of the Daesh supporter community on
Tumblr. ERGMs are a family of statistical models that allow for statistical inference about social processes such as mutuality or homophily.[56] These models take a given graph as a starting point (in this case
the Daesh supporter community and an unrelated Tumblr community)
and generate randomized graphs based upon the structural characteristics provided. These graphs provide a distribution of alternative
graphs, which share structural elements with the provided data but
are estimated stochastically. By comparing the rate of occurrence for
specific behaviours such as mutuality or homophily in the established
graphs with a distribution of random counterparts, it is possible to
make statistical assessments about whether the patterns in the former
are different from a randomized process.

Figure 9.2 Daesh-supportive network.

ERGMs have several advantages: first, unlike regression, they embrace the interdependent nature of a social graph. Using regression to predict the presence or absence of an edge would violate the assumption of independence within that model, yielding suspect results. Additionally, ERGM allows us to compare between different graphs, such as those of a Daesh supporter community and a non-supporter community, to determine if the structural characteristics of either graph are different from those of its counterpart.[57]

As Table 9.2 suggests, multiple comparative axes are applied in ERGM. We compare Daesh-supportive blogs to standardized Tumblr blogs, which is to say those bloggers who have been neither tagged nor flagged during the coding process as supportive of Daesh ideology. We also compare blogging patterns between male and female

Table 7.2

ERGM of ISIL supporter subgraph and standard Tumblr subgraph

	Dependent variable	
	ISIL supporter subgraph	Standard Tumblr subgraph
Edges	-5.623***	-3.854***
	(-6.696, -4.551)	(-4.009, -3.699)
Out-degree – zero	8.056***	6.556***
	(7.281, 8.831)	(5.888, 7.224)
Out-degree – one	4.832***	3.341***
	(4.107, 5.558)	(2.671, 4.012)
Out-degree – two	2.751***	1.913***
	(2.016, 3.486)	(1.276, 2.550)
Mutual connection – female	1.133**	2.298***
	(0.244, 2.022)	(0.786, 3.811)
Mutual connection – male	2.329***	2.283***
	(1.369, 3.289)	(1.780, 2.787)
Absolute difference – posts	-0.00001***	0.00000
	(-0.00001, -0.000001)	(0.00000, 0.00000)
Gender homophily – female	0.380***	0.284*
	(0.202, 0.559)	(-0.035, 0.603)
Gender homophily – male	0.041	0.188**
	(-0.155, 0.236)	(0.031, 0.344)
Ideological homophily – ISIL supporter	-0.927	–
	(-3.256, 1.403)	
Ideological homophily – non-supporter	2.076***	–
	(1.033, 3.118)	
Ideological homophily – ISIL tag user	-0.265	–
	(-1.740, 1.211)	
Posting rate – supporter [a]	2.134***	–
	(1.150, 3.117)	
Posting rate – tag user [a]	1.947***	–
	(0.981, 2.913)	
Akaike information criterion	6,223.572	6,425.272
Bayesian information criterion	6,349.664	6,506.550

All coefficients are logged odds of the probability of an edge.

Notes: * $p<0.1$
** $p<0.05$
*** $p<0.01$
[a] Reference category = non-supporter

users in both Daesh-supportive and standardized communities. We can consider the terms in Table 9.2 using an example involving two hypothetical, Daesh-supportive users with blogs titled "Vanilla-ISIS" and "Green-Daesh." In this example, the *edges* and *out-degree* variables would simply be used as controls for how frequently Vanilla-ISIS and Green-Daesh reblogged Tumblr content compared to a standardized Tumblr subgraph. The gendered *mutual connection* refers to the likelihood that a mutual relationship will be developed between persons of the same gender. In other words, if Vanilla-ISIS and Green-Daesh were both coded as female, will they be more likely to reblog each other's content? And does this likelihood deviate significantly from standardized Tumblr users? Next, *absolute difference* refers to the likelihood that a blogger will reblog someone who has used Tumblr more or less than them. For example, if Vanilla-ISIS creates content every day, and Green-Daesh only blogs content biweekly, is Green-Daesh more or less likely to reblog content shared by Vanilla-ISIS? And again, does this likelihood deviate significantly from that of standardized Tumblr users? As mentioned above, ideological and gender *homophily* refers to similarities in the actual content of the blogs. In this instance, have these users been coded as male or female? Ideologically speaking, do they contain material tagged or flagged as Daesh-supportive? If so, are Vanilla-ISIS and Green-Daesh more or less likely to reblog a user with similar ideological content or gender? And in what way do these patterns differ from that of a standardized Tumblr user? Finally, *posting rate* refers to the frequency with which tagged and flagged users reblog content as compared to a standard Tumblr user.

Limitations of Findings

We encountered two primary challenges in conducting this study. First, it is the nature of online communities to be highly transitory; this is particularly true of dark networks.[58] While the bloggers we analyzed made no effort to conceal their activities or support for Daesh, their blogs were frequently deleted, either because Tumblr banned them or because the bloggers simply chose to delete their blogs. We were frequently required to rework our approach during the coding process to accommodate shifts in the network. Relatedly, coding hundreds of blogs is a time-consuming process and requires several researchers working simultaneously to code the nodes of the

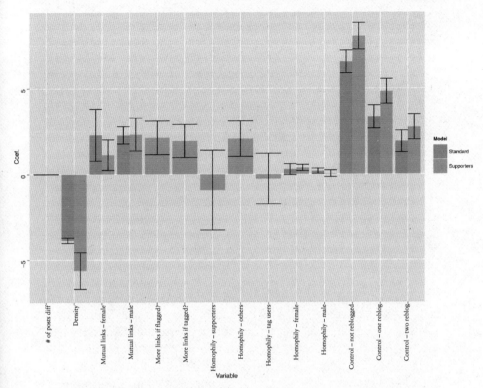

Figure 9.3 Coefficients with 95% confidence intervals for both ERGM models.

social network before blogs begin disappearing or, worse, entire web-sites are taken down by government cybersecurity forces. Second, this method required that we code each blog for a male-female binary – likely a contentious choice to any social scientist who rejects a sim-plistic male-female dichotomy. To overcome this challenge, we maintain that our results are true of a *feminized* or *masculinized* network. Regardless of whether or not *woman* and *man* are legitimate material constructs – and we do not argue that they are – we have no way of knowing with certainty that a given blogger that we selected was biologically male or female. We took great care to ensure that a blog would only be coded as female in the event that the blogger self-identified as female, either explicitly in the "about me" section or through the use of a feminized moniker or profile photo. Furthermore, all of these characteristics were examined in accordance with gendered Islamic cultural norms. For example, we would identify bloggers by *Umm* (mother of) or *Abu* (father of). As stated earlier,

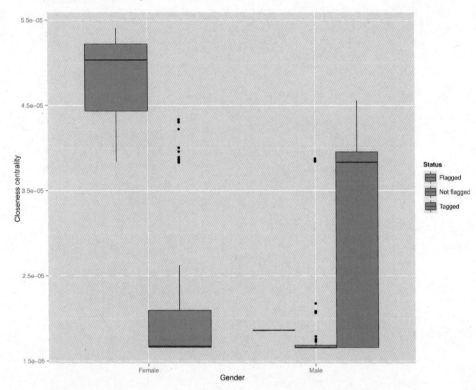

Figure 9.4 Relative centralities within the supporter Tumblr subgraph.

the gender performance of the blogger is more important to this study
than the so-called biological sex.[59]

Analysis

Our hypothesis was that there would be observable effects of gender
in the social graph produced by this analysis. Furthermore, we
expected that Daesh-supportive networks would differ in structure
from non-supportive networks. We expected to find gender homophily
in our analysis – in other words, women being more likely to reblog
the posts of other women, and men being more likely to reblog the
posts of other men – and that this would create gendered communities
among Tumblr bloggers. We also expected that women would have
dense networks of associational ties and that their networks would
be centralized. To test the validity of these hypotheses, we examined
the social graph for a number of factors, including mutual connection,

absolute difference, gender homophily, ideological homophily, posting rate, centrality, and average number of ties. Each measure will be explained in greater detail below.

MUTUAL CONNECTION

Female Daesh-supportive Tumblr users had slightly fewer mutual connections than average female Tumblr users, but given the margin of error, the difference is not significant. This suggests that mutual reblogging relationships among female Daesh-supportive networks are no different than among standardized Tumblr female networks. Similarly, male Daesh-supportive Tumblr networks did not demonstrate a significantly different rate of mutual reblogging from average Tumblr networks. This means that the tendency of female Daesh-supportive users to engage in mutual reblogging within their social network is the same as women in the non-supportive networks; and the same inference can be made about male users. It also suggests that users maintain relatively weak ties to other users.

ABSOLUTE DIFFERENCE

There was a marginal tendency for Daesh supporters to reblog prolific users more than we had expected, based on the standard Tumblr network. This suggests that less-experienced Daesh-supportive Tumblr users are linking with more-experienced Daesh-supportive Tumblr users. However, this may be due to a high rate of blog turnover in our Daesh-supportive graph. It is possible that Daesh-supportive users are more frequently banned because their blog contents violate Tumblr's terms of use. In this instance, previous users may have had their blogs deleted and could be re-establishing their links to prolific community members, contributing to the appearance of a higher overall rate of blogging.

GENDER HOMOPHILY

The Daesh-supportive graph shows that women are more likely to reblog posts by other female users rather than by male users within the community, but this coincides with a high degree of gender homophily in the standard Tumblr community. Similarly, male Daesh-supportive Tumblr users were more likely to reblog posts by other male Daesh-supportive users, though not at a rate that differs from what we could expect based on patterns within the standard Tumblr network. Unlike the *mutual connection* measure, which indicates

mutual reblogging, gender homophily only indicates a one-way relationship. This finding suggests that there are clear networks of female
and male associational ties within Daesh-supportive communities,
but that these gendered ties are no different than what we might
expect among non-supportive communities.

IDEOLOGICAL HOMOPHILY

We found that across the Daesh-supportive Tumblr community, Daesh-
supportive bloggers were as likely to reblog a non-supportive blogger's
content as they were to reblog that of a supportive user. In other
words, when controlling for gender, there was no strong tendency for
links among supporters. Furthermore, there were more links than we
expected between non-supportive users. This suggests that networks
that are supportive of Daesh are non-exclusionary, and diffuse across
a variety of other Tumblr networks. There is also the possibility that
this is the result of the small number of "seed blogs" we worked with,
and that we might have gleaned different results had more Daesh-
supportive blogs been available throughout the coding process.

POSTING RATE

We found that Daesh supporters posted more than non-supporters
within their social network, as did users that the algorithm tagged.
This suggests that Daesh supporters may use Tumblr to communicate
with their social network more than non-supporters, though we cannot infer the content of that communication.

CENTRALITY

We found that female Daesh supporters had a higher closeness centrality than non-supporters. This suggests that, with the exception of a
few outliers, female Daesh-supportive communities are far more centralized than non-supporter female communities. Similarly, the tagged
male Daesh-supportive network showed a higher degree of centralization than the male non-supportive network. However, the male supportive network was not nearly as centralized as the female supportive
network. From this, we can infer that the female Daesh-supportive
network is more centralized than its male counterpart, and that both
are more centralized than their non-supportive counterparts.

RESULTS OF HYPOTHESES

H1. Partially Confirmed   In both male and female Daesh-supportive
communities, we found a greater degree of closeness centrality than

among their non-supportive counterparts. This suggests that Daesh-supportive communities on Tumblr are more centralized than non-supportive networks. We also found that Daesh-supportive bloggers were more active than non-supporters, which demonstrates a more prolific use of Tumblr as a forum for social engagement. However, we did not find that Daesh-supportive groups had greater mutual connections than non-supportive groups, and there was no strong tendency toward ideological homophily. This suggests that although membership in Daesh-supportive communities is centralized around gender, ideologically they are very diffuse and non-exclusionary with relation to non-supportive groups.

H2. Partially Confirmed Significant gendered effects were visible on Daesh-supportive Tumblr networks. We found a high degree of gender homophily among both Daesh-supportive and non-supportive networks. We also found that female Daesh-supportive bloggers had far more centralized networks than male Daesh-supportive bloggers. Furthermore, the female Daesh-supportive network was more centralized than either male or female non-supportive networks. We expected that the female Daesh-supportive blog would have stronger ties than the male supportive blog, but in this regard our hypothesis was not supported. There was no significant difference in the rate at which flagged male and female users reblogged other flagged male and female users.

Gender Networks

Female Daesh-supportive community members are highly centralized and exhibit gender homophily, being likely to reblog other female users in the Daesh-supportive blog community. They are also likely to reblog other women that are identified as non-supportive. They do not have significantly stronger associational ties than non-supporters or male users. Male Daesh-supportive members of the community are less centralized than female-supportive communities, but still demonstrate gender homophily. Although flagged male users did not have significantly stronger ties than non-flagged male users, tagged male users had stronger ties than flagged and non-flagged users, whether female or male.

RESILIENCE IN ONLINE DARK NETWORKS OF WOMEN
From the study results, we can expect dark networks to stand apart from their "real world" counterparts in a number of ways. First, unlike

drug-smuggling rings or airplane-hijacker networks, participation incurs next to no risk and cost.[60] The threats usually associated with high visibility were absent in our networks and, indeed, many of these bloggers flaunted their support of Daesh by posting violent imagery and conspicuously reblogging the Daesh flag. Second, these networks are highly transitory; if a blog is deleted, a user can simply create a new one to take its place. Nevertheless, these networks are essential for providing the gendered element of the Daesh nation-building process. Certain attributes of Tumblr – its low participation cost and transitory nature – may also lend online women's dark networks greater resilience. When examining weak ties in dark networks, scholars often refer to Granovetter's "strength of weak ties" argument.[61] Granovetter's work suggests that weak ties are essential in connecting disparate clusters of strongly connected actors, as weak ties are far more likely than strong ties to bridge strongly connected communities that are divided by factors such as religion, race, or gender.[62] As a result, communities characterized by weak ties may actually be quite strong as a result of their ability to bridge a variety of different communities and thereby draw on the resources of numerous groups. Since our findings illustrate that weak ties characterize the female Daesh-supportive subgraph, and since women within the Daesh-supportive tend to post more frequently than their male counterparts, it is reasonable to infer that Granovetter's argument applies here, especially given the ephemeral nature of a Tumblr reblog as opposed to, for instance, co-membership in an Daesh-supportive organization. The abundance of weak ties may also make these networks more flexible and adaptive, increasing their resilience. Adaptive networks are more likely to remain connected in the event that a key node is removed, and are therefore less vulnerable to attack by security forces.[63] Further, the "strength of weak ties" argument may be significant for the study of combat motivation as a whole, and may underlie "swift trust" cohesion in military units (see Robert Engen's chapter in this volume).

Centralization can also play a key role in a social network's resilience. Central actors have proven important to the degree of network integration, which, according to Milward, "in this context is therefore generally understood as the extent of structural and cognitive-cultural inclusion of actors within a network to accomplish some type of collective output – public goods like health care or public bads like a terrorist attack."[64] These centralized actors are crucial for coordination and often serve as key players in dark networks.[65] The low-risk nature of online Daesh support radically changes the traditional incentive structure of centralization. The female Daesh-supportive Tumblr network can afford to be more centralized, since centralization carries few risks and considerable rewards. Our findings illustrate that Daesh-supportive female Tumblr networks are more centralized than any other subgraphs under examination in this study. Relationally at least, this suggests that women in the Daesh-supportive subgraph maintain closer ties to central actors and may therefore distribute information more effectively than other bloggers on Tumblr.

A DEEPER DIVE:
UMM LAYTH AND BIRD OF JANNAH

To exemplify the contents of these blogs, we selected two of the most infamous bloggers on Tumblr.[66] Countless Western media outlets – including the popular entertainment website BuzzFeed – have published articles exploring the lives of female Daesh members and supporters. Some articles provide detailed accounts of horrific instances of rape and torture at the hands of male Daesh members.[67] Still others describe the motivations of Western Muslim women who, no longer wishing to live under the laws of *kufar* (unbelievers), have chosen to make the *hijrah* (journey) to *Dar al-Islam* (the world's Muslim regions).[68] In this milieu, two female pro-Daesh bloggers – Umm Layth and Bird of Jannah – have garnered significant attention from media outlets and other bloggers. Claiming to be written by female Daesh insiders, the bloggers offer unique, firsthand insights into the role of women within Daesh. The section that follows endeavours to explore these two blogs/bloggers in greater detail. We conclude with a brief discussion of the blogs as a key part of Daesh's larger, gendered nation-building agenda.

Perhaps the most famous female pro-Daesh blog is that of Umm Layth. The name is a pseudonym; she is believed to be Scottish citizen Aqsa Mahmood, a young woman who left her Glasgow home in November 2013 to join Daesh in Syria. Umm Layth has made a name for herself by offering advice to Western Muslim women considering making the same hijrah to Syria. To this end, her blog posts contain practical advice to other "sisters." In a series of blog entries titled "Diary of a Muhajirah" (a *Muhajirah* is one who has made the hijrah), Umm Layth provides her readers with tips to make their journey to

Dar al-Islam easier. Her entry for 9 April 2014, for example, advises sisters to bring "clothes, shoes etc. from the West," because the quality of Syrian-made clothes "is really bad." She also urges them to bring their own religious clothing (hijabs, niqaabs, etc.) as the Syrian view of veiling "is a complete joke." Umm Layth goes on to complain that "the abayas are skintight and [the Syrian-made] niqaab starts from their forehead and ends at their nostrils."

Material concerns notwithstanding, Umm Layth understands that the decision to leave the comfort and security of one's home in the West is not an easy one. "To live a completely different kind of life," she writes, "means completely changing your outlook on life and researching as much [as] you want until you feel content with what you are about to do and know is right." She recounts how leaving her family "for the sake of Allah was the biggest sacrifice" that she had made in her "selfish life so far."

A number of Umm Layth's posts are devoted to describing the "day to day" responsibilities of women in al-Sham (the region encompassing Syria and the Levant). In another post, from her "Diary of a Muhajirah" series, she describes the normal day for a muhajirah as "revolving around the same duties as a normal housewife." She continues: "your day will revolve around cooking, cleaning, looking after and sometimes even educating the children." She concedes that days can sometimes feel "mundane," but reminds her sisters to "truly value every minute here [in Syria] for the sake of Allah."

The lives of women in al-Sham are not limited to cooking and cleaning, however. In her post of 1 July 2015, Umm Layth reminds her sisters, especially those who married a mujahid (a person engaged in jihad), to "respect their husbands." She writes: "A woman by nature is someone who is loving and caring and every man needs this, especially a Mujaahid. A Mujaahid needs someone who he can share his life with. He needs someone who he can take comfort and enjoyment with during his days off from front lines ... Let him find peace and solace in you and try to understand what he has been through."

In writing about the realities of marriage in the Islamic State, Umm Layth notes – in her post of 22 January 2015 – that a marriage to a mujahid "comes with the great acceptance and hefty reality, which is that ... we will most probably have to sooner or later hear the news of our [husband's] success which is his shahadah [martyrdom]." Her advice on the difficulties of marriage in the Islamic State also extends to men: "Ikhwan [brothers], fear Allah. You are responsible for your wife. You make sure to give her all her rights to her and under this comes one of the most important duties of yours brother, and this is to educate your wife! ... Brothers make sure you don't do any zulm [injustice/cruelty] on your wife."

In further describing the role of women in jihad, Umm Layth is "straight up and blunt": "There is absolutely nothing for sisters to participate in Qitaal [fighting] ... No amalia istishadiya [martyrdom operations] or a secret sisters katiba [militia/battalion]. These are all rumors you may have heard through some sources who themselves are not actually aware of the truth ... Please sisters, do not believe anything you hear or see online where apparently sisters are fighting feesaabeelilah [in the service of Allah]."

We argue that these blogs contribute to Daesh's larger nation-building project. Daesh strives to articulate a coherent "Islamic national identity" that not only differentiates the organization from the "unbelieving" West, but also from various Islamic countries in the Middle East (notably Iran and Saudi Arabia). We also argue not only that such differentiation requires the participation of women in the Islamic State, but that the status of women actually serves as one of the primary factors that sets the IS apart. Put differently, rigid gender hierarchies and separation are integral components of the foundation upon which Daesh's "imagined Islamic community" is built.

Perhaps the most detailed articulation of Daesh's official stance on women and their role within the "organization" can be found in the *Manifesto on Women of the Islamic State*, published by the Al-Khanssaa Brigade. Released in early 2015, the manifesto (originally published in Arabic) has been translated into English by the Quilliam Foundation, a London-based anti-terrorism think tank in February 2015. In its opening lines, the Manifesto explicitly states that its aim is "to clarify the role of Muslim women and the life which is desired for them, that which makes them happy in this world and the hereafter."[69] True to its word, the manifesto offers a scathing critique of the "Western model" of feminism and women's emancipation: "The model preferred by infidels in the West failed the minute that women were 'liberated' from their cell in the house."[70] This failure, they argue, stems from the nature of both men and women. Women, by God's design, are meant to live lives of "sedentariness, stillness and stability," while men crave "movement and flux." When these roles are challenged, we are told that "humanity is thrown into a state of flux and instability," ultimately leading to the "crumbling" and "collapse" of society.[71] The solution to this problem – that of societal collapse – is to return to the *gendered* plan ordained by God, wherein women are able to fulfill their "fundamental role" and kept in their "rightful place."[72] This fundamental role and place, we are told, is motherhood. "The purpose of her existence is the Divine duty of motherhood."[73] In the Islamic State, we are told, "women have been returned to their Rightful jilbabs [loose-fitting clothing designed to conceal body shape] and sedentary lifestyle."

Interestingly, the language used throughout the document to describe women's integral role within the community as "future mothers" is not unique either to Daesh or to the Al-Khanssaa Brigade. The very same gendered appeals are also made in the blogs. In the words of Umm Layth herself: "Sister's [*sic*] don't forsake this beautiful blessing being able to raise the future Mujahideen of Shaam ... It is a part of our Fitrah [human nature] to be wives and mothers, and we are not created like man." The similarities between the blogs and the Daesh manifesto on women are significant in that they complement one another and cooperate to offer a coherent stance on the organization's view of women and their role within Daesh's idealized Islamic society: women are mothers, caregivers, and housewives.

Yet, the attention devoted to describing the role of women as mothers and "reproducers" of the newly minted Islamic State is not without explicit political purpose. Indeed, the gendered dimension of nation-building projects and national movements is well documented. In *Gender and Nation*, her seminal text on gender and nationalism, Nira Yuval-Davis argues, "it is women ... who reproduce nations, biologically, culturally and symbolically."[74] Yuval-Davis's point regarding *women's* active participation in nation-building projects is an important one for our purposes here.

What the blogs, certain other social media locales, and even the Al-Khanssaa manifesto demonstrate is that women are not only active (even gleeful) participants in the dissemination of Daesh's worldview, they are explicitly targeting other women. It is, in other words, an online network of women speaking about women to women. What Daesh has created via social media, therefore, appears to be a virtual community of women promoting a unified (or at least somewhat coherent) message about an idealized way of life in the Islamic State to other women around the world. But as Anderson reminds us, the boundaries of the nation are always limited, because no nation imagines itself to be coterminous with all of humankind.[75] Thus, the repeated references to the "failures of Western civilization" and the various shortcomings of the laws of "unbelievers" in the West serve not only to differentiate the Daesh worldview from its so-called "western counterpart," but to demarcate further the boundaries of Daesh's online "imagined community" of women. The authors of these blogs, tweets, and Facebook posts may never meet their readers, but in each of their minds exists not only a sense of their communion, or sisterliness, with other Muslim women around the world, but also of those who are *not* included in this community, the online female *ummah* (community). In the words of the Al-Khanssaa manifesto: "Throw the sputum of [Western] culture, [Western] civilisation and your thinking into the sea. God fights you and *you are not of us and we are not of you.*"[76]

CONCLUSION

As Robert Martyn argues in his chapter in this volume, understanding the connections and motivations of adversaries is central to the critical examination of the present and future threat environment. One of the most unsettling challenges in the security field today has been the deterritorialization of threats entailed by the rapid migration of networked communities away from territorial boundaries and toward the cyberworld. Communities in cyberspace cannot be attacked with bullets and bombs; we cannot point guns at them and demand their surrender. As the blogger Bird of Jannah has said, "some are martyred in the land of jihad, whilst others get martyred on social media networks." However, in the case of Daesh, these online networks work toward attaining a very territorial objective. Women's Daesh-supportive dark networks lend strength to the organization's gendered narrative, which has proven essential to nation building in its corporeal territory. We have argued here that female Daesh-supportive communities exist on Tumblr, and that they may be highly resilient and capable of rapid diffusion of information. If this is indeed the case, then it should be a cause of great concern among security scholars and practitioners alike. Our deep-dive content analysis reveals that many of the blogs espouse a rigid gender hierarchy, adhering to a vision of sisterhood and femininity premised upon a radical and vicious ideology. This ideology connects women through shared hatred and violence while encouraging them to sever their ties with the contemporary feminist movement. Rather than undermine the importance of the agency debate within feminist security scholarship, these findings underscore its continued importance as a key element in researching relational ties within female dark networks. Continued research will better inform our understanding of what motivates women to form dark networks and the gendered dynamics of terrorism more broadly.

NOTES

1 Mala Htun and S. Laurel Weldon, "The Civic Origins of Progressive Policy Change: Combating Violence against Women in Global Perspective, 1975–2005," *American Political Science Review* 106, no. 3 (2012): 548–69; Drude Dahlerup and Monique Leyenaar, eds., *Breaking Male Dominance in Old Democracies* (Oxford: Oxford University Press, 2013).

2 Brooke Ackerly and Katy Attanasi, "Global Feminisms: Theory and Ethics for Studying Gendered Injustice," *New Political Science* 31, no. 4 (2009): 543–55.

3 Mia Bloom, *Bombshell: The Many Faces of Women Terrorists* (Toronto: Penguin Canada, 2011); Tuty Raihanah Mostarom and Nur Azlin Mohamed Yasin, "The Internet: Avenue for Women Jihadi 'Participation,'" *RSIS Commentaries* CO10088, 3 August 2010.

4 On types of jihad, see: Anita Peresin and Alberto Cervone, "The Western *Muhajirat* of ISIS," *Studies in Conflict & Terrorism* 38, no. 7 (2015): 495–509; and Joel Day and Scott Kleinmann, "Combating the Cult of ISIS: A Social Approach to Countering Violent Extremism," *Review of Faith & International Affairs* 15, no. 3 (2017): 14–23.

5 David Cook, "Women fighting in Jihad?", *Studies in Conflict & Terrorism* 28, no. 5 (2005): 375–84; Nelly Lahoud, "The Neglected Sex: The Jihadis' Exclusion of Women from Jihad," *Terrorism and Political Violence* 26, no. 5 (2014): 780–802.

6 Katharina Von Knop, "The Female Jihad: Al Qaeda's Women," *Studies in Conflict & Terrorism* 30, no. 5 (2007): 397–414.

7 Ibid.

8 Lahoud, "The Neglected Sex."

9 Peresin and Cervone, "The Western *Muhajirat*."

10 Heidi Basch-Harod, "The Right to Choose: Women of al-Qaeda," *Tel-Aviv Notes*, 9 February 2012.

11 Marne L. Sutten, *The Rising Importance of Women in Terrorism and the Need to Reform Counterterrorism Strategy* (Fort Leavenworth, KS: School

of Advanced Military Studies, Army Command and General Staff College, 2009).

12 Von Knop, "The Female Jihad," 409.

13 Manuel Ricardo Torres-Soriano, "The Dynamics of the Creation, Evolution, and Disappearance of Terrorist Internet Forums," *International Journal of Conflict and Violence* 7, no. 1 (2013): 165.

14 Ibid.

15 Ibid.

16 Geoff Dean, Peter Bell, and Jack Newman, "The Dark Side of Social Media: Review of Online Terrorism," *Pakistan Journal of Criminology* 3, no. 3 (2012): 113.

17 Torres-Soriano, "Dynamics," 168.

18 Dean et al., "The Dark Side," 113.

19 Ibid.

20 Benjamin Ducol, "Uncovering the French-speaking jihadisphere: An exploratory analysis," *Media, War & Conflict* 5, no. 1 (2012): 51–70.

21 Gabriel Weimann, "Cyber-Fatwas and Terrorism," *Studies in Conflict & Terrorism* 34, no. 10 (2011): 769.

22 Scott Shane and Ben Hubbard, "ISIS Displaying a Deft Command of Varied Media," *New York Times*, 30 August 2014.

23 Ariel I. Ahram, "Sexual Violence and the Making of ISIS," *Survival* 57, no. 3 (2015): 66.

24 Ibid.

25 Shane and Hubbard, "ISIS Displaying a Deft Command."

26 Peresin and Cervone, "The Western *Muhajirat*," 506.

27 Mrinalini Sinha, "Gender and Nationalism," *Women's History in Global Perspective, Vol. 1*, ed. Bonnie G. Smith (Urbana: University of Illinois Press, 2004).

28 Quilliam International, *Women in the Islamic State – Manifesto and Case Study*, trans. Charlie Winter (Quilliam International, 2015), 1–41.

29 Ibid., 37.

30 Ibid.

31 This chapter was drawn from a paper written for the 2016 American Political Science Association (APSA) Annual Meeting.

32 Bloom, *Bombshell*, 152.

33 Brenda Stoter, "Islamic State's female bloggers draw women to Syria," *Al-Monitor*, 30 August 2014.

34 Peresin and Cervone, "The Western *Muhajirat*," 495–506.

35 Ibid.

36 Alessandra L. González, Joshua D. Freilich, and Steven M. Chermak, "How Women Engage Homegrown Terrorism," *Feminist Criminology* 9, no. 4 (2014): 344–66.

37 Arie Perliger and Ami Pedahzur, "Social Network Analysis in the Study of Terrorism and Political Violence," *PS: Political Science & Politics* 44, no. 1 (2011): 45–50.

38 H. Brinton Milward and Jörg Raab, "Dark Networks as Organizational Problems: Elements of a Theory," *International Public Management Journal* 9, no. 3 (2006): 349.

39 Daning Hu, Siddharth Kaza, and Hsinchun Chen, "Identifying significant facilitators of dark network evolution," *Journal of the American Society for Information Science and Technology* 60, no. 4 (2009): 656.

40 Milward and Raab, "Dark Networks," 334.

41 Carrie Paechter, "Young women online: collaboratively constructing identities," *Pedagogy, Culture & Society* 21, no. 1 (2013): 118.

42 Ibid., 112.

43 W. Lance Bennett and Alexandra Segerberg, "The Logic of Connective Action: Digital Media and the Personalization of Contentious Politics," *Information, Communication & Society* 15, no. 5 (2012): 744.

44 Renée C. van der Hulst, "Introduction to Social Network Analysis (SNA) as an investigative tool," *Trends in Organized Crime* 12, no. 2 (2009): 107.

45 Olson argued that rational actors would not aggregate into large groups. This is primarily because, as group size increases, optimal allocation of resources will decrease. In exclusive groups (where resources are finite, unlike inclusive groups that enjoy infinite resources), a rational actor would "free-ride" off of the investment of the other actors within the group. In order to achieve any measure of group cohesion in a large latent group, where opportunities to advance social esteem would be limited, the state (or labour union, interest group, etc.) would have to incentivize actors so that those that did not participate would not receive any of the collective good being bargained for, such as higher wages, better health benefits, and so forth. This argument no longer holds as participation costs in online communities reach zero. Mancur Olson, "The Logic of Collective Action [1965]," *Contemporary Sociological Theory* (2012): 124.

46 Bennett and Segerberg, *Logic of Connective Action*, 752.

47 Michael Szell and Stefan Thurner, "Measuring Social Dynamics in a Massive Multiplayer Online Game," *Social Networks* 32, no. 4 (2010): 313–29.

48 Ibid.

49 Judith Butler, *Gender Trouble* (New York: Routledge Classics, 1990).

50 van der Hulst, *Introduction to Social Network Analysis*, 108.

51 Ibid.

52 Swati Agarwal and Ashish Sureka, "A Topical Crawler for Uncovering
    Hidden Communities of Extremist Micro-Bloggers on Tumblr,"
    5th Workshop on Making Sense of Microposts, #Microposts2015,
    Florence, Italy, 18 May 2015; Munmun De Choudhury, "Anorexia
    on Tumblr: A Characterization Study," DH: *Proceedings of the 5th
    International Conference on Digital Health*, May 2015, 43–50.

53 Stanley Milgram, "The Small World Problem," *Psychology Today* 1,
    no. 1 (1967): 61–7.

54 Vincent D. Blondel, Jean-Loup Guillaume, Renaud Lambiotte, and Etienne
    Lefebvre, "Fast Unfolding of Communities in Large Networks," *Journal
    of Statistical Mechanics: Theory and Experiment* 10 (2008): P10008.

55 Andrew P. Bradley, "The Use of the Area under the ROC Curve in the
    Evaluation of Machine Learning Algorithms," *Pattern Recognition* 30,
    no. 7 (1997): 1145–59.

56 David R. Hunter, Mark S. Handcock, Carter T. Butts, Steven M.
    Goodreau, and Martina Morris, "ERGM: A Package to Fit, Simulate and
    Diagnose Exponential-Family Models for Networks," *Journal of Statistical
    Software* 24, no. 3 (2008): nihpa54860; Peter R. Monge and Noshir S.
    Contractor, *Theories of Communication Networks* (Oxford: Oxford
    University Press, 2003).

57 Brian Keegan, Muhammad Aurangzeb Ahmad, Dmitri Williams, Jaideep
    Srivastava, and Noshir Contractor, "What can gold farmers teach us
    about criminal networks?", XRDS: *Crossroads, The ACM Magazine for
    Students* 17, no. 3 (2011): 11–5.

58 van der Hulst, *Introduction to Social Network Analysis*.

59 Butler, *Gender Trouble*.

60 Valdis E. Krebs, "Mapping networks of terrorist cells," *Connections* 24,
    no. 3 (2002): 43–52; Mark A. Lauchs, Robyn L. Keast, and Vy Le, "Social
    Network Analysis of Terrorist Networks: Can It Add Value?", *Pakistan
    Journal of Criminology* 3, no. 3 (2012): 21–32.

61 Mark S. Granovetter, "The Strength of Weak Ties," in *Social Networks:
    A Developing Paradigm*, ed. Samuel Leinhardt (Cambridge, MA: Academic
    Press, 1977), 347–67; van der Hulst, *Introduction to Social Network
    Analysis*, 107; Hugh Louch, "Personal Network Integration: Transitivity
    and Homophily in Strong-Tie Relations," *Social Networks* 22, no. 1
    (2000): 45–64; González et al., "How Women Engage"; Jonathan
    Kennedy and Gabriel Weimann, "The Strength of Weak Terrorist Ties,"
    Terrorism and Political Violence 23, no. 2 (2011): 201–12.

62 Stuart Astill, "The Strength of Weak Ties," in *Encyclopedia of Power*, ed. Keith Dowding (London: Sage, 2011).

63 Lauchs, "Social Network Analysis."

64 Milward and Raab, "Dark Networks," 345.

65 van der Hulst, *Introduction to Social Network Analysis*.

66 We selected two of the most radical Daesh bloggers on Tumblr because they typified best the gendered ideology of Daesh and are irrefutably supportive of the organization. We can make this claim with certainty due to prolific, in-depth reporting on the two users. Many blogs contained less-radical messages and simply integrated Daesh-supportive imagery and ideology into their daily blogging.

67 Liam Corcoran and Simon Carr, "The reality of life as an ISIS bride: Former jihadi wives give shocking account of gang-rapes and torture," *Mirror* (UK), 18 July 2015.

68 Nadim Roberts, "The life of a jihadi wife: Why one Canadian woman joined ISIS's Islamic state," *Huffington Post*, 7 July 2014.

69 Quilliam International, *Women in the Islamic State*, 12.

70 Ibid., 19.

71 Ibid.

72 Ibid, 18.

73 Ibid.

74 Nira Yuval-Davis, *Gender and Nation* (Thousand Oaks, CA: SAGE Publications, 1997), 2.

75 Benedict Anderson, *Imagined Communities: Reflections on the Origin and Spread of Nationalism* (London: Verso, 2006), 6–9.

76 Quilliam International, *Women in the Islamic State*, 41. Authors' emphasis.

"We're going to Afghanistan so that we get a decent deal on softwood lumber": The CIDP Combat Motivation Workshop Concluding Roundtable

Sonia Dussault and Robert C. Engen

On 2 November 2016, a crowded Korea Hall at Fort Frontenac, in Kingston, was the site of the Combat Motivation Workshop, which brought together all of the scholars who contributed chapters to this volume to speak on their respective topics of research. The final event of the day was a roundtable discussion involving panelists Ian Hope, H. Christian Breede, Robert C. Engen, and Allan English on the subject of "The future: how new concepts in combat motivation will impact on the Canadian Armed Forces." Audience members asked questions and commentary was offered by roundtable participants and other experts attending the workshop (in particular Dr Lee Windsor and Dr Robert Williams). Attendees posed four main questions during the space of the roundtable's one-hour duration.

Given the importance of the topic of combat motivation to the Canadian Armed Forces, the editors of this volume believe that the inclusion of an edited, unabridged account of this roundtable event, transcribed from the original audio recordings provided by CIDP and inspired by the proceedings report, would be a fitting way to conclude the book.[1] These questions and answers bridge several thematic gaps in the chapters of *Why We Fight*, but also underscore some of this volume's most prominent themes, such as: the impossibility of universal statements about combat motivation, which is as grounded in historical context and circumstance as the individuals who possess it; and the fundamental importance of understanding the variability of motivation within Canadian operations. In his introduction to the conference, Allan English quoted Milan Vego's observation that culture has "a significant effect on how military organizations judge their own actions and those of others: perceived irrationality is often the reflection of one's cultural values in evaluating the enemy's actions and reactions. An enemy commander is a product of a different society, traditions, and culture. Hence, he may make decisions that are considered irrational although they are fully consonant with his own societal values and military culture."[2] The same applies to every level of motivation, as the preceding chapters suggest.

Question

Very little has been done on the combative, physical, psychological, and moral dimensions of motivation since Sam Stouffer's studies during the Second World War. Combat is a harsh mistress. It is about death, destruction, and killing, and there are dilemmas involved that are at the heart of combat motivation, which are the dilemmas between personal survival and organizational success. As we look to the future, are we being honest about what combat is and what it entails, from a Canadian Armed Forces perspective?

Ian Hope

No, we are not being honest. We're not learning from Afghanistan. We're not doing the surveys, or interrogating ourselves on performance. Instead, everyone who went is a hero, and there are no cowards. We are not actually doing what is professionally necessary to do to learn from that conflict. And therefore, we're ignoring the brutality of the experience of combat in Afghanistan.

Going back: in a course he gave in 1998, Roger Spiller exposed me to the ideas of *combat* being a highly personal experience [and] *battle* being a collective one. Battle is easy to study and quantify, but the personal experience is *really difficult* to get at. And I don't know that our armed forces are getting into the cognitive, the emotive effects of combat. I think we're deliberately *not* studying Afghanistan, which I have a problem with, because we're now in a time of persistent conflict. It's not going away. In fact, it's only going to get worse. And we may want to go peacekeeping in Africa, believing in a narrative that peacekeeping is something we idealize and should do. The reality, however, is a lot harsher and, in the future, we will be drawn into heavier conflicts, which *will* involve combat. But when I visit combat training centres today, I don't see the training happening that I think is necessary.

Robert Engen

This lack of learning is, unfortunately, nothing new. It was also the case with the Canadian Army after the Second World War. Hundreds of detailed tactical questionnaires on combat behaviour and experience were filled out by Canadian junior officers during the fighting, which have served as the basis for a lot of my own studies. At the end of the war, there was talk in the Department of National Defence about doing some in-depth analysis of these questionnaires, and even of tabulating their results through some of the primitive computers of the time, to make certain that something was learned from the experience of close-combat fighting that we had during the war. Nothing ever came of that; the minister judged the whole idea to be too expensive, and the questionnaires mouldered in the archives for seventy years. Whether in Afghanistan or Normandy, Canada has not been good about learning from available experiences. Even when the intention and ability to gather the data is there, the inability to do anything with it is a longstanding problem.

Question

Many people who went to Afghanistan, especially in the early rotos [rotations], were not prepared for the end-state – that they could be killed. How can we better prepare our troops for that reality?

Ian Hope

I might be wrong, but my impression is that we might have given up what we knew before. When the Cold War ended, we adopted peacekeeping as our go-to. We did peacekeeping before that, and we were seen as great peacekeepers, but we didn't have peacekeeping *doctrine*. We had combat doctrine, but we were great peacekeepers. And that combat focus allowed us to scale back to peacekeeping and do other things from a position of having the fundamentals covered. We have not moved back to that combat focus after Afghanistan. We're doing more conventional training – harder, more demanding – to enable us to do something less than combat. Until we push back – and it's a lot of money to do that – but until we push back to that level, we may not be prepared for those kinds of missions. That's the only way I can see, personally – of getting an all-around good organization, set to go anywhere and do anything – is to do the hard stuff first.

H. Christian Breede

I totally agree. The answer is stellar military training, and advanced degrees and postsecondary education. And the higher up you are on the officer side, or on the non-commissioned member side, for that matter, the more postsecondary education needs to be required. That's the only way you're going to be able to wrap your head around the cultural nuances that you're facing. We don't have the resources available to make area specialists, as they do in the US. For the conventional forces, however, we can become generalists, we can become smart enough to recognize what we don't know – and that's half the battle right there. So, like Colonel Hope said, the question of preparation for combat should focus in terms of individual training, which we did – which I hope we continue to do – and then really double down on the education side, which I think is one area where we're falling short.

Question

The CAF Peace Support Training Centre [at CFB Kingston] is very interested in motivation, especially now that the CAF is being deployed into Latvia and Africa. As we're working in a coalition environment, what are your thoughts on maintaining or achieving the best motivation we can, when we're working in a multinational environment in which partner nations might have an adverse effect on individual motivation?

Ian Hope

It's great to draw distinctions between Latvia and Africa. The Canadian soldiers, the men and women going into these places, will do well because we have the best individual training system in the world. We train for redundancy. They'll adapt. The Canadian makeup, our psychological character, will bring value to the mission. We are bridge-builders in coalitions; people like to work with us, because we're not threatening.

The difference will be that in Latvia, we are part of an established alliance and we know the enemy. It's empirical, all of the information is right there: we know what equipment and capabilities they have, we know our own equipment and capabilities – it'll be easy. It will move the army to a warfighting doctrine, which is easier. But we don't know what we're getting into in Africa. We can't appreciate its layers of complexity, and we'll once again put young Canadian soldiers, ill-prepared, into environments that are not just ethnically complex, they are religiously complex, they are drug- and crime-oriented ... and frankly, we don't train well for that because we aren't really experienced enough to do that. Maybe that's the future. Maybe in five years, or ten years, the organization will have all of those capabilities, but we don't have them right now.

Robert Williams

To me, it speaks to the motivation of the allies involved. We've been on missions all over the planet where some allies are motivated by money, or are motivated by the desire to simply survive the mission. I was in Croatia with the UN in the 1990s, and I worked with the Russians. Their troops in Croatia were taking a break from Chechnya – that was their R&R deployment! So, in terms of motivation, you have to ask: is it mission success? Is it survival? Is it money? Is it staying on the NATO food chain?

As to what Ian said, just to use an example: what will motivation look like in Latvia? In an alliance, we will have trusted partners – the "swift trust" case – who are the ones that share our values, and are the ones we want to go to war beside as our allies. It's important that we have many of the same fundamental motivations as our closest allies: mission success, not money, not survival, not personal aggrandizement, not financial remuneration – that's not what we want. So, the government will have to be advised by military leaders about whom we actually trust, and mesh that with the political element of whom the government wants us to go on deployment with. Being able to correctly identify that others aren't motivated by the same things that we are is going to be increasingly important. To return to the example of the Polish Armoured Division during the Second World War: during the drive on Falaise, General Stanisław Maczek and the

Poles had different motivations than the British and the Canadians. Simonds and Montgomery were, by that point, in the war making decisions based around a need to minimize casualties in the Anglo-Canadian forces, for political and manpower reasons. This was not a motivation shared with the Poles – but this was not clear to everyone at the time. When motivations are different between alliance partners, frank honesty is needed.

H. Christian Breede

In the spirit of honesty, it's also important that we understand, and even problematize, what we mean by "success." What does success look like? It's very different depending upon the context that we're looking at. In Afghanistan, success for Canada really didn't have a lot to do with Kandahar or the Kandaharis themselves, and had everything to do with *being seen as a good alliance partner*. It's what Joel Sokolsky called "doing the least we can do to get by" – that nice little bumper sticker of Canadian foreign policy. We do the minimum. In Stéfanie von Hlatky's book *American Allies in Times of War*, she looks at middle powers and their strategies for dealing with the United States within alliance constructs.[3] In her understanding, Canada's Afghanistan mission was largely compensatory: we didn't go to Iraq, so we compensated and went to Afghanistan. That was success for us. Just the fact that we were there, in Afghanistan, was success.

That necessitates a very different set of motivation strategies for soldiers on the ground in Afghanistan. Soldiers in my company, when we were getting ready to go, would come up to me and ask: "Why are we going to Afghanistan, sir?" And I would say to them: "We're going to Afghanistan so that we get a decent deal on softwood lumber. It's to keep the Americans happy, to be seen as being a good partner. And *that* is our lot as professional soldiers."

That takes us straight back to my discussion of professionalism and warrior culture, and that's why the professional is the archetype that we want to focus upon, and that we want our soldiers to identify with. I think that when bringing in the warrior image, success becomes very different. Success is always mission success, and mission success is defeating the opponent – which sometimes is needed, but that's not always success in terms of why we're there in the first place. That can be hard to wrap your head around as a soldier, and that's the challenge.

Question

Do soldiers need "good" reasons to fight? How do we help soldiers wrap their heads around complex national goals? When we tell them that they're there fighting for softwood lumber, do we not run the risk of soldiers adopting a stay-in-the-bunker mentality of just trying to get through the mission alive?

Ian Hope

Everything that the commander says to the soldiers is recorded in their heads. It's extremely important. You can't lie to them. You don't need to tell them the entire truth, but you do need to speak truthfully. In Afghanistan, I had many soldiers come up to me and say: "What are we coming back to this place *again*? We've taken it three times!" And the answer, after a few months – and they figured it out themselves, too – was: "To buy time for someone else up higher to figure out what the heck's going on so that we can be relieved of this duty. But until then, there's only us." They get that. They understand that. We bought time, even if the higher-ups never did figure out how to use the time we bought.

Lee Windsor

I think we're finally getting to the heart of the matter. It strikes me as extraordinary that we've spent a whole day talking about combat motivation without talking about the cause for which soldiers put themselves in harm's way. Those of us who are historians working on the two world wars, we have an easy time because the cause is clear: there's a big, dark, evil enemy across the Atlantic that's got to be stopped in order to restore international law. Everything else is a little greyer.

Or is it? Because there are some common themes in Canadian Forces deployments which go right back to South Africa in the Second Anglo-Boer War in 1899–1902, when a lot of Canadians thought that they were going on a mission to oppose a state that held slaves in bondage and which was in gross violation of international law. The Canadian government also committed us to the First World War for a combination of altruistic reasons and reasons of national interest. So, too, with the Second World War. And so, too, with the many stability-building missions, including Afghanistan. There were many reasons to go into Afghanistan and, for a time, our troops were told that our being there made sense to the people of Afghanistan, and that we would make the region more stable, because that's what we do: Canada's interest is in creating a more stable global environment because that makes sense for all humankind. Does that sense of purpose need to be there for Canadian soldiers to fight? Is that an essential ingredient for combat motivation in this country? Does the Prime Minister's Office have to communicate to Canadian soldiers that there is a reason for going? Perhaps in Afghanistan we suffered from that as a problem; we had a national election right in the middle of things getting hot, and we had a change of government after one government had initiated this mission, and then another government changed the rules on what the cause was.

So, to what extent do you think the *cause* is part of the combat motivation equation?

H. Christian Breede

For a professional soldier, it doesn't matter what the cause is. They're going to do what they're told because they're a professional, because it's part of the job, part of the description. I know that's a bit flippant, but in the short strokes, it doesn't really matter because professional soldiers will do what they're told. They have an intrinsic motivation to do what their profession asks them to do. That's the civil-military dynamic we have in Canada and the civil-military dynamic we enjoy in Western liberal democracies. It doesn't make it any easier, but that is essentially how you remain apolitical: you remain professional. A warrior's mindset, in which you need a real, just cause for what you're doing, is where you're going to start to have problems.

Question

There's also a significant difference between professionals and short-service soldiers, which we see in the two world wars. Lee is absolutely right about the buy-in among Canadian soldiers, the vast majority of whom were short-service volunteers during the Second World War. The cause of toppling the Nazi regime was widely accepted, and there was a real sense of necessity among the troops, that this was something that had to be done. It was a highly legitimate cause. But during the autumn of 1944 and, again, in the spring of 1945, some of the greatest problems that the Canadian Army had with morale – as tracked by the field censors who were reading the soldiers' mail – was when rumours began that after the defeat of Germany, the Canadians were going to be sent to the Pacific, or to Burma, to fight the Japanese. These rumours caused tremendous unease and anxiety among soldiers, and there was plenty of talk about resisting such a redeployment, with soldiers openly saying, "well I, for one, am not going," and suggesting that they would fight the Germans to the end, but would desert before being sent off to fight the Japanese. Being redeployed to the Pacific was not, at least in First Canadian Army, seen as being legitimate. The short-service troops had joined to fight the Germans and saw it as a violation of their contract, or covenant, with the army for them to afterward be required to fight what they viewed as a separate war.

In the end, the Canadian military decided to form a Canadian Pacific Force on an all-volunteer basis, and soldiers in Europe were offered the chance to *re*-volunteer for the force, with the offer of generous home leave en route to the invasion of Japan (which never happened anyway). So, that problem was ultimately circumvented. It's also very likely that the attitude was quite different among Canada's professional soldiers of the day. But among the short-service soldiers, I think it's notable that a very clear distinction could be drawn between the cause of fighting against Germany and then the cause of being told to go and fight against the Japanese. The tension and the resistance there might be an important element of motivation.

Ian Hope

We also shouldn't discard the fact that medals are important to soldiers, that the check in the box of operations and experience is important to soldiers, and that financial allowance benefits are important to soldiers. The soldier will go almost anywhere, for any reason, to get those six or eight months of extra money.

Allan English

That segues nicely into a historical example, as well. If you look at the First World War and what the soldiers were writing about and saying, there were no Nazis in the First World War – there was no great, giant German threat. The best you could do in 1918 was that we were fighting against Prussian militarism. But in terms of it being a cause to fire people up – who's going to go over the top and into no man's land for *that*? Actually, for the Canadians, motivation had a lot to do with the fact that pay and allowances had increased fifteen times from their original size, back in 1914. These might seem like prosaic motivations by today's standards, but perhaps they would ring true for the soldiers that Ian just spoke about as well. I think that's where historians can add a lot of value to this sort of research: when you see what the troops were saying at the time, the reality is extremely complex. The greater part of research on combat motivation in the Canadian context remains to be done.

NOTES

1 Sonia Dussault, "Combat Motivation: Past, Present and Future – The Canadian Context," Proceedings Report (Kingston, ON: Centre for International and Defence Policy, 2016): 26–8. The following transcript has been edited and rearranged for clarity and brevity, on the basis of the original audio recording and the proceedings report. The identities of those who asked questions, unfortunately, is not recorded, either in the proceedings or the audio log, so they have been left anonymous.
2 Milan Vego, "Science vs. the Art of War," *Joint Force Quarterly* 66 (Fall 2012): 69.
3 Stéfanie von Hlatky, *American Allies in Times of War: The Great Asymmetry* (Oxford: Oxford University Press, 2013).

Contributors

H. CHRISTIAN BREEDE is an associate professor of political science at the Royal Military College of Canada, cross-appointed with the college's Department of Political Studies. He is also deputy director of the Centre for International and Defence Policy at Queen's University and associate chair of RMC's Master of Public Administration program. Breede holds a PhD in war studies from RMC and has published on the topics of foreign and security policy with a research focus on societal cohesion and technology. He has deployment experience with the Canadian Army in Haiti and Afghanistan.

CLAIRE COOKSON-HILLS is a professional historian who lives and works in Kingston, Ontario. She holds a BA (hons) from the University of Calgary and an MA and a PhD from Queen's University. Her dissertation, "Engineering the Nile" (2013) was an exploration of British military engineers and their work on civil engineering projects in Egypt between 1882 and 1914. Her current research explores sexual assault and sexual violence against German women by Canadian soldiers in the Second World War. Cookson-Hills is currently an adjunct professor in the Department of History at Queen's, where she researches and teaches modern British and military history.

KAREN D. DAVIS is a defence scientist with the Director General Military Personnel Research and Analysis, Defence Research and Development Canada, and the Chief of Military Personnel. Formerly as a commissioned officer and currently as a civilian scientist, she has conducted research on human resources issues in the military for more than twenty-five years, and has published numerous reports, journal articles, and book chapters related to the integration of women into the military, and gender, leadership, and culture in the military, including her PhD dissertation, "Negotiating Gender in the Canadian Forces, 1970–1999." Dr Davis has provided expert testimony and presentations to numerous domestic and international bodies, including committees of the Canadian Senate and House of Commons, the Australian Defence Force, the Australian Human Rights Commission, the United States Defense Advisory Committee on Women in the Services, the US Marine Corps, and Women in International Security. She currently leads a research team conducting various projects related to military leadership and culture, leads the team's delivery of international gender, peace, and security workshops, and is co-lead of a NATO Research Task Group on the Integration of Women into Ground Combat Units.

SONIA DUSSAULT is currently pursuing her PhD in history under the supervision of Dr Allan English at Queen's University. She is a regular visiting professor at the Bader International Study Centre (UK) where she teaches on genocide, war crimes, and crimes against humanity as part of BISC's program in international law and politics. She was recently appointed director of the program.

ROBERT C. ENGEN is an assistant professor in the Department of Defence Studies at the Canadian Forces College in Toronto. He is the author of two major studies on human behaviour and motivation in the Canadian Army: *Canadians Under Fire: Infantry Effectiveness in the Second World War* (McGill-Queen's University Press, 2009) and *Strangers in Arms: Combat Motivation in the Canadian Army* (MQUP, 2016). Engen teaches on Canadian history, human behaviour, force health protection, defence policy, and artificial intelligence. His recent work includes co-editing a volume on military education titled *Military Education and the British Empire* (UBC Press, 2018) and a forthcoming two-volume study of disease prevention in the Second World War.

ALLAN ENGLISH is associate professor of Canadian military history in the Queen's University History Department. His book *Understanding Military Culture: A Canadian Perspective* was published in 2004, and he continues to research and publish in that area. Dr English has taught courses related to human behaviour, command, leadership, and ethics and the military profession at the undergraduate level to cadets at the Royal Military College of Canada, and at the graduate level to senior and general officers at the Canadian Forces College in Toronto. In November 2015, he received the Queen's University Award for Excellence in Graduate Supervision in the Social Sciences and Humanities.

IAN HOPE has thirty-six years of service in uniform, including eighteen years in leadership roles with infantry battalions. His operational experiences include the first Gulf War in 1991, multiple tours in the Balkans, Africa, and Afghanistan, and domestic operations. He commanded the 1st Battalion, Princess Patricia's Canadian Light Infantry Battle Group (Task Force Orion) in Kandahar in 2006, earning the Meritorious Service Cross. In 2012, he commanded the Afghan National Army Collective Training (Fielding) Centre in Kabul, earning the Meritorious Service Medal. He is a graduate of the Canadian Land Forces Command and Staff College, the US Army's Command and General Staff College, the School of Advanced Military Studies, and the US Army War College. Hope has served on the faculty of the US Army War College and as an associate professor at the Royal Military College of Canada. He holds a BA in history (hons) from Acadia University, and an MA in military arts and science, an MA in strategic studies, and a PhD in history from Queen's University. He is the author of *A Scientific Way of War* (University of Nebraska Press, 2015), *Dancing with the Dushman* (Canadian Defence Academy Press, 2008), three monographs, and a dozen articles and chapters on military history and strategic studies. Colonel Hope is now serving on faculty at the NATO Defense College in Rome.

ROBERT MARTYN is a fellow of the Centre for International and Defence Policy and the Canadian Institute for Military and Veteran Health Research, both at Queen's University, where he earned a PhD in military history. Following a year-long post-doctoral fellowship at Carleton University's Norman Paterson School of International Affairs researching issues of intelligence and "small wars," he conducted funded terrorism research at the College of William & Mary in Williamsburg, Virginia. Martyn's previous degrees include a BA in political studies from the University of Manitoba and an MA in war studies from the Royal Military College. In addition to providing subject-matter expertise to the Department of Justice on the 2001 Canadian Anti-Terrorism Act, he wrote the initial draft of a counterinsurgency doctrine for the Canadian Army. Further writings include an edited volume on military aspects of domestic operations, and book chapters on future military interventions, peacekeeping, and intelligence. Martyn is a former member of the Canadian military's Regular Force, having served in armour and search-and-rescue before commissioning into intelligence. His operational deployments include Cyprus, Bosnia, Kosovo, and Afghanistan. Martyn remains active as a reserve infantry officer, having recently transferred from Special Operations Forces Command to the Brockville Rifles. His current research is on insurgent and terrorist motivation.

ROGER SPILLER was the George C. Marshall Professor of Military History, emeritus, US Army Command and General Staff College. He was a founding member of the college's Combat Studies Institute and a member of the faculty from 1978 to 1982, and 1985 to 2005. From 1982 to 1985, he served as special assistant to the Commander-in-Chief, United States Readiness Command, and from 1992 to 1995, he served as personal historian to the Chief of Staff, US Army. Most recently, he served as an affiliate member of the graduate faculty at the University of Kansas. His published works include a new translation of Ardant du Picq's *Études sur le combat* (University of Kansas Press, 2017), *In the School of War* (University of Nebraska Press, 2010), and *An Instinct for War* (Harvard University Press, 2005). Since 2004, he was associated with documentary filmmaker Ken Burns's Florentine Films and served on the advisory boards of the PBS documentaries *The War* (2007) and *The Vietnam War* (2017). Dr Spiller passed away in 2017, shortly after attending the CIDP Combat Motivation Workshop which inspired this volume.

VICTORIA TAIT completed her BA (hons) and MA in political studies at Queen's University in Kingston. Her MA research examined how asymmetric engagement changed the gendered roles of female combatants in insurgent organizations and in the Canadian military. During this research, she interviewed twenty members of the Canadian Combat Arms to determine how female soldiers and combatants were perceived by their peers while on deployment to Afghanistan. Victoria's PhD research examines the apparent disconnect between Canada's strong presence in framing and adopting Resolution 1325 at the United Nations Security Council and NATO, and the notable dearth of female personnel in the Canadian Combat Arms. She is particularly interested in how the normative and practical goals of UNSC Resolution 1325 and NATO/EPAC Directive 40-1 have been translated and communicated to Canadian soldiers during gender sensitivity training. She was an executive editor for the journal *Federal Governance*, is an active reviewer for *Armed Forces & Society*, and serves as vice-president of social affairs for the Political Science Graduate Committee at Carleton University. She is currently working as a collaborator, with Dr Maya Eichler, on a Social Sciences and Humanities Research Council of Canada (SSHRC) Insight Grant on the experiences of female veterans. Victoria's research is funded by SSHRC and the Carleton University Department of Political Science.

ROBERT WILLIAMS received his PhD from Queen's University in Kingston in 2017, while working full-time. While serving with the Canadian Army, he was deployed on overseas operations in Croatia, Bosnia (several times), and Afghanistan. A multi-linguist, he has experienced the reality of coalition military operations, where communications with allies and within operational environments present many challenges beyond the linguistic hurdles. Robert retired from the Canadian Army as a brigadier-general.

Index